LEFT BEHIND

A Historic and Ongoing Blackopolypse

by

Eric M. Betts

ISBN: 978-1960853-62-2

Liberation's Publishing LLC
Columbus - Mississippi

LEFT BEHIND

A Historic and Ongoing Blackopolypse

Table of Content

Left Behind—A Historic and Ongoing Blackopolypse

This text offers a revolutionary critique of white evangelical eschatology, challenging the predominant paradigm that interprets current and future tribulations as largely concerning the loss of existing comfort and stability, a perspective deeply rooted in privilege. Left Behind compellingly argues that the tribulations envisioned by many in these communities, pale in comparison to the systemic racism and enduring hardships faced by Black communities—not in some distant, apocalyptic future, but in the everyday now. Drawing from a rich historical tapestry that spans from the Transatlantic slave trade to modern-day injustices, Additionally, this text illuminates how these ongoing struggles against institutionalized racism have been, and continue to be, the real tribulations of our times. Contrary to seeing these as insurmountable woes reserved for an eschatological resolution, Left Behind— advocates for recognizing and combating these injustices in the present, guided by a more inclusive and culturally sensitive understanding of biblical teachings. This book is not just a critique; it's a clarion call for change, urging the reader towards a deeper, action-oriented faith that challenges deceitful narratives and works tirelessly for equality and justice, truly reflecting what it means to be made in the image of God, in his thought-provoking analysis serves as a call for a more culturally sensitive and inclusive understanding of eschatology, one that genuinely acknowledges and respects the unique tribulations of Black communities throughout history."

-Eric Betts

INTRODUCTION

The denominations that primarily emphasize prophecy as their core attraction emerged from the Advent movement of the 1830s and 1840s. Adventism, religious systems that originated in the United States during the 19th century, focuses on teachings about biblical prophecy. It frequently discusses the Dark Ages that plagued Europe over a millennium. However, how does this relate to our culture, ancestral heritage, and the horrors of our own Dark Ages, which commenced with the transatlantic slave trade and the subsequent atrocities? These religious groups often speak of a future time when Christians will face persecution. Yet, Christians outside of the Western world have historically endured persecution, including the unimaginable suffering of human enslavement, genocide, and lynching. The belief in Jesus' return should not be based on worsening circumstances for Europeans alone. Some American evangelicals claim that Jesus will return because of the perceived erosion of their religious freedom, while neglecting the fact that Africans enslaved in the Americas were chained since 1619 and denied religious freedom. They were forbidden from playing drums, praying, worshiping, or preaching without the supervision of a White church or an approved white minister. Many were forced to practice their faith and pray in secret. As we look to the future, it is essential that we acknowledge and learn from the pain of our past. The global church must understand that these horrors are not isolated incidents, but still present realities in many parts of the world where Christians suffer for their faith.

In order to create a better future, we must recognize the injustices of the past. We can no longer rely on a European-centered approach to eschatology and biblical prophecy. Instead, we must strive for a comprehensive understanding of the world that includes all voices, even those silenced by the power structures of centuries ago. Through this, we can ensure that the dark ages don't recur in the future. It is only then that we will be able to envision a world where all people have access to religious freedom and can live out their faith freely. This is an important step if we are to understand God's ultimate plan for humanity, no matter our background or nationality.

Although the past is painful, we are obligated to remember in order to keep those painful histories from happening again. We need to ensure that conversations on eschatology and biblical prophecy include people of all nationalities, backgrounds, experiences, and beliefs so that we can have a more inclusive approach. Only then will we be able to create an understanding of the future that takes into account the pain of our past. By doing this, we can create a future where all people are free to practice their faith without fear of persecution or oppression.

Reductionist theology of White evangelicalism asserts that the ministry of Jesus is a completed endeavor, urging believers to simply await the tribulation and second coming. However, this theology reveals a lack of awareness and a certain blindness to the historical tribulations endured by black and indigenous people of color, as well as a deficiency in efforts to alleviate their suffering. The core message is that we should focus on preaching that Jesus died on the cross, and that through belief in Him, we can be saved from the consequences of sin. Some proponents of this perspective argue that by preaching the gospel, we can address all societal issues, including racism and colonization. They contend that concerns about environmental pollution, air, and water quality, and even climate change are unnecessary because Jesus will ultimately renew all things. However, this viewpoint has been criticized for neglecting the importance of caring for the current world in which we live.

One particular resource, Scofield Reference Bible, widely acclaimed for its role in nurturing contemporary interpretations of the rapture and evangelical eschatology, carries a lamentable legacy of promoting a racist eschatology surrounding the 'curse of Ham'. Deeply ingrained in its pages is a narrative that not only misinterprets the course of humanity but also fuels racial hierarchy. The 'curse of Ham' has been erroneously interpreted as a divine justification for the enslavement and oppression of people of African descent. This deeply damaging belief, propagated by this Bible edition, has been used to normalize racial disparities and support nefarious practices such as slavery and racial segregation. It is thus essential to critique and reevaluate such harmful theological interpretations, bearing in mind the profound impact they've had on societies and the perpetuation of structural forms of racism.

A widely sold text, The Scofield Reference Bible holds significant influence among Evangelicals.[1] However, it is crucial to acknowledge that this influential work contains racist sentiments that were met with indifference by White Christians. It is worth noting that Cyrus Scofield, the author, served as a Confederate soldier. His work served to bolster a Eurocentric mindset and contributed to the normalization of religio-political anti-blackness. The article "A Famous Evangelical Book Was White Supremacist" exposes Scofield and his connection to white supremacy.[2]

The Church must remain vigilant in incorporating an anti-racist stance into its theology, pushing back against any narrative that perpetuates racial injustice and inequality. We must reject teachings such as those advocated for in the Scofield Reference Bible and other supremacist discourses, recognizing them to be contrary to the Gospel of Christ. We must always strive for a more just world, and this effort starts with recognizing the wrongs of our past and vowing to never repeat them. It is only through humble dialogue and honest self-reflection that we can learn from our

---

[1] Scofield, C. I. (Ed.). (1917). *The Scofield Reference Bible: The Holy Bible, containing the Old and New Testaments*. Oxford University Press.

[2] A Famous Evangelical Book was White Supremacist | by Jonathan Poletti | I blog God. | Medium

errors and move forward towards true unity in Christ.

Cyrus Scofield's racial bias seeped into his theological interpretations, which is evident in several ways. Firstly, the Scofield Reference Bible, his most influential work, upholds a Eurocentric worldview by presenting white societies as the pinnacle of civilization and the primary actors in God's plan for humanity. This ethnocentric perspective systemically marginalizes people of color, relegating them to the periphery of theological discourse and effectively erasing their significance in biblical narratives.

Secondly, Scofield's theology inherently supported the notion of racial hierarchy. His interpretation of the "Curse of Ham" - a biblical passage often misused to justify slavery and racial segregation perpetuated racial stereotypes and laid the groundwork for systemic racism. Lastly, Scofield endorsed the theology of Manifest Destiny, a 19th-century ideology that posited the divine right of white Americans to expand westward across North America, leading to the displacement and genocide of indigenous peoples. This belief, rooted in white supremacy, underpinned the violent colonization and oppression that characterized American expansionism, with Scofield's theology providing a religious justification for such atrocities.

In these ways, Cyrus Scofield's theology exhibited a profound racial bias that has had enduring impacts on the Christianity's approach to issues of race and equality.

The interpretation of the Curse of Ham found in Genesis 9:18-29 has been marred by historical misuse, particularly during the era of the transatlantic slave trade and the institution of slavery in the antebellum South. In an attempt to rationalize the inhumanity of slavery, the Curse of Ham was manipulated and read with modern notions of scientific racism. This racialized reading of the biblical text positioned Africans as cursed descendants of Ham, justifying their enslavement and subjugation.

But the narrative surrounding the Curse of Ham served a dual purpose in constructing a racial hierarchy. More than just providing a prooftext for the subjugation of people of African descent, it offered a biblical basis for the superiority of whiteness, personified in the figure of Japheth. This interpretation suggested that the descendants of Japheth, implicitly linked with Europeans and their descendants, were divinely destined for supremacy. It is important to state that there is no biblically anthropological case for Japheth being the ancestor of Europeans.

In this light, the interpretation of the Curse of Ham in the antebellum period not only rationalized a system of oppression, but also reinforced a deracialized whiteness, biblically produced, and sanctioned with divine authority. The proslavery rationalization of Christian antebellum writers, thus, was rooted in this deracialized whiteness and the biblical narrative they manipulated to uphold it. This insidious use of scripture has had enduring impacts on the trajectory of racial discussions within Christianity.

To justify Negro slavery based on the prophecy surrounding the Curse of Ham, proponents had to establish four criteria. Firstly, they needed to prove that all of Canaan's descendants were predestined for slavery. Secondly, they had to demonstrate that African Negroes indeed descended from Canaan. Thirdly, they needed to assert that each descendant of Shem and Japheth held a moral right to enslave any Canaanite descendant. Lastly, they had to confirm that every slaveholder was directly descended from either Shem or Japheth.

However, none of these four criteria could be substantiated with irrefutable evidence. Allowing such practice, so starkly opposed to the universal principles of divine law, would require an explicit grant from the highest authority. Yet no such conclusive authorization exists. Theologian and scholar, Wongi Park, addressed the failure to provide proof for any of the four criteria, which would nullify the entire argument rationalizing Negro slavery based on the Curse of Ham. [3]

This type of forced pseudo-biblical interpretation with the aim to justify racism and oppression is sadly still alive today. We must

---

[3] *The Blessing of Whiteness in the Curse of Ham: Reading Gen 9:18–29 in the Antebellum South,"* published in the journal *Religions* in 2021

make a conscious effort to understand our history better, so that we can move toward a more just and equitable society where everyone is seen as equal in the eyes of God. In learning from our past mistakes, we must strive to create an environment in which everyone is seen as an important and valuable part of our global community. Until then, the dark legacy of racism will continue to haunt us.

In doing so, we can begin to undo the damage that has been done by centuries of white supremacy and systemic injustice. We must actively work toward dismantling oppressive systems and structures and creating a world where everyone is treated with dignity and respect. In order to do this, we must first start by understanding the complex history of eschatology and how it has been used to justify racism and oppression in previous centuries. Only then can we ensure that such injustices are never allowed to occur again.

We must also continue to educate ourselves about how anti-Africanness still exists today, and how it affects people of all ages and backgrounds. We must recognize the ways in which racism still pervades our society and actively work against it. This includes having difficult conversations about race, dismantling oppressive systems, creating safe spaces for marginalized communities, listening to the stories of those who have experienced discrimination, and standing up for what is right — even when it is not popular.

The past 500 years of colonialism have created a legacy of racism and oppression that still affects us today, but we must remember that change is always possible. We must continue to learn from our history, speak out against injustice, and actively work toward creating a more equitable world — one in which everyone can live free from the fear of discrimination or oppression. During the antebellum period, a distinct biblical understanding of race emerged, aligning with prevailing racial theories of the time. However, it diverged in its explanation of race's origins, rejecting climate, geography, or contemporary theories. Instead, it traced race back to a biblical myth involving

Noah and his sons, who symbolized three racial archetypes.

Within this framework, Ham and his descendants were characterized as Black in two ways: either through divine creation or as a consequence of the curse itself. Some antebellum writers suggested that the curse extended beyond skin color, affecting other traits like hair. Others argued that the curse impacted the character, mind, and personhood of Ham and his descendants. Simultaneously, whiteness was glorified in the deracialized figure of Japheth, portrayed as a superior embodiment of humanity, contrasting with the racialized blackness of Ham.

This interpretation served to justify the antebellum institution of slavery under the guise of biblical prophecy and divine authority, marking Black people for subjugation while sanctifying whiteness. As Ibram X. Kendi argues, racial inequity results from policies and ideas that perpetuate disparities between racial groups, reinforcing the notion of racial superiority and inferiority. [4]

Thus, the biblical interpretation of the antebellum period sanctified the reprehensible practice of slavery as a divinely ordained institution, perpetually condemning Blackness while affirming the eternal blessing of whiteness. This perspective underscores the crucial role of biblical scholars, Christian institutions, and society at large in recognizing historical misinterpretations and actively working to dismantle the enduring impact of biblical racism. If racism's modern legacy stems from biblical origins, then we all bear a profound ethical responsibility to address these fundamental issues, challenge racial hierarchies, and foster human flourishing.

Likewise, it is essential that we recognize the moral and spiritual costs of racism and injustice, both past and present. We cannot begin to repair the damage caused by racial violence without first acknowledging its scope and intensity in our own histories. To move forward in love, justice, and unity, our conversations must grapple with the reality of slavery's impact on

---

[4] Ibram X. Kendi, *How to Be an Antiracist* (New York: One World, 2019)

Black lives throughout the centuries. We may never undo the harm that has been done, but we can strive to create a more equitable and just future for all people, regardless of complexion, ethnicity or creed. In doing so, perhaps we can finally begin to move beyond our dark past toward a brighter tomorrow.

Additionally, it is important to remember that racism is not solely rooted in Europe's Dark Ages. Colonialism and imperialism across the globe have perpetuated racial violence, subjugation, and oppression throughout the modern era. The same forces that justified colonization in Africa and the Americas continue to drive policies of exclusion and exploitation today. It is our responsibility to recognize this pattern of behavior for what it truly is, condemn its use wherever we find it, and strive towards a better world.

Ultimately, we must recognize that racism is not a problem of the past; it remains very much alive in our present day. We live with its systemic consequences and legacies every single day. It is up to us to take ownership of this difficult history and ensure that all people are treated equitably and justly moving forward. We can strive for a brighter future by actively working to eliminate racism in our institutions, homes, and communities. Only then can we seek true justice and healing for all of us.

Once we examine the long legacy of racial oppression, we can more fully recognize the importance of taking action against it today. As difficult conversations about race continue to unfold, we must remain mindful that this is not a new struggle, but a continuation of a fight for justice that began many centuries ago. We have the power to learn from our history and create a better world where everyone can live with dignity and respect.

In the realm of eschatology, the interpretations of the "Curse of Ham" found in both Scofield's biblical commentaries and traditional Mormon theology share some notable similarities. Both rely on a historically fraught biblical interpretation used to justify racial hierarchies and oppression, particularly against Black individuals and communities.

Similarly, traditional Mormon theology has invoked the Curse of Ham to explain the dark skin of Black individuals, associating it with a divine curse and a mark of disfavor. This belief, although disavowed by the Church of Jesus Christ of Latter-day Saints in more recent times, was used for a long period to deny priesthood and temple blessings to Black Mormons.

These parallels underscore how religious interpretations, both in Scofield's works and in Mormon theology, have been manipulated to validate systemic racism and marginalization. Recognizing and challenging these distortions is crucial to dismantling the intertwining structures of religious belief and racial prejudice.

The Scofield Reference Bible continues to be a widely used resource in many seminaries, churches, and Christian bookstores today. Although the controversial interpretation of the "Curse of Ham" is not universally accepted, the Scofield Bible's influence in shaping theological perspectives is undeniable. Despite its historical context and the controversies, it has sparked, its comprehensive cross-referencing system, concise notes, and ease of use, make it a favored study tool among many Christian scholars and laypersons alike. As we engage with such texts, it is crucial to approach them with a critical lens, being mindful of historical distortions that may have been employed to justify oppressive ideologies like racism and colonialism.

The perpetuation of the Scofield Reference Bible in religious circles can be largely attributed to a pervasive indifference towards racial harm within the White evangelical community. Rooted in a lack of empathy for the experiences of those who have been othered and oppressed, this indifference allows the problematic aspects of Scofield's interpretations to be glossed over.

Despite the Bible's diabolical and dehumanizing stance on Africanness, it remains in circulation as the focus remains predominantly on its theological utility, rather than its historical and sociopolitical implications.

The reluctance to universally denounce or reject the Scofield Reference Bible indicates a disregard for the deep-seated pain inherited by those subjected to centuries of racism, slavery, and colonialism. The ongoing acceptance of a text that was used to endorse racial prejudice and marginalization manifests an alarming complacency towards these damaging ideologies. It is a stark reminder of the need for ongoing education and critical discourse to challenge such deep- seated biases in religious teachings and interpretations.

John MacArthur, a pastor, author, and a well-known and influential figure in contemporary evangelical Christianity, has faced criticism for his theological perspectives, particularly those that intersect with issues of race and eschatology. Critics point to his staunch adherence to a 'colorblind' theology as evidence of implicit racism. This view, while seemingly promoting equality, can inadvertently perpetuate systemic racism by failing to acknowledge and address the distinct experiences and challenges faced by people of color. It effectively erases the history of racial discrimination and its ongoing effects on marginalized communities.

Furthermore, in his eschatology, MacArthur advocates a dispensationalist perspective, an outlook on end-times associated with a predominantly Eurocentric world view. Such a framework has been criticized for indirectly validating a colonialist mentality, often to the detriment of non-European cultures and societies. Critics argue that this approach can perpetuate harmful stereotypes and power dynamics, reinforcing systemic racial inequalities rather than challenging them.

Finally, MacArthur's antagonism and moral superiority on issues of racial justice, such as the Black Lives Matter movement, has been interpreted by some as a reflection of complacency towards racial injustice, which sets the stage for anti-black violence. For most of his ilk, while not openly promoting the KKK or the use of the N-word, their support of Donald Trump-a leader of white domestic terrorism- and what can be described as a white's only immigration policy, anti-DEI initiatives, and attempts to erase black history, while simultaneously supporting the white supremacist theory of white genocide, is none other than obvious acceptance and normalization of such ideas and policies.

In a sermon titled *How Should Christians Respond to the*

Riots? delivered in 2020, MacArthur expressed concerns about the BLM organization's principles. He highlighted aspects such as the movement's stances on transgender and queer issues, its approach to family structures, and its perceived anti-authority sentiments. MacArthur argued that these positions are contrary to biblical teachings and described the organization as "anti-God, anti-Scripture, anti-Christ. [5] Amazingly, McArthur and leaders who theologize as he does, have no issue with embracing the quest for liberty by the "founding fathers," who were racists, kidnappers, family separationists, traders in African humanity, and rapists. They condemned BLM for the reasons they did, but do not condemn the "founding fathers." They uphold them as godly persons due to their mentions of "God" and their advancement of white world domination, which they believe serves the greater good. They are not regarded as anti-Christs.

Furthermore, MacArthur has been associated with the "Statement on Social Justice and the Gospel," also known as the Dallas Statement, which he co-authored in 2018. This statement addresses concerns about the influence of social justice movements, including BLM, on evangelical Christianity. It emphasizes that the gospel should not be conflated with social justice ideologies, which the authors believe can undermine scriptural authority. Historically, the 'Curse of Ham' theory found traction among certain segments of American evangelicalism, especially during periods of intense racial tension. While most contemporary influential American evangelicals have disavowed the theory, there were prominent figures in the past who did propagate this fallacy.

For instance, Jerry Falwell Sr., a dominant figure in the American evangelical movement and founder of the Moral Majority, was known to have used the 'Curse of Ham' theory in sermons during the Civil Rights movement. Bob Jones Sr., the

---

[5] John MacArthur, "How Should Christians Respond to the Riots?" *Grace to You*, June 7, 2020, YouTube video, 1:05:32, https://www.youtube.com/watch?v=WKXAykFtehY.

founder of Bob Jones University, also enforced segregationist policies at his institution based on the same doctrine. This belief system became the theological underpinning for a conservative Christian resistance to racial integration in the 20th century America.

In the present day, it's crucial to note that most mainstream evangelicals have distanced themselves from such doctrine and view it as a gross misinterpretation of the Bible. Yet, the impact of such teachings lingers, and it's crucial to recognize this historical context in order to fully understand and address the racial issues that still permeate American evangelicalism today.

The Black Hebrew Israelites, a group known for their provocative street preachers and controversial beliefs, interpret Deuteronomy and other biblical texts in a manner that paradoxically suggests that black people are under a divine curse. They posit that African Americans are the true descendants of the biblical Israelites, and their current state of social and economic hardship is a result of their disobedience to God's Levitical laws. This interpretation mirrors the problematic concept of racial cursing seen in the discredited 'Curse of Ham' theory.

The group selectively highlight verses from Deuteronomy, like chapter 28, which outlines blessings for obedience and curses for disobedience, to suggest that the plight of black people in America is a fulfillment of these curses. They argue that the transatlantic slave trade, centuries of racial discrimination and systemic oppression are part of the divine punishments foretold in these texts. This idea suggests that Europeans are somehow justified in the numerous atrocities and genocides they have committed against racialized individuals, as if they are merely fulfilling a divine curse.

This is a falsehood that needs to be uprooted and removed from public discourse. The 'Curse of Ham' theory, and its modern variant as presented by the Black Hebrew Israelites, serves only to perpetuate anti-Blackness, Anti-Africanness, oppression, and the modern enslavement structures in the prison for profit complex. We must ensure that this dangerous fallacy has no place in our minds or hearts. We should instead focus on celebrating the strength, resilience and achievements of African descended peoples, despite centuries of systemic racism. This calls for a re-examination of our history and the legacy of violence that accompanies it. We must understand how colonialism, slavery and mass displacement have shaped the world we live in today.

Certain sects within the Black Hebrew Israelites propagate the troubling and problematic belief that, in the heavenly afterlife, they will enslave those who have historically oppressed them.

This notion is deeply rooted in a desire for justice and recompense for centuries of suffering, yet it mirrors the very structures of systemic oppression and racism that have caused such immense harm. In fact, it fails to denounce the evil of slavery itself and embraces it as a legitimate institution to be inflicted upon deserving groups.

While it is significant to acknowledge the anger and pain underlying such beliefs, it is also crucial to note that this is not a universally accepted doctrine among all Black Hebrew Israelites. Many followers vehemently reject this teaching, advocating instead for unity, reconciliation, and mutual respect.

The notion of heavenly retribution, as propagated by some Black Hebrew Israelites, illustrates the dangerous potential for misinterpretation and misuse of religious doctrines. It reinforces the need for ongoing dialogue, education, and critical analysis of our religious texts and beliefs. It underscores the importance of challenging any teachings that perpetuate divisions, hatred, and violence, regardless of their origin.

Critics of the Black Hebrew Israelites' interpretations of Deuteronomy, particularly the verse "The LORD will send you back in ships to Egypt on a journey I said you should never make again" (Deuteronomy 28:68), argue that the correlation made between this verse and the transatlantic slave trade is a form of eisegesis. They suggest that the group's members are reading their own experiences of pain, suffering, and displacement into this ancient text.

In an ironic twist, the doctrine proposed by the Black Hebrew

Israelites inadvertently places America at the epicenter of a major biblical narrative by interpreting "Egypt" as a metaphor for the United States. This interpretation not only results in a Eurocentric reading of a crucial biblical text, but it also elevates America to a status akin to that of the ancient kingdoms referenced in the Bible. This, in many ways, serves as a stark reminder of the pervasive influence of Western-centric perspectives on theological interpretations. By recasting America as the 'New Egypt', the doctrine reinforces the very Euro-American centrism it seeks to critique, and further underscores the complex interplay of power, oppression, and theological interpretation that characterizes contemporary discussions on eschatology. Amazingly, most who belong to the sect criticize mainstream Christians for following the doctrines of "Esau," who they interpret as the Europeans.

Some Black Hebrew Israelites, in their effort to propagate their positions, resort to controversial methods that include disparaging Africans. They maintain their distinct identity and the belief in their direct descent from the ancient Israelites by drawing a clear line between themselves and Africans. They argue that their ancestors were only temporary sojourners in Africa, effectively distancing themselves from the African identity. In doing so, they create a hierarchical system of racial and ethnic superiority within their doctrines, with the Black Hebrew Israelites at the apex and Africans at the base. This attitude perpetuates the dangerous stereotypes and Anti-Africanness already prevalent in society, further exacerbating harm. Such practices, while they may bolster the group's unique identity claims, simultaneously undermine the broader struggle for racial equality and unity among people of African descent.

This view aligns with their broader eschatological doctrine, which anticipates an imminent liberation from oppression, akin to the exodus of the Israelites from Egypt. This liberation, as foretold in their prophecy, will be marked by the downfall of their oppressors, symbolized by America, or "Babylon" and the ascendance of the Black Hebrew Israelites to their rightful place as God's chosen people, which some claim, as a time when they will be able to enslave Europeans.

The Seventh-day Adventist Church has a unique interpretation of Revelation 13 and America's role within it. They believe that the second beast, often referred to as the 'earth beast,' represents the United States. The prophecy states that this beast would rise from 'the earth,' which Adventists interpret as a sparsely populated area, as opposed to 'the sea,' a metaphor for heavily populated regions in Europe. This aligns with America's historical development, emerging as a world power from a relatively unpopulated continent.

It's fundamentally inaccurate, and ethnocentric, to depict America as emerging as a global power from a relatively unpopulated continent. This perspective not only overlooks but also erases the mosaic of Native American history that spanned thousands of years before European colonization. At the time of European contact, the Americas were populated by millions of indigenous people with diverse cultures, languages, and societies. These people had intricate trade networks, advanced agricultural practices, and sophisticated political systems. Presenting America as a sparsely populated continent, the narrative consciously or unconsciously propagates the 'terra nullius' myth - a Latin expression meaning "nobody's land."

It was a myth that was used to justify the colonization and oppression of indigenous people. This distortion of history perpetuates a form of cultural genocide and historical erasure and furthers the systemic racism and inequities that have long been a part of American society. Therefore, a critical reassessment of these interpretations is necessary to ensure that eschatological discussions are inclusive, just, and accurately represent historical reality.

Adventists, along with other eschatologists, interpret the term 'waters' or "Seas" in Revelation as symbolic of the populated and significant nations of Europe. This understanding has its roots in a Eurocentric worldview, which often marginalizes or completely overlooks the indigenous lands of the Americas. This interpretation, in effect, positions European nations as the center of the world and the primary players in the end times, while everyone else is a pawn in the drama of destiny, thereby ignoring the significant indigenous civilizations that existed in the Americas.

Contrary to the belief that the Americas were sparsely populated and lacked great nations, historical evidence paints a different picture. The Aztec, Maya, and Inca civilizations, among others, had built populous cities, intricate social and political systems, and made significant contributions to art, science, and technology long before the arrival of Europeans.

The interpretation of 'waters' as representing the vast populations of Europe while ignoring the robust indigenous nations of the Americas is tied to a white supremacist framework. This perspective is a reflection of the systemic racism that disregards non-white histories and cultures. It reinforces the narrative that the significant events of human history and the future unfold primarily in the context of the European or Euro-American world, thus perpetuating cultural erasure and historical inaccuracy in eschatological interpretations.

The concept of 'terra nullius,' has roots in Roman Law, which established the principle of 'res nullius' - denoting things capable of being acquired through occupation. This idea was later manipulated by European colonizers to legitimize their acquisition of new territories across the globe during the Age of Discovery. According to this distorted perspective, any land that was not "civilized" by European standards, i.e., unused, or uninhabited by peoples they considered "civilized," was deemed 'terra nullius' and hence ripe for the taking.

Such a doctrine was inherently dehumanizing and promoted white supremacy. It essentially invalidated indigenous peoples' rights to their ancestral lands, asserting that only European methods of land use were legitimate. It relegated indigenous societies as inferior or non-existent, thereby justifying the colonizers' so- called 'right' to take over. The 'terra nullius' myth propagated a harmful narrative that indigenous peoples were less than human, as it denied their sophisticated cultures, education, governance structures, and relationships with the land. These ideas facilitated the whitewashing of colonial violence, including dispossession, displacement, and genocide, under the guise of 'civilizing missions.'

Ultimately, the 'terra nullius' concept is a manifestation of white supremacy, used as a tool for colonization and oppression. Acknowledging its origins and implications is crucial in the ongoing fight against systemic racism and in efforts to decolonize our understanding of history.

Before the arrival of Christopher Columbus, the indigenous population of the Americas was staggering. Although estimates vary, some sources suggest that the population may have been as high as 112 million. [6] These figures are based on various data, including archaeological evidence, recorded historical accounts, and demographic modeling. It is essential to note, however, that these estimates are contentious and subject to ongoing debate among scholars due to the lack of precise records. Despite this, it is universally accepted that the indigenous population was significantly reduced following the European invasion, primarily due to violence, disease, forced labor, and social disruption. Some prophecy expositors will admit that the population was reduced due to genocide, but such a travesty against humanity could never lay the foundation for the rise of a "godly" or Lamb like nation which would perpetuate such evils.

In 1619, when the first Africans arrived on North American shores, the indigenous population was already significantly diminished from its pre-Columbian peak. Although there are no precise census numbers, research estimates suggest a population of approximately 5 million to 6 million indigenous peoples in what is now the United States. This decrease was primarily due to the catastrophic impacts of foreign diseases, warfare, and forced labor

---

[6] David Michael Smith, "Counting the Dead: Estimating the Loss of Life in the Indigenous Holocaust, 1492–Present," in *A-NAS-2017 Proceedings*, Southeastern Oklahoma State University, 2017, https://www.se.edu/native-american/wp-content/uploads/sites/49/2019/09/A-NAS-2017-Proceedings-Smith.pdf.

imposed by the European colonizers. Nevertheless, the indigenous communities continued to demonstrate resilience, maintaining their cultural traditions and societal structures amidst the onslaught of European colonization. As the Africans were brought to these shores under the brutal conditions of slavery, they encountered a native population that had already been enduring the harsh realities of colonial oppression and genocide for over a century.

Before colonization, North America was home to numerous great indigenous nations, each boasting its unique culture, societal structure, and rich historical legacy. The Apache, known for their formidable warrior culture, roamed the Southwest, while the Sioux established a far- reaching empire across the Great Plains. Eastern woodland nations like the Iroquois and Cherokee developed highly organized societies with sophisticated agricultural systems and myriad social structures. To the far North, the Inuit people adapted to the harsh Arctic conditions, demonstrating remarkable resilience and resourcefulness. The Hopi and Zuni, amongst other Pueblo cultures, thrived in the arid Southwest, constructing intricate cliff dwellings and developing advanced irrigation systems. These are but a few examples of the diverse and resilient indigenous nations that flourished across the continent prior to the advent of European colonization.

The Doctrine of Discovery embodies a stark example of institutionalized racism, and the foundational ideas of white supremacy, originating in the era of European colonial expansion. Rooted in a series of papal bulls issued by the Catholic Church in the 15th century, this doctrine granted European Christian monarchs the 'divine' right to claim lands they 'discovered' for their own, disregarding the indigenous peoples who had been living there for centuries. The doctrine, under the guise of religion, essentially legalized the colonization, subjugation, and even eradication of non-European, non-Christian societies, by declaring them 'inferior'. This doctrine laid the groundwork for a global wave of colonization, ultimately leading to the countless instances of genocide, forced displacement, and cultural erasure. In many respects, this doctrine can be seen as the historical precursor to modern forms of systemic racism and inequality. Its impacts reverberate to this day, as indigenous peoples worldwide continue to fight for their rights to land, resources, and cultural recognition.

Following the Doctrine of Discovery, came the concept of Manifest Destiny in the 19th-century United States. This ideology, similar to the Doctrine of Discovery, held that American settlers were divinely ordained to expand across North America, spreading their institutions and civilization. Much like the Doctrine of Discovery had disregarded the rights of indigenous populations in favor of European colonizers, Manifest Destiny also justified the displacement and oppression of Native Americans, Mexicans and others. This ideology served as an extension of the Doctrine of Discovery, with the belief in divine sanction continuing to fuel European- American expansion, ultimately leading to widespread genocide, slavery, and lynching of non- European societies. Through Manifest Destiny, the Doctrine of Discovery found new expression, paving the way for the United States' westward expansion and the continued subjugation and erasure of indigenous cultures.

The consequence of such atrocities has been profound; the indigenous peoples of the Americas have suffered under centuries of racism, discrimination, and marginalization. This legacy can still be felt today in high rates of poverty, illness, incarceration, and suicide among indigenous populations. It is essential to recognize that this suffering did not occur in a vacuum; it is directly linked to generations of abuse and oppression.

If we are to truly understand the present state of the world, we must confront our history honestly and without reservation. We must ask ourselves difficult questions about the consequences of colonialism, racism, and discrimination. Facing these uncomfortable truths is essential if we are to create a more equitable future for all people. As scholars continue to grapple with eschatology, it is vital that the legacy of colonialism and oppression be addressed honestly and with compassion. Only by doing so can we ensure that dark chapters in history are never repeated.

Colonial powers, predominantly from Europe, advanced the narrative that their colonization was a fulfillment of the Christian mission to spread the Gospel, as outlined in the Great Commission (Matthew 28:16-20). Consequently, indigenous populations weren't just considered uncivilized due to their differing cultural practices or lack of formal land ownership structures, they were also viewed as heathens in need of religious enlightenment. This provided a dual justification for the invasion and occupation - the 'civilizing' of supposedly barren lands, and the 'saving' of purportedly lost souls. Some still argue that the enslavement of Africans and the religious colonization they endured, was for their own good. The idea is that it is better to have been a slave and make it to heaven, then to remain in Africa and go to hell. Sadly, they do not recognize that the actions of their forbears were both hellish and worthy of hell.

Chapter 2

THE DOCTRINE OF DISCOVERY IN AMERICAN ESCHATOLOGY

Impetus behind European colonizers disseminating their religious beliefs in other countries is multifaceted, rooted in a mix of self-righteous sense of duty, supremacy, and economic exploitation. While they professed their actions to be guided by a noble intention of 'saving souls,' it is crucial to examine this impetus within the context of the era's sociopolitical landscape. Within Christianity, the concept of the 'Great Commission,' as stated in Matthew 28:16-20, is often cited as a divine directive to share the Gospel globally. This scripture was interpreted by Europeans as a mandate not just for personal faith but for collective societal responsibility. This mandate, in conjunction with a Eurocentric world view that deemed non-European cultures as 'inferior' or 'uncivilized,' created a justification for their colonial endeavors.

However, these religious justifications were often a veneer for the economic and political benefits accrued through colonial expansion. The propagation of Christianity often went hand- in-hand with the acquisition of foreign lands, resources, and power. Thus, while the spreading of the Gospel was purported as the primary goal, it was, in reality, intertwined with the establishment of dominance and control over colonized populations.

This manipulation of religious doctrine to legitimize land theft and cultural eradication was a stark perversion of Christian teachings. It effectively allowed colonizers to commit atrocities, including forced conversions, cultural genocide, and physical violence, all under the banner of Christianity.

Sadly, stories of oppression and bigotry in the name of religion are not limited to colonial times. Even today, religious sects across the world continue to exploit and manipulate theology with malicious intent.

Denominational teachings such as those of the Mormons, Jehovah's Witnesses, and certain evangelical Christian sects, for instance, also infer that America has a prophetic role in the spread of Christianity and freedom. The Church of Jesus Christ of Latter-Day Saints (Mormons) teach that the United States was divinely prepared for the restoration of the Gospel. Jehovah's Witnesses view America as part of 'Anglo-America', a significant player in biblical prophecy.

Similarly, certain evangelical factions, influenced by the teachings of Puritan colonizers, consider America a 'city on a hill', an example of Christian morality for the world. However, this narrative can be viewed as a manifestation of white supremacy. The implied premise here is that America - predominantly led by white Europeans - has been chosen to spread Christianity and freedom, thus implicitly bestowing a divine status to white Americans. This narrative perpetuates a Eurocentric worldview, positioning the West as the savior, and everyone else as those in need of saving. It ignores the atrocities committed in the name of spreading Christianity, such as the forced conversions, cultural erasure, and physical violence against indigenous populations. When critically examining these interpretations of prophecy, we can uncover the underlying biases and begin to challenge the structures that uphold these oppressive narratives.

The Adventist Church further teaches that the 'earth beast' would initially present as lamb-like, symbolizing innocence and gentleness, which they associate with the early principles of religious freedom and democratic governance foundational to the United States. However, the prophecy warns that this beast will speak like a dragon, signifying oppressive behavior and an abandonment of its foundational idealism. The Adventists believe that America, with its significant global influence, will lead in enforcing religious practices contrary to the teachings of the Bible, resulting in global spiritual oppression.

However, it's important to consider that theological interpretations can vary, and debate continues among scholars about the specific meaning of these prophecies. This interpretation is among many others in the broad spectrum of Christian eschatology and should be considered in its theological and historical context.

While the "earth beast" is often associated with innocence and gentleness in its early stages, symbolizing the principles of religious freedom and democratic governance that the United States was built upon, this narrative both oversimplifies and overlooks crucial aspects of American history. The inception of the United States was not marked by universal innocence and gentleness, particularly towards Indigenous peoples and Africans.

From its earliest days, America's history is steeped in oppressive practices, despite the popular narratives of it being a beacon of freedom and democracy. For Black and Indigenous people of color, the narrative of America as an oppressor is not a futuristic prophecy, but a historical reality. The colonization of the Native American lands by European settlers was marked by violent displacement, forced assimilation, and disease epidemics. This genocidal undertaking decimated Indigenous populations and cultures.

Simultaneously, the transatlantic slave trade brought millions of Africans to America under the most inhumane conditions. Those who survived were subjected to a life of brutal slavery, where they were treated as property rather than human beings. The legacy of slavery continued in the form of lynching, segregation, and systemic racism, which is still evident in today's society.

In this regard, America's historical development is not merely a shift from innocence and gentleness to oppression. Instead, it has continuously perpetuated oppressive practices since its inception. This alternate interpretation presents a more inclusive view of eschatology, challenging the traditional Eurocentric perspective that aligns the worsening of conditions with the Second Coming of Christ. It is a sobering reminder that for many marginalized communities, 'the worst' is a lived historical and present reality, not a future prophecy.

Contrary to the principles of freedom and democracy,

Indigenous communities were subjected to forced displacement, cultural erasure, and genocide as European settlers colonized their lands. Similarly, Africans were not beneficiaries of the proclaimed freedoms but victims of a brutal system of slavery that served as the economic backbone of the new nation. These oppressed groups did not enjoy the religious or political freedoms that were foundational to the United States, revealing a contradiction between the nation's espoused principles and its actual practices.

Thus, the interpretation of America's rise as entirely innocent and gentle is significantly flawed, as it disregards the experiences of marginalized communities and the oppressive systems they were forced to endure. The understanding of these historical realities is essential in providing a more nuanced and accurate perspective on eschatological interpretations related to America.

John Hagee, a prominent figure in the Christian evangelical movement, indeed purports that America holds a special place in biblical prophecy. He contends that the nation was divinely chosen and established by God to serve as a beacon of freedom and righteousness in the world. However, this interpretation is infused with a Eurocentric bias that overlooks the historical injustices committed by the nation, including colonization, oppression, and racial discrimination. While Hagee's teachings may resonate with some, they risk perpetuating a narrative that glosses over America's complex and often troubling past, thus potentially hindering a more inclusive understanding of eschatology.

Highly regarded as an eschatology expert by many in the evangelical world, John Hagee has made several statements that emphasize America's role in prophecy. He argues that America is God's base of operations in the world, and that America was God's idea, and that God divinely founded it. He further asserts, "America has been blessed by God like no other nation on the face of the earth. God birthed America to be a praise to His Glory."[7] These quotes exemplify Hagee's belief in America's divine

---

[7] John Hagee, *Can America Survive?* (New York: Howard Books, 2010).

ordination and special role in the world. However, they also underscore the Eurocentric bias present in his teachings, as they distinctly overlook the historical injustices committed by the country. Such statements, while espousing a patriotic sentiment, risk painting an oversimplified and skewed picture of America's place in eschatology.

Apart from John Hagee, several other evangelical pastors emphasize America's special role in Prophecy. Pat Robertson, founder of the Christian Broadcasting Network, would often intertwine current American scenarios with biblical prophecy, suggesting a divine plan for the nation.

David Jeremiah, the founder of Turning Point Radio and Television Ministries, frequently explores themes of America in prophecy, linking national events to end-times predictions. Perry Stone, the host of Manna-Fest, is also known for his teachings on the significance of America in biblical prophecy, interpreting contemporary issues through an eschatological lens. These figures, like Hagee, tend to interpret the scriptures from a Eurocentric perspective, often neglecting the historical injustices inflicted on marginalized populations. This underscores the need for a more inclusive approach to eschatology that acknowledges these injustices and challenges the dominant narrative.

In the 1800s, various restorationist groups emerged, each asserting their divine mandate to restore the Church to its supposed biblical purity. Key amongst these were the Millerites, the Stone-Campbell movement, and the Latter-Day Saint movement. They all carried a firm conviction that their small American congregations were chosen by God to restore the Church, mirroring the ethnocentric and white supremacist ideologies that permeated society during that period.

These groups based their belief system on the notion of "manifest destiny," a doctrine deeply rooted in white supremacy that justified the colonization and oppression of non-European cultures. The concept of manifest destiny suggested that it was God's plan for the American nation, predominantly white Europeans, to spread their influence and institutions across North

America. This belief, while appearing religiously motivated, was inherently ethnocentric, attributing a special divine favor to a particular ethnic group while marginalizing others.

This Eurocentric bias is a reflection of the broader societal context of the time, where white supremacy was both overt and systemic. Thus, it is crucial to challenge and reevaluate these ethnocentric interpretations of eschatology, emphasizing a more inclusive approach that acknowledges the historical injustices and oppression perpetuated by such beliefs. If God was indeed calling believers to restore the church, why was he only choosing white Americans. Why not Africans? Why not Syrians? Why not Aboriginals? It is essential to examine the implications of this theology and its contemporary relevance, especially in terms of how we view injustice today.

Our interpretation of eschatology affects our view of reality, shapes our attitudes towards others, and informs our understanding of justice. We must strive to understand it from a multi-cultural perspective that takes into account the history and legacy of racism, colonialism, slavery, and genocide. It is only then that we can begin to reconcile our beliefs with a more equitable view of humanity for which justice prevails. We must be willing to reexamine our theology from the perspective of those who have been historically marginalized by Western Christianity in order to develop a richer understanding of God's plan for redemption.

The prophecy of Daniel 2, specifically the dream of the statue with feet of iron and clay, has been interpreted by many experts as symbolizing European nations. This Eurocentric interpretation, however, is a manifestation of the arrogant assumption that eschatological prophecies must revolve around the Western world. Historical and scholarly analysis suggests that these prophetic symbols could very well refer to the Maccabean period, during which the Jewish people were subject to Greek rule and influence.

Scholars see the symbolism of iron and clay in Daniel 2 as corresponding to the tumultuous Maccabean period for several compelling reasons. First, the mixture of iron and clay implies an unstable amalgamation, reflecting the volatile political climate of the Hellenistic kingdoms during the Maccabean era. The Seleucid Empire (iron) had sought to impose Greek culture and religious practices on the Jewish people (clay), creating a tense and unstable sociopolitical environment. Second, the Greek empire's attempt to blend with the Jewish nation mirrored the futile effort to merge iron with clay, as narrated in the prophecy. Both elements maintain their distinct identities despite the forceful efforts to combine them, echoing the Jews' resilience in preserving their faith and culture amidst Greek domination. Lastly, the prophetic vision of a stone destroying the statue can be seen as symbolic of the Maccabean revolt, which eventually led to the downfall of the Hellenistic influence over the Jews. Therefore, the iron-clay symbolism in Daniel 2 provides a potent metaphor for the Maccabean period, illustrating the indomitable spirit of the Jewish people and their resistance against cultural and religious assimilation.

This interpretation places the prophecy in a context relevant to the writer and the original audience, rather than projecting it onto the future as yet unrealized at that time.

Understanding the dream in relation to the Maccabean period provides a fresh perspective that challenges the conventional, Eurocentric interpretation. Moreover, it aligns with the historical-critical approach to biblical interpretation, which seeks to understand the texts in their original historical and cultural contexts. Dismissing these earlier interpretations, prophecy experts not only reveal a lack of humility in their reading of the scriptures but also perpetuate the Eurocentric bias that has long dominated eschatological discourse.

Brodrick D. Shepherd is a renowned scholar in the field of eschatology, specializing in non- Eurocentric interpretations of biblical prophecy. His groundbreaking analysis of Daniel chapters 2 and 7 brings forth a fresh perspective in which he associates these chapters directly with the Maccabean period. Shepherd posits that the prophecies in Daniel were not forecasting far-off future events but rather were directly related to the immediate historical and cultural context of the Jewish people.

In his interpretation, Shepherd suggests that the dreams and visions narrated in these chapters symbolize the Jewish revolt against the Hellenistic influences attempting to suppress their faith and culture. He argues that the symbolic images - the statue in chapter 2 and the beasts in chapter 7 - are metaphors for the oppressive Greek empire, while the stone and 'one like a son of man' represent the Jewish nation and their successful rebellion.

Regarding the Jewish interpretation of the Antichrist, Shepherd articulates that it is not centered around an individual figure, as is often depicted in Protestant America. Instead, he maintains that the concept of the Antichrist in Jewish eschatology is symbolic of oppressive powers and systems that go against God's will - a perspective that speaks volumes to the experience of those subjected to colonization, slavery, and genocide throughout history. This interpretation continues to challenge conventional Eurocentric views, broadening our understanding of eschatology beyond a narrow, ethnocentric lens.

Broderick D. Shepherd further extends his ground-breaking analysis to the book of Esdras, reinforcing his conviction that the apocalyptic scenes in Daniel are rooted in the historical and cultural context of the Maccabean period rather than the Roman era. He scrutinizes the intricate symbolism within Esdras, connecting it back to the imagery found in Daniel. Shepherd argues that the visions of the three-headed eagle and the rampaging lion echo the imagery of the beasts in Daniel, effectively symbolizing the Hellenistic forces that sought to suppress Jewish faith and culture during the Maccabean revolt.

Shepherd's examination of Esdras also uncovers distinctive parallels with the Maccabean period. Drawing on the vision of the lion in Esdras, which mirrors the 'one like a son of man' in Daniel, Shepherd underscores the lion's decisive victory as a symbolic representation of the successful Jewish rebellion against Hellenistic oppression. This interpretation firmly places the apocalyptic scenes from Daniel within the context of the Maccabean period rather than projecting them into a Roman future.

Shepherd's analysis of Esdras thus serves to substantiate his non-Eurocentric interpretation of biblical prophecy, further challenging traditional views and expanding our understanding of eschatology beyond ethnocentric boundaries.

In his book 'Beast, Horns, and Antichrist', Broderick D. Shepherd presents a detailed critique of Antiochus, a figure heavily associated with the atrocities committed against the Jewish people. Shepherd posits Antiochus as a symbol of oppressive forces, drawing parallels with the apocalyptic images of beasts described in biblical prophecy. He suggests that Antiochus, with his reign of terror, fits the biblical description of the beast or horn that sought to annihilate the Jewish faith and culture.[8]

Shepherd further delves into the depiction of Michael the Archangel, a figure revered in Judeo- Christian tradition. He correlates Michael's image to the defeat of Antiochus's forces, interpreting it as a prophecy of hope and liberation amidst persecution. In his analysis, Shepherd interprets Michael the Archangel as a spiritual warrior, symbolizing divine intervention against oppressive forces. Michael's triumph over the beast, as depicted in the apocalyptic texts, signifies the ultimate defeat of Antiochus and his forces. This interpretation provides a reassurance of faith's victory over oppression, a central theme in non-Eurocentric eschatology.

Broderick Shepherd elucidates the historical events of the Maccabean Revolt, a pivotal moment in Jewish history, marked by the brutal repression of the Jewish faith and culture under Antiochus IV Epiphanes, the Seleucid Greek king. Antiochus perpetrated unthinkable atrocities, including the desecration of the Jerusalem temple, outlawing of religious practices, and execution of those who refused to renounce their faith.

Shepherd interprets these historical events as fulfilling Daniel's prophecies. Daniel's vision of a beast symbolizes oppressive rulers, and Shepherd identifies Antiochus as this beast. The king's heinous acts, his attempt to eradicate Jewish culture and faith, embodies the beast's actions as prophesied by Daniel.

---

[8] Brodrick D. Shepherd, *Beasts, Horns and the Antichrist: Daniel, A Blueprint of the Last Days* (Grassy Creek, NC: Cliffside Publishing House, 1994)

Ultimately, however, it is the story of the Jewish people's resilience and triumph that takes center stage. Shepherd emphasizes the victory of the Maccabees, a small but fierce group of Jewish fighters who led the revolt against Antiochus. This triumph, Shepherd asserts, aligns with the prophecy of Michael the Archangel's victory over the beast in the apocalyptic texts.

Correlating these historical events with the prophecies in Daniel's vision, Shepherd extends the interpretation of eschatology beyond Eurocentric views. He emphasizes the universal application of biblical prophecies, recognizing that the struggle against oppression and the ultimate triumph of faith is a common theme shared by all cultures and historical contexts.

Gene L. Green, a notable scholar and theologian, is renowned for his extensive work on eschatology, particularly within the framework of the majority of the world. In his groundbreaking book, "All Things New: Eschatology in the Majority World," Green challenges the Eurocentric interpretation of eschatology.[9]

Green posits that the European perspective of eschatology has, for centuries, been viewed through a lens of privilege and power, often overlooking the experiences of the colonized, oppressed, and erased. He argues that the "end times" as portrayed by the Protestant America, characterized by widespread immorality and global crises, are not novel phenomena for those who have endured the brutality of colonization, slavery, and systemic racism.

For these communities, eschatological struggles are not an impending reality but have been an ongoing part of their history. Green suggests that a more inclusive understanding of eschatology must recognize these experiences, thus broadening the scope of eschatological interpretation beyond the confines of Eurocentric thought.

In "All Things New," Gene L. Green poignantly remarks, "The Eurocentric lens of eschatology, often steeped in privilege, has been woefully blind to the struggles and triumphs of those

---

[9] Gene L. Green, Stephen T. Pardue, and K. K. Yeo, eds., *All Things New: Eschatology in the Majority World* (Carlisle, UK: Langham Publishing, 2019)

outside its immediate sphere. The suffering of Africa, a result of centuries of colonization and oppression, is not an impending apocalypse but an enduring reality. The inability of European scholars to empathize and acknowledge this fact speaks volumes about the inherent biases that skew our understanding of eschatology."

Dr. Wil Gafney is a renowned womanist Hebrew scholar, an ordained Episcopal priest, and a professor of Hebrew and Old Testament at Brite Divinity School. She is renowned for her work that merges scholarly exegesis with contemporary concerns, particularly focusing on the experiences of marginalized communities.

Gafney's critique of Eurocentric eschatology echoes Green's sentiments, especially highlighting its inability to adequately address or respect the experiences of non-European cultures and individuals. She is particularly critical of the popular 'Left Behind' doctrine, a Eurocentric interpretation of eschatology that suggests that faithful Christians will be raptured or taken to heaven, leaving behind those who do not subscribe to these beliefs.

Gafney argues that this doctrine is inherently problematic, presenting an oversimplified worldview that neglects to account for the complexities of individual experiences across different cultures and races. She suggests that such doctrines perpetuate the cycle of exclusion and privilege that characterizes much of Eurocentric theology, reinforcing the idea that eschatology – and by extension, divine salvation – is a concept reserved for a select few, rather than a universally applicable belief.[10]

In the realm of eschatology, there exists a commercialization and fearmongering industry that capitalizes on sensationalism surrounding teachings on the rapture, tribulation, last days, revelation, and Antichrist. This industry, often propagated by televangelists, best-selling books, and blockbuster movies,

---

[10] Wil Gafney, "Holy Blackness: The Matrix of Creation," sermon delivered at All Saints Church, Pasadena, CA, December 1, 2019, https://www.wilgafney.com/2019/12/01/holy-blackness-the-matrix-of-creation/.

monetizes fear and apprehension about the end times. It stokes anxiety by promoting an eschatology that is centered around cataclysmic events, evoking images of mass destruction, global chaos, and supernatural warfare.

The 'Left Behind' series, a popular franchise of novels that depict the rapture and subsequent tribulation, is a prime example of this industry. The series, which has sold millions of copies worldwide, propagates a specific interpretation of eschatology that capitalizes on fear and uncertainty. By doing so, the authors have not only profited financially but also shaped the theological understanding of countless readers, engraining a Eurocentric and exclusionary interpretation of the end times.

Such teachings often overshadow the profound, hopeful messages inherent in eschatology, trading depth and nuance for spectacle and drama. This is particularly concerning as it obscures the broader themes of justice, liberation, and restoration that are central to eschatological discourse, especially from the perspective of oppressed and marginalized communities.

In this context, it becomes clear how the economics of fear can drive theological discourse, steering it towards sensationalism and away from transformative, inclusive understandings of eschatology. It's a reminder of the need for ongoing scrutiny of such teachings and the forces that shape them, particularly in their potential to reinforce oppressive structures.

This is especially true in terms of the end times beliefs which have been embraced by American Protestantism. In equating increased immorality, war, disease, and sexual sins as signs that Jesus is coming soon, they neglect to consider the centuries of racialized violence and oppression suffered by those colonized and erased by Europeans and Americans. Dismissing these experiences as less relevant or worthy of consideration, they perpetuate a dangerous narrative that ignores the reality of injustice experienced by non-Europeans throughout history.

At its core, eschatology should be an open and inclusive dialogue, rooted in humility and respect for all human experience. Such discourse can help to shift our perspective on end times beliefs away from a Eurocentric view towards one that is more informed by a global perspective. In this way, we can begin to create a shared eschatological narrative that is truly reflective of the diverse experiences and perspectives of people across the world.

Our interpretation of eschatology may have far-reaching consequences, and thus it's essential that we take steps to ensure our views are inclusive and respectful. This includes understanding the dark history of colonialism and its legacy of oppression, as well as recognizing our privilege in being able to take part in a discourse that is too often dominated by those with Eurocentric perspectives. Only then can we begin to move towards an eschatology that truly reflects the complexity and diversity of human experience.

As we turn our attention away from the Eurocentric view of eschatology and towards a more inclusive perspective, it is important to remember the lessons learned from the dark chapters of history. We must reckon with the reality that those who have been colonized, oppressed, and erased throughout history are owed justice, and their experiences should not be overlooked or minimized in any conversations related to end-time beliefs.

Eric Betts

Chapter 3

SURVIVING "THE LAST DAYS"

In the first century, the concept of "the last days" was deeply rooted in the socio-political and religious context of that era. It was a period marked by immense upheaval and uncertainty, with the early followers of Christ experiencing intense persecution. Hence, the eschatological narratives of the first century anticipated an imminent cosmic upheaval and divine judgement primarily connected to their own historical and existential crises, rather than any distant future era. This perspective contrasts markedly with modern interpretations that apply these ancient prophecies to our current times or the future. It's crucial to understand that these texts were written by specific people, at a specific time, facing specific circumstances.

The early church believed that the book of Revelation applied to their own days, viewing it as a prophetic commentary on the struggles and persecution they were undergoing in their time. This interpretation was largely based on the prevailing socio-political context, with the Roman Empire as the antagonist and the Christian community as the oppressed. They perceived the visions recorded by John of Patmos as coded messages, providing hope and assurance that their suffering was not in vain, and that divine retribution awaited those who oppressed them. The vivid imagery of beasts, dragons, and cataclysmic events were understood symbolically, representing the oppressive forces of their time and the imminent divine judgement. This perspective maintained a focus on their immediate existential realities rather than projecting onto indeterminate future events. Such an understanding underscores the need to interpret eschatological texts within their original historical and cultural contexts, revealing their relevance to the contemporary audience in a different light.

This principle applies equally to the history of racism and oppression. The legacy of colonialism, slavery, genocide, lynching, segregation, and other forms of institutionalized racism has been overlooked in a lot of popular eschatological discourse. This neglect has perpetuated a false narrative that these atrocities do not weigh heavily on God's divine judgement in the final days. For many, the history of racism has been conveniently relegated to a distant past, existing only in textbooks and archives instead of being acknowledged as an ever-present reality that we still grapple with today. In this way, uncomfortable conversations about systemic injustice are avoided, while dominant narratives about world events remain unchallenged. This distortion is damaging to those who suffer the brunt of the consequences and ultimately deny the full scope of eschatological truths.

As we move forward in our exploration of this theology, it is important to remember that no population should have to endure such suffering for centuries before receiving God's justice. Preterist interpretation of Revelation, originating from the Latin term "praeter", meaning "past", is a theological perspective that views many or all prophecies of Revelation as having already been fulfilled. This approach asserts that the apocalyptic events detailed in Revelation are not prophetic visions of the future, but rather metaphorical descriptions of historical events that took place in the past.

Preterists view emerged primarily as a response to the historical context of the early Christian church. The first followers of Christ were living in a time of intense persecution and tribulation, much of which was inflicted by the Roman Empire. According to preterist interpretation, the dramatic imagery and catastrophic events depicted in Revelation are symbolic references to these historical experiences, rather than predictions of end times yet to come.

Such an interpretative lens challenges the traditional eschatological views that project cataclysms into the future and instead urges us to confront the tangible injustices of the past and present. Interpreting Revelation in this light, we can better understand and address the legacies of racism, oppression, and genocide, which continue to shape our world today. The preterist view of Revelation, which interprets the book as a symbolic representation of historical events in the first century CE, seems to be more consistent with gospel, due to its inclusiveness of non-European groups such as African descendants within the historical narrative over the past two-thousand years. This perspective allows for an understanding of the so-called "end times" as an ongoing process of societal decay and upheaval, rather than a singular future event. It aligns more closely with the lived experience of many non-European groups who have faced continuous forms of oppression spanning centuries. It acknowledges the long-standing suffering of these groups, validating their experiences rather than downplaying them as mere preludes to a distant cataclysmic event. This viewpoint offers a more equitable rendering of eschatology, one that underscores the urgency of addressing systemic injustices in the here and now, rather than deferring action until the perceived end of days.

African American theologians who adopt the preterist view offer an insightful perspective that directly challenges Eurocentric interpretations of eschatology. They posit that eschatology should not only be about future prophecies but also about the reality of systemic injustices borne out of European colonialism and white supremacy. It validates their suffering, acknowledging it as a form of 'end times' in itself, rather than an antecedent to an abstract future catastrophe.

Furthermore, African American preterists emphasize that this theological understanding encourages an active struggle against racism and oppression in the present. They argue that for those who have been victims of slavery, lynching, and systemic racism, the 'end times' is not a distant future event but a lived reality. This reframing of eschatology from the perspective of the oppressed destabilizes Eurocentric interpretations. It shifts the focus from a distant, individualistic salvation to a present, collective liberation, underscoring the urgency of rectifying systemic injustices in our immediate context.

In her groundbreaking book, "Stand Your Ground: Black Bodies and the Justice of God" (2015), Douglas interrogates the pervasive influence of white supremacy within American Christianity and the implications it has for eschatology. She writes, "The stand-your-ground culture's god sanctions the erasure of black bodies. Indeed, this is a god of their own making, which reflects the white self's will to dominance. This god is not the God of the cross. The God of the cross is a God of love who desires that all humanity, and all creation, have life and have it abundantly." Douglas' words echo her strong critique of a Eurocentric eschatological perspective and her call for a theological shift towards a more inclusive, justice-oriented view.[11]

In his seminal work, *The Cross and the Lynching Tree*, James Cone presents a profound exploration of the relationship between the crucifixion of Jesus and the lynching of Black individuals in the United States. According to Cone, the cross and the lynching tree hold a mirror to the horrific reality of systemic racial violence. Concerning eschatology, Cone bridges the gap between divine justice and human suffering, suggesting that the last days are not merely a future event, but a present reality for the oppressed. He elucidates, "The cross was God's critique of power—white power—with powerless love, snatching victory out of defeat." Cone challenges the Eurocentric eschatological perspectives that often disconnect eschatology from the lived experiences of the oppressed, inferring that the 'last days' are as much about the here and now as they are about the future. He emphasizes that the Christian narrative of salvation is not complete without recognizing and rectifying the injustices faced by marginalized communities.[12]

Cone's theology of the cross, thus, offers a significant correction to eschatological thinking, highlighting that the divine promise of a better future must propel believers towards procuring

---

[11] Kelly Brown Douglas, *Stand Your Ground: Black Bodies and the Justice of God* (Maryknoll, NY: Orbis Books, 2015)

[12] James H. Cone, *The Cross and the Lynching Tree* (Maryknoll, NY: Orbis Books, 2011).

justice in the present.

Brian K. Blount is a renowned African American biblical scholar and theologian known for his critical analysis of New Testament texts and emphasis on apocalyptic theology. He is currently the president and professor of New Testament at Union Presbyterian Seminary. His cutting- edge works incorporate themes of eschatology with racial justice, challenging traditional Eurocentric interpretations of Biblical texts. Blount's approach to eschatology underlines the urgency of tackling systemic racial oppression and injustice in the present age, drawing from the apocalyptic language of the New Testament. His academic contributions, especially his interpretive analysis of the Book of Revelation, have significantly enriched discussions within the field of eschatology.[13] Blount's scholarly interpretations of the book of Revelation, presents a preterist perspective, emphasizing that much of the prophetic narrative was fulfilled in the first century A.D., specifically in the context of Roman oppression. He argues that the vivid apocalyptic imagery and intense symbolism found in the book of Revelation were not meant to foretell distant future events, but rather to convey the realities of the socio-political situation faced by the early Christian communities under Roman rule.

Blount's preterist viewpoint advises against a futuristic reading of Revelation. Instead, he guides us to understand the text as a coded language of resistance against the oppressive Roman regime, intended to inspire and embolden the followers of Jesus in their struggle for liberation and justice. This perspective diverges from a Eurocentric eschatological reading that typically disconnects the prophetic narrative from its historical context and instead aligns it with the lived experiences of those who were oppressed in the past, emphasizing the urgency of justice in the present.

In essence, Blount's preterist interpretation of the book of Revelation underscores that prophecies are not only about

---

[13] Brian K. Blount, *Revelation: A Commentary* (Louisville, KY: Westminster John Knox Press, 2009).

predicting the end times, but also about addressing the current state of affairs, particularly from the standpoint of marginalized communities. His work thus contributes to a more nuanced, inclusive, and socio-politically aware understanding of eschatology.

In his exegesis, Brian K. Blount highlights that the book of Revelation portrays Rome and Asia Minor officials as embodiments of evil and oppressive powers. He identifies Rome with the symbol of the "beast" from the sea, an image resonating with the predatory and destructive nature of the Roman Empire. Correspondingly, Asia Minor officials, who were complicit with Rome in oppressing the early Christians, are represented by the "second beast" or the "false prophet". This beast, arising from the earth, signifies the local authorities who enforced the imperial cult and exacerbated the persecution of the believers. These symbolic representations, in Blount's view, serve to unmask the oppressive structures of the time and to rally the oppressed communities towards resistance and hope for ultimate divine justice.

Exercising theological brilliance, Blount's iinterpretations and assertions about the book of Revelation offers an in- depth exploration of the ties between the apocalyptic narrative and the experiences of those oppressed by imperial powers, challenging conventional Eurocentric readings of eschatology.

In a compelling exploration, Blount draws parallels between the symbols in the book of Revelation and the historical and ongoing struggles of African Americans. He sees a striking similarity between the "beast from the sea" - representing the oppressive Roman Empire, and the systemic racism and oppression that African Americans have endured. Just as the beast wreaked havoc and destruction, so too have policies of racial segregation, discrimination, and violence devastated the lives of African Americans. Similarly, the "second beast" or the "false prophet" is likened to institutions and individuals within society who perpetuate racial disparities and injustice. These entities, while appearing benign or even beneficial, have in reality inflicted immense harm by upholding and enforcing an unjust status quo.

Blount's interpretation of Revelation thus serves as a potent metaphor for the African American experience, reinforcing the fundamental message of hope and liberation that underlies eschatological teachings.

In his own words, Brian K. Blount states, *Just as John of Patmos preached an apocalyptic message to seven churches facing the threat of the Roman Empire, African American preachers today must prophesy against the 'beasts' of racism, poverty, and disenfranchisement. Like the ancient community of John, we are called not only to resist but to bear witness, to stand firm in the face of systemic horror and proclaim a different world is possible.*[14] This powerful quotation underscores the resonating parallels between the apocalyptic narrative and the African American experience, highlighting the necessity for a daring and vocal stand against racial injustices.

Historicism and futurism represent two key viewpoints within eschatology. Historicism interprets biblical prophecies as continuous, connected events throughout history, usually from the time of the prophet to the end of the world. Futurism, on the other hand, proposes that these prophecies predominantly pertain to events that will occur in the future, often linked with the end-times.

While distinctly different in their interpretation of biblical prophecies, historicism and futurism often align in their Eurocentric perspectives. They frequently ascribe key dates and times in the books of Daniel and Revelation to significant European and American historical or future events. Historicists, for instance, may link the "time, times, and half a time" prophecy in Daniel (Daniel 7:25; 12:7) and Revelation (Revelation 12:14) to the 1260 years of the Middle Ages — a period of significant European ecclesiastical authority. Similarly, the "seventy weeks" prophecy (Daniel 9:24-27) is often applied to a timeline that culminates in events central to European Christian history, such as the crucifixion of Christ or the destruction of Jerusalem by a

---

[14] Ibid.

Roman emperor.

Meanwhile, futurists tend to project the prophecies of Daniel and Revelation onto anticipated events that often revolve around Euro-American geopolitics. The rise of the Antichrist, the tribulation, and the Battle of Armageddon are frequently anticipated as events directly impacting or even originating from Europe or America.

Thus, both historicism and futurism in eschatology tend to centralize European and American experiences, often overlooking or minimizing the struggles and realities of marginalized communities around the world. This Euro-American focus, while not inherent to these interpretative methods, has been a consequential trait in their mainstream applications.

The issue with both these perspectives arises when they are interpreted through an Anglo- centric lens, which lies at the heart of their racial problematic. Historicism, by tracing a continuous line through history, can inadvertently validate colonial narratives and perpetuate the erasure of non-European histories. Focusing on a Eurocentric historical trajectory, this view tends to sideline or dismiss narratives of colonization, slavery, and genocide, treating these as peripheral rather than integral to the development of Christian history.

Futurism, on the other hand, can be problematic by cultivating a sense of complacency towards present-day injustices. When the eschatological focus shifts towards an anticipated future, often portrayed as a predominantly white, western world, it can lead to a disengagement from the immediate realities of racial and social injustice. This can result in a theology that is neglectful of the suffering experienced by oppressed communities in the present, while it waits for a distant, idealized future.

In essence, both historicism and futurism, when filtered through an Anglo-centric worldview, can contribute to an eschatology that marginalizes non-European experiences and struggles, thereby reinforcing systemic racism within theological discourse.

The casting of Barack Obama, the first black president, as the

Antichrist by some evangelicals is a clear manifestation of this ethnocentric and racially biased eschatology. Despite Obama's reputation as an upstanding family man and leader, the predominately white evangelical community chose to frame him in an antagonistic role within their end-times narrative, a move that reeks of racial and ethnocentric prejudice.

Several evangelical leaders, perhaps driven by political and ideological differences, implicated Obama in their end-time narratives. Prominent among them was Pastor Wiley Drake, former vice-president of the Southern Baptist Convention, who publicly prayed for Obama's death, hinting that he could be the Antichrist.[15] Similarly, Pastor Robert Jeffress, a vocal supporter of Donald Trump, likened Obama's policies to paving the way for the future reign of the Antichrist.[16] In the media universe, televangelist Jack Van Impe and radio host Alex Jones also propagated theories linking Obama to the Antichrist archetype.[17] It's crucial to note that these views are not representative of all evangelicals, and many within the community have denounced such racially tinged eschatological interpretations.

This bias becomes even more apparent when compared to their response to Donald Trump, a man renowned for his extravagant and lavish lifestyle, marked by extramarital affairs and morally questionable decisions. Trump's associations with porn stars and his admission, captured in one recording of delighting in non-consensual advances towards women, including forcible kissing

---

[15] Larry Keller, "Pastor Asks God to Smite President Obama," Southern Poverty Law Center, June 25, 2009,

https://www.splcenter.org/hatewatch/2009/06/25/pastor-asks-god-smite-president-obama.

[16] Robert Jeffress, *Perfect Ending: Why Your Eternal Future Matters Today* (Colorado Springs, CO: Worthy Publishing, 2014)

[17] Jack Van Impe, *Revelation Rumblings* (Troy, MI: Jack Van Impe Ministries, 2013), DVD.

and groping, are well-known. Space does not allow one to speak of Trump's many convictions and felonies, in addition to his attempt to bully state officials to skew the 2020 elections in his favor. Despite these revelations, many evangelicals hailed him as a savior, a symbol of hope within their eschatological narrative. Moreover in 2024, they elected him a second time when given the option of electing a qualified prosecutor, vice president and Howard University graduate, Kamala Harris.

Given the fact that evangelicals have chosen to overlook his questionable morality, while vilifying Obama in their eschatological interpretation of current events, speaks volumes about the cultural and racial biases ingrained within certain strands of evangelical theology. It suggests a theological framework that prioritizes whiteness over other racial identities; one that chooses to overlook the sins of those who identify with white culture and

Such a distortion, favoring a white man over a black man, despite their respective moral orientations, illustrates a deep-seated racial bias within evangelical eschatology. It reaffirms the notion that Eurocentric perspectives dominate these theologies, relegating narratives and figures that do not conform to this Eurocentric worldview to the sidelines or casting them in a negative light. This contributes to the perpetuation of systemic racism within theological discourses, reinforcing the marginalization of non-European experiences and perspectives.

Within the turbulent socio-political landscape of recent times, certain evangelical pastors have drawn upon eschatological narratives to interpret events such as the Black Lives Matter protests and the rollout of COVID-19 vaccines. They've framed these events as existential threats to their perceived freedoms, indicators of an approaching apocalyptic end.

The Black Lives Matter protests, advocating for racial justice and equality, have been mischaracterized by these pastors as a challenge to their societal position. Instead of recognizing the cries for justice and systemic change, they perceived these movements as an attack on their freedoms. They viewed the rallying calls for racial justice as a social disruption, fitting into an eschatological narrative of societal moral degradation preceding the last days. COVID-19 vaccines, a scientific achievement aimed at curbing the pandemic's devastating impact, were similarly misconstrued. Some pastors interpreted the widespread vaccination campaigns as a coercive measure infringing on their individual liberties, echoing conspiracy theories of a looming totalitarian rule. In their eschatological perspective, these vaccines were seen not as a life-saving tool, but as a harbinger of the apocalypse, a sign of the encroaching 'end times'.

Such interpretations reflect an eschatology that is not only Eurocentric but is also marked by a refusal to acknowledge realities that challenge their worldview. Much irony lies in the selective perception of the evangelical community, particularly in its interpretation of 'signs of the last days.' They focus on events they deem a direct threat to their societal status, while overlooking systemic tragedies that disproportionately affect marginalized communities. Police brutality against African Americans, the prison-industrial complex primarily targeting poor communities and people of color, inadequate healthcare for minorities, and high mortality rates among pregnant Black women are issues deeply rooted in structural racism and economic disparity. These are profound societal ills that inflict immeasurable suffering and should invoke a sense of moral urgency. Yet, they are tragically disregarded in the evangelical eschatological narrative. It's a stark contradiction that while they fear an encroaching apocalyptic end, they fail to recognize the 'apocalyptic' conditions that many marginalized communities already endure. This blindness to the 'apocalypse already in progress' exposes a profound bias in their eschatological interpretation and highlights the necessity for an eschatology that is cognizant of diverse experiences and systemic injustices.

Stephen Charleston, an esteemed Native American bishop, and theologian, lends a distinct perspective to eschatology in his groundbreaking work, "We Survived the End of the World." A member of the Choctaw Nation, Charleston brings forth the experiences and understandings of Indigenous peoples, thus shedding light on a vastly overlooked area in the discourse of eschatology.[18]

In his book, Charleston posits that Indigenous communities have already experienced their apocalypse through the harrowing events of colonization – the forced removal from their ancestral lands, the eradication of their cultures, and the systemic genocides. He explores the concept of "surviving the end of the world," the resiliency of Indigenous communities who have withstood their apocalyptic events and continue to thrive, despite ongoing oppression and marginalization. Through his lens, the apocalypse isn't a future event but a historical and ongoing reality for these communities.

Charleston's work challenges the mainstream, Eurocentric view of eschatology, urging us to see the apocalypse not as a single, universal event but as a series of unique experiences that differ greatly among communities, particularly those that have suffered under colonialism. His insights underscore the need to broaden our eschatological perspectives to include those outside the dominant cultural narrative.

---

[18] Steven Charleston, *We Survived the End of the World: Lessons from Native America on Apocalypse and Hope* (Minneapolis: Broadleaf Books, 2023).

Chapter 4

THE RAPTURE AND BLACK TRIBULATION

David Currie, renowned theologians, raises significant concerns about the commonly popularized rapture doctrine. They argue that this doctrine, in fact, leaves people behind, countering the very principle it professes to uphold. According to Currie, the rapture doctrine promotes a vision of salvation that is selectively exclusive, effectively leaving behind those who do not conform to its narrow interpretations or who have been marginalized by oppressive systems, such as racism and colonialism.[19]

This critique asserts that the rapture doctrine eliminates the concept of the cross or suffering. Rapturism, in its essence, advocates for an escape from tribulation and hardship, which starkly contrasts with the biblical teaching that calls for believers to bear their crosses. The concept of bearing one's cross is synonymous with enduring trials and challenges which are associated with unexplainable human suffering and standing up against injustice. Currie contends that the rapturists' evasion of enduring hardship contradicts the lived experiences of many communities, notably those who have survived oppression and genocide. Consequently, they encourage a re-evaluation of the rapture doctrine to encompass a more inclusive theology that does not leave the oppressed and marginalized behind and acknowledges the reality of suffering in the world.

Ultimately, Currie's critique of the rapture doctrine serves as a reminder that eschatology must be rooted in justice, especially for those who have been historically and systemically left behind. To this end, it is imperative to consider the experiences of all people when discussing eschatological events or concepts: those living

---

[19] David B. Currie, *Rapture: The End-Times Error That Leaves the Bible Behind* (Manchester, NH: Sophia Institute Press, 2003)

under oppressive systems, indigenous populations.

Donald Akenson, in his seminal work "Exporting the Rapture," raises profound concerns about evangelical teachings on the rapture.[20] Akenson underscores that the rapture doctrine's narrative of an imminent apocalyptic event, triggered by escalating immorality and global crises, tends to overlook the longstanding tribulations of colonized populations. He argues that these communities have already endured their own version of 'apocalypse' through centuries of oppression and genocide, yet their experiences are often eclipsed in mainstream eschatological narratives. According to Akenson, the teaching of the rapture, therefore, necessitates a comprehensive re-examination to develop an inclusive, global perspective that acknowledges and validates the histories and experiences of all populations, not just the Euro-American viewpoint.

Confronting the limitations of Eurocentric eschatology, this analysis enables us to develop a more nuanced and holistic understanding of how our religious beliefs can shape our worldviews. This is especially essential for those seeking to understand the ramifications of their faith in an increasingly globalized world. Ultimately, it is necessary to internalize the harsh truths about our past in order to foster our more inclusive, equitable, and just futures. By doing this we can move beyond a narrative that solely centers around the "end of days" to one that seeks to realize a better tomorrow for all people.

Akenson powerfully asserts, "In the conventional narrative, the apocalypse is a future event, a cataclysm to befall the privileged Euro-American societies. But for the colonized, the oppressed, the 'apocalypse' is not an impending event; it is a historical reality, a lived experience of past centuries. Their 'end of days' has already been endured and survived, yet this truth is conspicuously missing

---

[20] Donald Harman Akenson, *Exporting the Rapture: John Nelson Darby and the Victorian Conquest of North-American Evangelicalism* (New York: Oxford University Press, 2018).

in our mainstream eschatological discourses."[21] He extends his critique to the African slave trade, a dark chapter in human history often overlooked in eschatological discussions. He argues that the harrowing experiences of African slaves – the forced labor, systemic oppression, and profound suffering – were, in essence, an 'apocalypse' of their own. Yet, this lived reality is rarely acknowledged within the predominant Euro-American narrative. The slave trade, Akenson asserts, represented a tangible 'end of days' for countless African communities; their societies were upended, their cultures erased, and their freedoms brutally snuffed out. This perspective challenges us to recontextualize our understanding of 'apocalypse', recognizing it not just as a potential future event for the privileged, but as a historical reality for the oppressed and marginalized.

Dr. Gene L. Green's seminal work, "Theology in the Majority World: A New Kind of Conversation", expands the discourse on eschatology by centering perspectives from the Majority World. Green challenges the Eurocentric narrative of 'end times' theology by arguing for a more nuanced understanding that acknowledges the experiences of those who have lived through societal upheavals and catastrophic events. He asserts that these communities have already endured their own 'apocalypses' – through colonialism, genocide, and systemic oppression – and their theological perspectives offer valuable insights into our understanding and interpretation of eschatology. Through this approach, Green's work prompts us to reconsider how we define and approach 'end times' theology, broadening our perspective to include the lived experiences of communities outside of the dominant Euro-American framework.

From the dark ages of colonialism, slavery and systemic racism has emerged deeper appreciation for different perspectives and an increased respect for all humanity. This is seen in the growing number of people who are calling for greater

---

[21] Ibid.

understanding and unity in the face of fragmentation. Similarly, the rising waves of awareness and activism around social justice shows that there is a growing desire to create meaningful change on a global scale.

Rev. Benjamin Cremer, a respected theologian and scholar, has shared insightful interpretations on the eschatological importance of '666' and being 'marked by the beast'. According to Rev. Cremer, the number '666', mentioned in Revelations 13:18 in the Bible, is not merely a sign of the apocalyptic end times. Instead, he posits that '666' is symbolic of man's imperfection and failure to attain divine completeness, represented by the number '7'. He asserts that it's a metaphorical indicator of the systemic evils of oppression, racism and colonialism that have been perpetrated in the name of religion and progress.[22]

Being 'marked by the beast', as per Rev. Cremer, does not refer to a physical mark. Instead, it refers to the societal and personal marks left by systems of oppression and dehumanization. Those 'marked' are the individuals and communities who have been marginalized and subjugated throughout history. For Cremer, understanding these symbols in their historical and sociopolitical context rather than literal interpretations is crucial for a more inclusive and justice-oriented understanding of eschatology.

Cremer extends his interpretation of the 'mark of the beast' to institutions, particularly the Church. According to him, a Church 'marked by the beast' is one that is complicit in global systems of oppression, racism, and discrimination. It has strayed from the original mission of love, peace, and justice that Christ advocated for, and has, instead, become a conduit for systemic injustice. This mark, he posits, is not visible to the eye, but is evident in a Church's actions and policies. Cremer cautions that such institutions, while professing faith, effectively perpetuate the very evils they are called to dismantle. For him, the challenge lies in acknowledging these marks, seeking redemption, and actively

---

[22] Benjamin Cremer, "The Mark of the Beast," Into the Gray, accessed May 23, 2025, https://benjamin-cremer.kit.com/posts/the-mark-of-the-beast.

working towards a church and society free of such marks.

For Cremer, the 'beast' of Revelation is not a literal monster as traditional interpretations may suggest. Rather, it symbolizes the power structures and systems of the world that perpetuate oppression, racism, and discrimination. These systems can take the form of governments, corporations, or even religious institutions. The 'beast', in his view, is an embodiment of the systemic evils that have been deeply entrenched in society, masked by an appearance of normalcy and acceptance. 'Bearing the mark of the beast' does not signify allegiance to a demonic entity, but participation, whether active or passive, in these unjust systems. As such, the 'beast' of Revelation is a metaphor, representing the pervasive and destructive forces of oppression and inhumanity that have been propagated under the guise of progress and civilization.

According to Cremer, resisting the mark of the 'beast' requires a fervent commitment to justice, love, and equality. It necessitates the will to scrutinize and confront our own compliance in these systems of oppression, and to challenge the status quo. Resisting the 'beast' is not a passive act, but rather, an active, ongoing struggle against systemic racism and discrimination. It demands a steadfast engagement in dismantling these oppressive structures, through advocacy, activism, and a commitment to the gospel of Christ, which liberates.

Furthermore, Cremer emphasizes the importance of reclaiming the Church's true identity and mission, to foster a community of love, peace, justice, and redemption, free from the taint of the 'beast'. Resistance, in this context, is an assertion of humanity and a refusal to partake in the perpetuation of systemic evils.

Only by recognizing and actively resisting oppressive forces can we hope to transcend the "dark ages" of human history and create a better future for all. For those who have been subjected to systemic racism, oppression, and the horrors of slavery, lynching, and genocide, the so-called "end times" have been a lived reality for centuries. Rather than perceiving worsening conditions in Europe or America as indicators of the last days, the focus should be shifted towards the relentless suffering endured by the colonized, oppressed, and erased peoples.

For Africans who were uprooted from their homelands and subjected to the brutality of the transatlantic slave trade, the concept of 'end times' was not an abstract future event, but a lived reality. Chancellor Williams, scholar and professor, powerfully captures the apocalyptic dimensions of what was lost. He asserts that the degradation of African civilization began well before the Transatlantic holocaust. He says, "The Land of the Blacks was a vast land, a big world unto itself covering 12,000,000 square miles."–emphasizing the scale and significance of lost civilizations. He further observes, "...that from time immemorial, stark greed, the desire for wealth, has overridden all humane considerations. Greed has served as a kind of anesthesia, deadening humane sentiments and breaking the bonds of affection that relate man to man."– pointing to systemic destruction rooted in exploitation.[23]

The relentless suffering endured during the Middle Passage, the inhumane conditions of slavery, and the continued systemic racism – these were and continue to be apocalyptic experiences. The Black experience is in itself a testament to an ongoing holocaust. Over 400 years of systemic oppression, from the horrors of the slave trade to the continual fight against racism and inequality, is a holocaust that has painted an apocalyptic picture for those who have lived through it. For the Black community, the 'end times' has been a protracted reality, marked by pain and resilience in the face of relentless adversity.

The countless episodes of Black genocide – from the brutalities of the slave trade to the malicious acts of lynching and the systemic oppression that persists today – these are not isolated events but a continuous holocaust that spans over four centuries. It's an ongoing catastrophe that has marked every generation of the Black community. Our history, filled with resilience and revolution, is inseparable from this backdrop of sustained horror.

---

[23] Chancellor Williams, *The Destruction of Black Civilization: Great Issues of a Race from 4500 B.C. to 2000 A.D.* (Chicago: Third World Press, 1987)

Our narrative, therefore, is one of survival amidst a protracted apocalypse.

Legacies from such a holocaust, and its profound effects on the Black community, is an integral part of our history. As we continue to confront this legacy today, it is paramount to recognize and acknowledge our collective trauma in order to move forward towards liberation and flourishing. Only then can we begin to heal and reclaim our narrative from the oppressive forces that have dictated our lives for centuries. Recognizing our traumatic history, we can better grapple with the present-day implications of the past and seek justice and true liberation in the future.

This understanding of Black history as part of an ongoing apocalypse is essential to challenging the preconceived notions of eschatology, while providing a more comprehensive view of our shared experiences. It allows us to move beyond the Eurocentric view of the world and acknowledge the unique struggles of those who have been colonized, oppressed, and erased. In turn, this opens up a new space for dialogue around eschatology which accounts for centuries of systemic inequity and recognizes that ultimately, liberation is our collective goal.

Such horrific experiences of Africans in the slave castles on the African coast was nothing short of apocalyptic. Captured and stripped of their rights, these individuals were held in deplorable conditions in these coastal fortresses. Living quarters were cramped, dark, and poorly ventilated, with hundreds of people packed into small spaces. Disease was rampant, and the fear of death was a constant companion. The cruelty of their captors was relentless, with physical and psychological abuse being a daily reality. The slaves endured gruesome punishments and endured a pervasive culture of dehumanization. Their identity, culture, and dignity were systematically eroded, leaving a legacy of trauma that echoes through generations. This is an important chapter in our understanding of the sustained horror endured by the colonized and oppressed, challenging the conventional narratives of eschatology.

The degradation and brutalization of African women in the slave castles extended far beyond the overarching oppressions of slavery. Solemnly, the current writer visited the Elmina Castle in Ghana in 2011 and heard the stories. Women were subjected to horrific sexual abuse, reduced to objects of gratification for their captors. They were routinely raped, their dignity and agency violently stripped away in acts of unspeakable violation. This sexual exploitation was not just a horrendous personal violation, it was an institutionalized aspect of the slave system, a tool used to further dehumanize and control. Female slaves lived in a constant state of terror, their bodies commodified, and their worth defined solely in terms of their sexual and reproductive utility. These women bore the additional burden of forced pregnancies, their children born into the cruel and relentless cycle of slavery. This devastating account of female slaves serves as a stark reminder of the gender-specific atrocities committed in the slave castles of the African coast, further reinforcing the need to challenge the prevailing Eurocentric narratives of eschatology.

Individuals who dared to rebel against the oppressive regime of the slave castles often faced extreme punishments as a means of instilling fear and maintaining control. The defiance of these brave souls was met with brutal torture, designed not only to break their will but also to serve as a deterrent for others contemplating resistance. Torture methods were unspeakably cruel, including flogging, branding, and mutilation.

Beyond physical torture, rebels were often subjected to severe deprivation, starved to the point of death. Denied even the basic necessity of food, they were weakened and made to suffer gradual, agonizing deaths. This cruel strategy served the dual purpose of quelling rebellion and conserving resources - a chilling example of the inhumane efficiency of the slave system. These brutal practices underline the unimaginable suffering endured by the enslaved, a dark facet of history that reminds us of the depths of inhumanity possible when power is unchecked. The recounting of these horrors serves as a powerful counter-narrative to traditional Eurocentric eschatological teachings.

Brutal effects of slavery extended beyond the physical and psychological torment of those held in bondage. The legacy of this system has left deep long-lasting scars on our society even today. The atrocities committed against African slaves led to a deeply entrenched racism that continues to plague us centuries later. The trauma inflicted on generations of people has been passed down through time, leading to a systemic inequality that persists in our society.

The Middle Passage represents one of the darkest chapters of human history, a testament to the horrifying depths of racial oppression. Slave ships were the harrowing vessels of this journey, where millions of African men, women, and children were packed like livestock into the suffocating bowels of these ships, stripped of their humanity. The conditions onboard were unimaginably cruel; the captives were shackled together in tight, confined spaces, forced to lie in their own waste. Disease was rampant, with dysentery, smallpox, and measles contributing to the terrifying mortality rates.

The despair and desolation that gripped those enslaved often led to acts of resistance, with some choosing death over the bleak prospect of life in bondage. Mothers clutched their babies and jumped overboard, sensing that it would be better to eaten by the sharks of the Atlantic than the barely human sharks on the other side. It was not uncommon for captives to leap overboard or starve themselves, preferring the cold embrace of the sea to the brutal existence on the slave ships. Slavers, in their cruel indifference, would often throw the ill and the dying overboard, considering them as nothing more than expendable cargo.

Indeed, it was common for enslaved Africans to be murdered and cast overboard during the transatlantic journey. This heinous act was not merely a consequence of the harsh and inhumane conditions on the slave ships; it was a calculated endeavor driven by the cold, profit-centric logic of the slave trade. Slave owners often took out insurance policies on their 'cargo'—the enslaved Africans. When disease or malnutrition threatened the life of an enslaved person, the slavers, in their twisted logic, would deem it more profitable to throw the dying overboard rather than risk the loss of the 'investment'.

In one of the most infamous cases, the Zong massacre of 1781, the ship's crew threw approximately 133 enslaved Africans into the Atlantic Ocean to claim insurance payouts. Through this horrific act, the enslaved were reduced to mere commodities, their lives worthless compared to the potential financial loss of their owners. The Zong massacre highlights the brutally mechanistic and financially driven nature of the transatlantic slave trade, showing that the commodification of human life reached terrifying extremes.

Historians estimate that over the course of the transatlantic slave trade, approximately 2 million Africans perished during the Middle Passage alone. This monumental loss of life is a chilling testament to the brutality of the slave trade, a stark reminder of the human cost of systemic oppression. The horrors of the Middle Passage, much like the atrocities of slavery, serve as a potent counter-narrative to Eurocentric eschatological teachings, underscoring the need for a more inclusive understanding of historical and future trajectories. The current writer remembers listening on the radio to the late right wing radio host Rush Limbaugh being tickled with laughter as he played the voice of an African American scholar lecturing on this atrocity.

The auction blocks, another horrific symbol of the dehumanizing slave trade, were where the enslaved Africans were sold like commodities upon their arrival in America. Stripped of their dignity and freedom, men, women, and children were paraded in front of potential buyers, their physical traits scrutinized and haggled over as if they were mere livestock. It was a marketplace of human misery, where families were torn apart, never to see each other again. Buyers would inspect the enslaved individuals, often in the most invasive ways, evaluating their 'worth' based on their physical strength, health, and age. This was the final phase of their commodification – from being captured in their homeland to surviving the brutal Middle Passage, only to be auctioned off to the highest bidder. The auction blocks stand as a stark reminder of the unimaginable trauma inflicted upon the African people, casting a long shadow on the Eurocentric view of eschatology, and highlighting the dire need for a more inclusive, global perspective.

Standing on the auction block, the enslaved Africans must have felt an overwhelming sense of helplessness and despair. Stripped of their humanity and dignity, they were reduced to mere commodities, their worth assessed by potential buyers with an indifferent, calculating gaze. The ground beneath them may have felt like a precipice, the very edge of their known world, beyond which lay an abyss of uncertainty and dread. The air around them, heavy with the collective fear, anticipation, and resignation of countless others like them, resonated with the unspoken pain of broken dreams and severed ties. Their hearts, once vibrant with hopes, dreams, and the warmth of their homelands, were now weighed down by the chains of their imposed servitude. This dehumanizing experience, a stark contradiction to the principles of human rights and justice, painted a grim picture of their future, challenging the Eurocentric eschatological assumption of a progressively worsening world preceding the end-times.

As the enslaved Africans set foot on the foreign soil of America, their world, as they knew it, ceased to exist. The familiar sights, sounds, and scents of their African homelands were replaced with the unfamiliar, the harsh, and the oppressive. Stripped of their cultural identities and forcibly distanced from their roots, their languages, religions, and customs were systematically erased. They were expected to adopt the language and religion of their captors, a cruel irony considering the latter's eschatological beliefs of deteriorating morality and growing sin, while they themselves were the perpetrators of such heinous crimes against humanity. Thus, the arrival of enslaved Africans on American soil not only signified the end of their free world but also marked the beginning of a prolonged era of violent anti-Africanness, oppression, and unspeakable suffering, a dark period in history that continues to impact the lives of their descendants. This narrative starkly contrasts the Eurocentric view of eschatology that associates the worsening of European or American societies with the impending end times, completely disregarding the apocalyptic experiences of the colonized and oppressed.

For the Africans, boarding the slave ships was tantamount to a collective human apocalypse. They were torn away from their families and communities, losing not just their freedom, but their entire world. Their societies, rich with diverse cultures, traditions, languages, and social structures, were irrevocably shattered. The long journey across the Atlantic, known as the Middle Passage, was a horrifying ordeal. They were forced into the cramped, filthy holds of the ships, subject to inhumane conditions, torture, and disease. Many perished before they even reached the American shores.

Their arrival in America signified the loss of their dignity, their identities, and their humanity. They were treated as property, subjected to unimaginable brutality and dehumanization. One slave narrative said that they were treated "worse than a dog." Their rich cultural past was forcibly replaced with the language, religion, and customs of their oppressors. The traditional knowledge, wisdom, and skills they possessed, fine-tuned over generations, were dismissed as primitive, and their contributions to human civilization were systematically erased from the annals of history. The echoing pain of this immense loss still reverberates through the centuries, a haunting reminder of the human capacity for cruelty and oppression.

The slave trade had an unimaginable and devastating impact on the economy and societal structure of Africa. Economically, the extraction of millions of able-bodied men, women, and children deprived Africa of its most valuable resource: its human capital. This led to a significant decline in agricultural productivity given that a substantial portion of the workforce had been removed and sold into slavery.

Moreover, the economies of many African societies, previously focused on sustainable subsistence farming, shifted towards the extraction of humans for trade. This change further disrupted traditional economic systems and eroded social cohesion, as tribes and communities turned against one another, lured by the prospects of wealth from the slave trade.

Societally, the slave trade resulted in the breakdown of traditional family structures and communities. With the young and strong taken away, the elderly and children were left vulnerable, unable to adequately fend for themselves or sustain their communities. This led to societal instability and a fragmentation of cultural norms and values that were passed down through generations. Additionally, the continuous threat of raids and kidnappings instilled a pervasive climate of fear, further damaging the social fabric of African communities.

Consequences of this brutal period in history are still apparent today, reflected in the socio- economic challenges faced by many African nations. Thus, the impact of the slave trade has been a sustained and systemic hindrance to the development and progress of Africa.

Brutal conditions of American slavery inflicted upon black men were not only physical but also profoundly psychological, eroding their sense of dignity, freedom and identity. These men were subjected to inhuman treatment and unbearable humiliation, often viewed and treated no better than animals.

Torture was a common tool used by the so-called slave masters, and it was often marked by a terrifying degree of creativity in the ways to inflict maximum pain. Whipping, branding, mutilation, and confinement in unbearable conditions were common forms of physical torture. These were not only punitive measures, but methods designed to break the spirit of these men, subduing any instinct of rebellion or resistance.

Psychological trauma experienced by these men was just as severe. Stripped of their names and identities, they were systematically dehumanized and reduced to mere property. This had a profound impact on their sense of self-worth and left deep psychological scars that endured long after physical wounds had healed. The enduring trauma was often perpetuated by the fear of being sold away from loved ones, an ever-present threat that caused constant anxiety and distress.

Moreover, the public humiliation they were subjected to, such as being displayed naked at auctions, further compounded their psychological suffering. This deliberate degradation served to reinforce their perceived inferior status in the minds of their oppressors and, tragically, in their own. The effects of this physical and psychological abuse have had long-lasting effects, resonating through generations, and continuing to impact the descendants of those who endured the atrocities of American slavery.

Women suffered unique and horrifying abuses during the era of American slavery. They were not exempt from the physical torture meted out to enslaved men; indeed, they were similarly subjected to inhumane practices such as whipping, branding, and confinement in squalid conditions. The dual burden of sexism and racism made enslaved women vulnerable to egregious sexual violence and exploitation by their enslavers, an unspeakable violation that was tacitly accepted and institutionalized within the slave system.

Enslaved women were forced into reproductive labor, their worth often measured in their ability to bear children, who were seen as additional property to increase the wealth of the slaveholder. This was a brutal form of psychological torture, as women lived in constant fear of their children being ripped away from them, sold to distant plantations.

Additionally, women were exposed to the same public humiliation and dehumanization as their male counterparts, subjected to naked displays at auctions, their bodies objectified and commodified. This endured humiliation served to reinforce their inferior status and left indelible psychological scars. Sadly, the legacy of this systemic abuse of women during slavery has had far-reaching consequences, resonating through the generations, and continuing to shape the experiences of their descendants today.

Another disturbing aspect of American slavery involved black enslaved women being coerced into wet-nursing white children, often at the expense of their own offspring. Enforced lactation became an extension of their enslavement, as their bodies were commodified not just for their labor, but also for their biological processes. This practice often meant that these women had to neglect their own children in favor of the children of their enslavers.

The psychological impacts of this forced wet nursing were profound. While their own children faced starvation or neglect, these enslaved women were expected to provide nourishment and maternal care to white infants. This cruel system further underscored the inhumanity of slavery, where basic maternal rights were denied under the guise of economic necessity. The legacy of this painful aspect of slavery continues to reverberate through generations, contributing to the complex tapestry of racial tension and social inequity that characterize contemporary American society.

In the brutal world of slavery, black women found themselves robbed of their autonomy, their bodies commodified as instruments of labor and sites of sexual exploitation. Enslavers exerted an unfathomable degree of control over their bodies, reducing these women to mere breeding machines to perpetuate the slaveocracy. The systematic rape of enslaved black women was an abhorrent aspect of this institution, serving as a means of terror, domination, and procreation.

This forced breeding is a stark testament to the grotesque dehumanization these women endured. Subjected to repeated violations, their bodies were used for the production of more enslaved people, adding to their enslavers' wealth. They became victims of a horrifically mechanized form of procreation that stripped them of their dignity and reduced them to mere vessels.

Perpetual cycles of sexual violence and forced breeding served two perverse objectives: maintaining a steady supply of labor and asserting racial control. The lingering scars of this brutal exploitation persist today, reflected in the pervasive racial and gender inequalities that continue to mark American society. This painful chapter of history underscores the need to confront the legacy of slavery in our contemporary discourse on race, gender, and power.

Enslaved individuals were cruelly objectified, their human essence effaced as they were commonly advertised alongside livestock in newspapers – a degrading practice that further entrenched their dehumanization. This was not a mere coincidence, but a calculated strategy designed to diminish their status to mere property, equating them with animals and cattle in a marketplace. This abhorrent practice laid bare the disturbing reality of the slave economy, where human beings, endowed with feelings, thoughts, and dreams were commoditized like farm animals in the pursuit of profit.

Human beings, whose worth is immeasurable and dignity inviolable, were reduced to mere commodities, their value determined by their perceived physical strength or fertility. These advertisements typically featured detailed descriptions of their physical characteristics alongside their 'productivity'. The enslaved were stripped of their identities, individuality, and humanity, referred to by mere numbers or depersonalized descriptions.

This chilling practice underscores the extent of the dehumanization and commodification perpetuated by the slaveocracy. It served as a stark reminder of the inhumanity inherent in a system predicated on the perception of certain human beings as property, and the brutal lengths to which this mindset was propagated in public discourse. This aspect of history further highlights the devastating legacy of slavery and the urgent necessity of acknowledging and addressing this past in our present-day conversations about racism and social justice.

Post Traumatic Slave Syndrome (PTSS) was first introduced by Dr. Joy DeGruy, an acclaimed researcher and educator. Her pioneering work argued that centuries of slavery, followed by systemic racism and oppression, had a profound and lasting impact not only on those directly subjected to these atrocities but also on subsequent generations. PTSS posits that the after-effects of such profound trauma can be transmitted across generations, thereby disrupting the mental and emotional wellbeing of descendants of slaves.[24]

---

[24] Joy DeGruy, *Post Traumatic Slave Syndrome: America's Legacy of Enduring Injury and Healing* (Milwaukie, OR: Uptone Press, 2005).

Historically, the genesis of PTSS lies within the horrific realities of slavery. The brutality and inhumane conditions of slavery—ranging from the forcible uprooting and trans-Atlantic transportation to the physical, sexual, and psychological abuse suffered—left indelible scars on its victims. These traumas did not end with the abolition of slavery but were prolonged through institutionalized racism, segregation, and violence, such as lynchings and police brutality.

PTSS provides a framework to understand the lingering psychological effects of such systemic trauma, acting as a lens through which we can understand the current socio-economic disparities, systemic inequities, and deeply rooted racial tensions that continue to reverberate in our society today. Dr. DeGruy combines historical analysis with clinical research to discuss how these traumas have led to adaptive behaviors that persist in African American communities today. Dr. DeGruy's work underscores the importance of historical context in understanding present-day issues, underscoring the dire need to rectify the injustices of the past to strive for a more liberated and compensated future.

Emasculation of Black males during the era of slavery was a deliberate and cruel act, wielded as a tool of oppression and control. Enslaved men were frequently subjected to public humiliation and degradation, often in front of their loved ones, to erode their sense of manhood and assert the dominance of the slave masters. In a horrifying display of power, these men were stripped of their clothing and dignity, subjected to brutal physical punishment, and degraded in the most profound ways. This was not simply a brutal act of violence; it was a meticulously calculated method to shatter their self-esteem, rob them of their masculinity, and reinforce the power dynamics of the time. By dehumanizing Black men in front of their women and children, so-called slave masters ensured the perpetuation of racial hierarchies, dehumanizing them and marking them as 'inferior'. This systemic humiliation has had far- reaching psychological impacts and has played a significant role in the generational trauma experienced by the descendants of those who endured slavery.

Cone presents a potent exploration of the horrifying experiences of the Black community, drawing parallels between the crucifixion of Jesus and the lynching of Black people in America. Cone asserts that the lynching tree was an instrument of terror that embodied the height of America's racial violence. It served not only to punish individuals but to intimidate and subjugate the entire Black community.

Cone reminds us, Both the cross and the lynching tree were symbols of terror, instruments of torture and execution, reserved primarily for slaves, criminals, and insurrectionists—the lowest of the low in society.[25] He emphasizes that the white supremacists who perpetrated these lynchings did so with an unfathomable sense of entitlement and righteousness, often justifying their actions by distorting and weaponizing Christian teachings.

In drawing this connection, Cone challenges traditional theological perspectives, proposing a reinterpretation of Christian symbols through the lens of Black suffering and resilience. This approach not only critiques the complacency of mainstream Christianity in the face of systemic racism but also highlights the strength and faith of the Black community in the face of horrific oppression.

Additionally, Cone asserts that Black people were often driven by the most trivial of reasons - *a perceived insult, an inappropriate glance, or simply the color of their skin. The objective was not merely punishment, but to instill a pervasive fear within the Black community, a fear designed to maintain the racial hierarchy and to silence any notion of resistance. It is a terrible thing to constantly live under the terror of death, the absolute power of someone else over your life,* Cone wrote, capturing the true horror and fear that was part and parcel of the Black experience in a racially segregated America. The lingering fear, the ever-present terror was a tool of oppression, a mechanism to uphold white supremacy and perpetuate systemic racism.

---

[25]James H. Cone, *The Cross and the Lynching Tree* (Maryknoll, NY: Orbis Books, 2011).

In a chilling account, Cone describes an incident where a Black boy was lynched purely for possessing a photograph of a white woman. The stark triviality of this provocation underscores the heinous depths of anti-Africanness. This young boy, the victim of a society pulsating with bigotry, was brutally murdered, not for a crime or an act of resistance, but simply for having an image—a mere piece of paper showcasing the likeness of a white woman. It was a terrifying demonstration of the extremes of white supremacy, a stark reminder of the constant danger lurking in the shadows for Black people, where even the most benign actions could be distorted into reasons for execution. It was this climate of ceaseless fear and violence that formed the horrific backdrop of Black existence during this era of American history.

James Cone presented a harrowing perspective on the frighteningly casual manner in which white society often treated the lynching of Black individuals. He recounted instances where white people, in a grotesque display of inhumanity, would derive pleasure and amusement from the brutal execution of innocent Black men. He detailed how these horrifying events were not merely executions, but rather community spectacles that were often treated as social events, complete with food vendors and photographers. In an egregious distortion of justice and morality, these acts of racial violence were recast as a form of entertainment for white spectators. This chilling normalization of such extreme brutality against Black people further underscores the horrifying depths of systemic racism and white supremacy that permeated this era.

Eric Betts

Chapter 5

OUR WORLD IS ON FIRE

Anti-African animus precipitated not only the deaths of countless Black individuals, but also the systematic destruction of thriving Black communities. These communities represented burgeoning symbols of Black success and autonomy, a stark contrast to the narrative of Black inferiority propagated by white supremacy. One of the most notorious instances of this is the obliteration of the prosperous Black community in Tulsa, Oklahoma, often referred to as "Black Wall Street". This community, flourishing with Black-owned businesses and affluent Black families, was razed in a violent episode in 1921, known as the Tulsa Race Massacre. White mobs, inflamed by unproven allegations against a young Black man, embarked on a rampage of arson and murder, effectively decimating the prosperous community.

The Tulsa Massacre, a devastating eruption of racial violence, was a living nightmare for its victims, many of whom never fully recovered from the trauma. Personal accounts from survivors and eyewitnesses chronicle the horrifying events with chilling clarity. Dr. Olivia J. Hooker, one of the last known survivors of the Massacre, vividly recalled the terror of that night in 1921. She was just six years old when mobs of white men stormed her family's home, destroying their possessions and forever shattering her sense of safety.

Mary E. Jones Parrish, another survivor, compiled numerous firsthand accounts in her book, "Events of the Tulsa Disaster". Her narrative, punctuated by the raw emotion of those who experienced the Massacre, encapsulates the full horror of the event. One man recounted hearing the blood-curdling screams of his neighbors as their homes were set ablaze, while another described the streets as a war zone, overrun by armed white mobs.

Buck Colbert Franklin, a notable Black attorney in Tulsa and father of acclaimed historian John Hope Franklin, recounted in his memoir witnessing a sea of white faces illuminated by the massive fires, a haunting image that underscored the racial animus underlying the attack.[26] These testimonials serve as stark reminders of the atrocities endured by the Black community during the Tulsa Massacre, an episode of history that underscores the depth and brutality of racial violence and systemic racism in America.

The Tulsa Massacre's devastating effects extended far beyond the immediate destruction and loss of life, leaving a generational impact that continues to be felt today. The Greenwood District, once a thriving epicenter of black economic power known as 'Black Wall Street', was reduced to ashes. Over 1,200 homes were destroyed, along with numerous businesses, leaving a once prosperous community in ruins.

The Massacre not only robbed the community of its wealth, but also of its sense of security and dignity. The trauma inflicted was not limited to that single horrific event, but instead rippled outwards, affecting subsequent generations. Many families were unable to rebuild their lives, trapped in a cycle of poverty and disenfranchisement that echoes to this day. The lack of justice and reparations further deepened the wounds, with the state and city authorities failing to hold any of the perpetrators accountable.

Achieving the economic prosperity of the Greenwood District, or 'Black Wall Street', was no small feat for those who dared to dream in a time of systemic racism and discrimination. The African American community, despite having faced the traumatic legacy of slavery and the oppressive institution of segregation, rose from the ashes and built a prosperous enclave. This was a monumental endeavor made possible by a collective determination to create a self- sufficient community where black excellence and economic empowerment were not only celebrated but also deeply ingrained in the fabric of daily life.

The community was a beacon of African American enterprise,

---

[26] John Hope Franklin, *Mirror to America: The Autobiography of John Hope Franklin* (New York: Farrar, Straus and Giroux, 2005)

marked by thriving businesses, well-established schools, and landmarks of cultural significance. Entrepreneurs, educators, craftsmen, builders, doctors, and lawyers collectively contributed to a vibrant socio-economic mosaic that was the envy of many. The success of 'Black Wall Street' was a testament to the resilience and tenacity of a community that chose to rise above the confines of racial oppression.

Yet, this remarkable feat of community-building was abruptly and tragically cut short by the ferocity of anti-African motivated hatred during the Tulsa Massacre. The burning down of 'Black Wall Street' represented more than the physical destruction of property; it was a violent attempt to dismantle the economic power of a thriving black community. The destruction of Greenwood remains a profound illustration of the enduring impact of racial violence and systemic racism, and a somber reminder of the lengths to which hate can go to suppress progress and autonomy.

Moreover, the Tulsa Massacre's historical erasure from national discourse until recent decades compounded the trauma. The silence and denial around these events served as an additional layer of violence, effectively erasing a significant instance of racial terror from collective memory.

This recognition is not just about rectifying historical records, but also about understanding the long-standing effects of racial violence and systemic oppression on African-descended communities, and how they continue to shape our present-day reality. Similarly, the thriving Black community of Rosewood, Florida, met with a tragic fate in 1923. A fabricated accusation against a Black man sparked a horrific spree of violence and destruction by white mobs. The once-thriving town was left in ruins, and the residents, terrorized and displaced, never returned.

Rosewood, Florida, was a testament to the resilience and tenacity of the Black community, having been established in the late 19th century predominantly by emancipated slaves and their descendants. Despite the harsh realities of the post-slavery era, they managed to build a self-sustaining community marked by flourishing businesses, churches, and a school. Rosewood had become a haven of Black prosperity in a segregated America, a beacon of hope and testament to the possibility of progress.

However, this beacon was abruptly extinguished in 1923. An unfounded accusation made by a white woman against a Black man provided the spark for an explosion of racial violence. White mobs descended on Rosewood, emboldened by a racially biased judicial system and prejudiced societal norms. Over a week, the mob unleashed a wave of terror that saw homes and businesses burnt to the ground, innocent lives lost, and an entire community displaced.

The horror of the Rosewood massacre lies not just in the physical violence inflicted, but also in the psychological terror it instilled in the survivors and the Black community at large. The incident demonstrated the precariousness of Black life and prosperity in a society deeply entrenched in systemic racism. It underscored the grim reality that their hard-won progress could be annihilated at a moment's notice based on a mere fabrication, leaving generations of trauma in its wake.

These are but two examples of the multitude of successful Black towns that have been erased from the American landscape due to anti-Black animus. The destruction of these communities represents a deliberate effort to dismantle Black prosperity, autonomy, and resistance—a chilling testament to the pervasive and enduring nature of anti-Black oppression in the United States.

Wilmington, North Carolina, was another thriving Black community that tragically fell victim to racial violence. The Wilmington massacre of 1898, often referred to as a coup, saw a mob of white supremacists violently overthrow the city's biracial government, causing the death and displacement of many black citizens.

Analyzing this event, we see that the Wilmington massacre was precipitated by a combination of factors rooted in the deep-seated racism and white supremacy prevalent during that time. Post-Civil War Wilmington had a thriving Black middle class and a majority-Black population, which was a source of resentment for many white residents. The city's biracial government, which included Black aldermen, judges, and police officers, was seen as a threat to white supremacy.

This tension was further escalated by the political landscape. The fusion coalition of Populist and Republican parties, which advocated for interracial cooperation and held significant political power in the state, was met with vehement opposition from the Democratic Party. The Democrats, in their quest to regain control, stoked racial tensions through a campaign of fear and misinformation, painting Black leadership as a threat to white women's safety.

Angry at the publication of an editorial by Alex Manly, a Black newspaper editor, European American retaliated. Manly challenged the white supremacy narrative and the stereotype of Black men as a threat to white women. His bold stance was twisted into an excuse for the white supremacists to organize a coup, systematically planning the massacre and overthrow of the biracial government.

Thus, the Wilmington massacre was a carefully orchestrated act of racial terrorism, driven by a desperate desire to reclaim white dominance and quash Black political and economic autonomy. This narrative underscores the fact that the true cause of the massacre lies in the fear of Black prosperity prevalent at that time, and the loss of social status by those racialized as white.

Elaine, Arkansas, was the setting of one of the deadliest racial conflicts in U.S. history. In 1919, an organized group of black sharecroppers who were seeking fair pay were attacked by white mobs. The Elaine Massacre resulted in the killing of an estimated 100-237 black people and five white people. This massacre was part of a wave of lynching and violence that followed the Great Migration of African Americans from rural areas to cities in search of economic opportunities. The mob had used false rumors, alleging that the sharecroppers were planning an insurrection, as justification for their actions.

The Elaine Massacre serves as a stark reminder of how racism and oppression have been deeply embedded in the history of this country, and how it continues to shape our present. It is a reminder of how those who are privileged have used fear and violence as tools of domination for centuries. We must confront these painful realities in order to move forward towards social justice and an equitable future.

Exploring the history of the Dark Ages of white terror shows that racism, oppression, genocide, and domestic terrorism are as American as apple pie. Ocoee, Florida, was a prosperous black community and the site of a violent racial episode in 1920. In an event now known as the Ocoee Massacre, black citizens were killed, and the entire black community was driven out following a black man's attempt to vote.

Building a prosperous city like Ocoee in the early 20th century was no small feat, especially for a Black community caught in the stranglehold of systemic racism and economic oppression. It required resilience, unity, and an immense amount of hard work. The people tilled the soil, established thriving businesses, built homes, and fostered an environment where education was valued, and communal bonds ran deep.

Such a Massacre, however, tragically uprooted this burgeoning community. The killings and subsequent displacement had a deep and lasting impact. Economically, the loss of property, businesses, and jobs was catastrophic. Socially, the fabric of the community was irrevocably damaged as families were torn apart, and friends lost contact. Culturally, a rich heritage was nearly extinguished as traditions, stories, and shared experiences were scattered with the wind.

Unquestionably, the Ocoee Massacre was a direct response to African Americans' attempts to exercise their legal and constitutional right to vote. This assertion of civic agency was perceived as a threat to the entrenched racial hierarchy, triggering a violent backlash from the white community. In their attempts to suppress the political voice of the Black community, white mobs unleashed a wave of terror and violence, resulting in the deaths of an unknown number of Black residents and the destruction of their homes and businesses.

The realities of displacement were severe and multifaceted.

The survivors of the massacre were left homeless, jobless and traumatized. They were forced to flee for their lives, leaving behind the ashes of their hard-won prosperity. This displacement was more than just physical; it was a seismic disruption of community ties, economic stability, and cultural continuity. Displaced residents scattered throughout the region, carrying with them the painful memories of loss and the lasting scars of racial violence. The trauma of the Ocoee Massacre passed down through generations, a haunting reminder of the destructive power of racial prejudice and fear. This event was a tragic illustration of how racism and oppression can destroy thriving communities and displace entire populations.

The long-term impact of such violence extends beyond the immediate loss. It creates a ripple effect, disrupting the socio-economic progression of generations. It also instills a deep-seated fear and mistrust that takes decades to heal. In the broader context of America's history, these events serve as stark reminders of the oppression and violence that mar the nation's past and continue to shape its present and future.

East St. Louis, Illinois, in 1917, witnessed a bloody race riot sparked by labor disputes. White workers, threatened by black migrants who were brought in as strikebreakers, initiated a brutal attack on their black counterparts, resulting in the deaths of hundreds. It marked one of the bloodiest episodes in the ongoing narrative of racial violence in America. Incited by labor tensions, white mobs unleashed a wave of brutal violence on the African American community. Over a few horrifying days in July, estimates of African Americans killed ranged into the hundreds. Property damage was catastrophic, with hundreds of homes and businesses owned by black residents set ablaze, effectively wiping out the wealth accumulated by these individuals.

With diabolical intent, the massacre inflicted deep psychological trauma on the survivors, many of whom were forced to flee their homes and start anew in unfamiliar places. The violence served not only to assert white dominance but also to curtail black economic competition. Such a massacre and the subsequent mass exodus exemplify the systemic nature of racial violence aimed at maintaining oppressive structures. Violent incidents such as these serve as a stark reminder of the corroding effects of anti-African hatred and the apocalyptic struggles African Americans have had to endure throughout American history.

Thibodaux, Louisiana, was the site of the Thibodaux Massacre in 1887. The massacre was the culmination of a three-week strike by sugar cane plantation workers seeking equal treatment and a wage. Violently, the protest ended in a horrific attack by white mobs, resulting in the death of an estimated 50-300 Black workers.

Viewing the Thibodaux Massacre of 1887 retrospectively, we find a stark example of the deadly intersection of anti-Black hatred and economic exploitation. At the heart of this tragic event was a dispute between Black sugar cane workers and their white employers in Thibodaux, Louisiana. For decades after the end of Civil War and the abolition of slavery, Black workers continued to toil in near-slavery conditions on Louisiana's sugar plantations. Fed up with this enduring exploitation, the Knights of Labor, a labor union that included Black members, organized a strike in November 1887, demanding fair wages and equal treatment.

However, the strike did not sit well with the white elites who saw it as a threat to their economic interests and a challenge to the racial hierarchy they were keen to maintain. Subsequently, the white community mobilized, leveraging their control of local government and law enforcement, and formed militias to suppress the strike. This led to the horrific events of November 23rd, when armed white mobs attacked the Black community of Thibodaux, killing an estimated 50- 300 Black workers, though the exact figure remains uncertain due to a lack of official records.

The Thibodaux Massacre illustrates the lengths to which the power structure would go to preserve its position of power. It exemplifies an oft-overlooked aspect of American history, where economic interest, racial prejudice, and violence intersected in a devastating manner. Continuing to explore and understand these events is critical in understanding the anti-Black violence embedded in America's past and its ramifications on the present day.

Historically speaking, the Thibodaux Massacre left an indelible scar on the socioeconomic fabric of the African American community, not just in Louisiana, but across the country. Its aftermath extended beyond the immediate loss of lives, systematically oppressing African Americans and perpetuating racial and economic inequalities. The massacre spread fear among black workers, effectively quelling further collective labor action for decades. This further entrenched the exploitative labor practices where black workers were paid a pittance for their toil.

Moreover, the massacre served to uphold the status quo of racial hierarchy, reinforcing the notion of white supremacy. It served as a brutal reminder to African Americans of the extent to which the system would go to sustain racial segregation and economic subjugation. This event, among others, continued the cycle of fear, violence and systemic oppression against African Americans. By casting a shadow of terror, it discouraged future generations from standing up for their rights.

Understanding this event's aftermath is therefore vital in addressing and dismantling the structures of racial inequality in modern America.

In the North, Chicago's African American community faced the 1919 Race Riot. An incident of racial violence spiraled into a week-long riot, leading to the death and displacement of many African Americans. The riot deepened the existing racial divide in the city, influencing housing and social policies that led to the systemic segregation and economic marginalization of the African American community.

Through these instances, it becomes evident that racial terror has had a profound impact on the displacement and destabilization of African American communities across the United States. Recognizing this history is crucial to understanding the deeply ingrained structures of racism and inequality that persist today.

Atlanta, Georgia, saw one of the bloodiest race riots in the nation's history in 1906. Triggered by newspaper reports of Black men assaulting white women, the Atlanta Race Riot lasted for four days and resulted in numerous Black citizens being killed or injured, and their properties destroyed or damaged.

Tragically, the Atlanta Race Massacre of 1906 was fueled by a potent combination of perceived racial threat and the manipulation of the white population's fear. The city was experiencing rapid demographic changes as Black citizens were moving into previously white areas, creating economic competition and social frictions. Anti-Black sentiments were exacerbated by the city's newspapers, which published sensational and often fabricated stories of Black men assaulting white women. These stories, aimed at selling papers, ignited white mob violence that lasted for four days. Thus, the Atlanta Race Massacre was not an isolated incident but part of a broader pattern of racial violence and oppression, deeply rooted in racism and economic competition.

In another anti-Black episode, the industrial town of Anniston in Alabama came under attack, and bears a tragic testimony to the devastating intersection of environmental ethics, poverty, and anti-Blackness. Predominantly African- American and economically disadvantaged, the town has been a victim of industrial pollution for decades. The Monsanto Chemical Company, now part of Bayer AG, dumped tons of polychlorinated biphenyls (PCBs) into local creeks for nearly 40 years, contaminating the soil and water and leading to a severe public health crisis. Illnesses, including various types of cancer, became frighteningly common among the residents, while their pleas for help went largely unheeded.

Despite the clear link between environmental pollution and the health crisis, the residents of Anniston have been unable to seek adequate redress or relocate due to financial constraints and systemic neglect. Their plight underscores the need for rigorous environmental ethics, including corporate responsibility and government accountability. It demonstrates the cruel reality of environmental racism, where the most vulnerable populations bear the brunt of environmental disregard and are left to suffer its long-term consequences.

Uniontown, another locality in Alabama, shares a similar story of environmental racism and its devastating health impacts. Deep in Alabama's black belt, Uniontown's citizens, predominately African American and poverty-stricken, have long suffered from an unhealthy environment. This can largely be attributed to the Arrowhead Landfill, a waste facility that accepts millions of tons of coal ash collected from across the country. This toxic waste, known to contain arsenic, mercury, and other harmful substances, seeps into the groundwater, polluting the local environment and posing severe health risks.

Residents have reported a range of health issues, including respiratory problems, skin rashes, and a higher incidence of cancer, presumably linked to the contamination. The case of Uniontown exemplifies environmental injustice, where Black people, who are socio- economically disadvantaged bear the health and environmental burdens of pollution.

Adverse environmental conditions in Uniontown have resulted in an unbearable quality of life for its residents. High rates of unemployment compound the issues at hand, with the majority of residents living below the poverty line. This socio-economic disadvantage makes it extremely difficult for inhabitants to relocate or seek legal recourse against the harmful environmental conditions perpetuated by the Arrowhead Landfill.

Moreover, Uniontown's problems extend beyond pollution. The town also hosts a correctional facility, which poses additional challenges. Aside from the moral implications of a largely African American population living in the shadows of a prison, the facility contributes to the town's overall health crisis. Inmates' basic human rights are often neglected, including access to clean water and sanitary living conditions. Furthermore, the prison contributes to the local pollution problem, further exacerbating the precarious environmental and health conditions faced by Uniontown's residents.

These elements of economic hardship, environmental racism, and systematic neglect coalesce into a dire situation for Uniontown, Alabama. It's a stark example of the egregious violations of human rights that marginalized communities, particularly those of African descent, face in their own homes. This narrative is not unique to Uniontown but is an agonizing repetition of the oppression and discrimination that these communities have suffered for centuries. The narrative of Uniontown underscores the urgency for a reevaluation of our environmental ethics, a call to action for those who have endured the long history of environmental racism. Like the residents of Anniston, the people of Uniontown have found themselves trapped, unable to escape their toxic surroundings due to financial limitations. They are yet another testament to the ongoing legacy of environmental racism that continues to plague the United States, further underscoring the urgent need for environmental justice reforms, corporate accountability, and stringent environmental regulations.

Historically, one of the darkest chapters in the United States' history is the era of lynching, a grisly form of public spectacle that disproportionately targeted African Americans. It's a painful topic, but necessary to address in the context of oppression and systemic racism. Lynching, often by burning, was used as a tool of terror and control over Black communities. This brutal act was not only a ghastly physical torment but also a psychological weapon to sow fear and maintain white supremacy. These horrifying crimes, carried out publicly and with impunity, exemplify the deep-seated racial hatred that has stained the fabric of American society. The legacy of this violence continues to reverberate through communities today and underlines the importance of acknowledging, confronting, and rectifying the injustices of the past.

These are just a few examples of the numerous horrific race riots, lynchings, and other forms of racial violence that have taken place throughout history. They serve as a vital reminder of how racism and oppression were -- and still are -- deeply entrenched in our society. If we commit ourselves to understanding our painful past, then perhaps we can create a future where all people are equally respected and protected. This is one of the most important lessons eschatology has to offer us: that justice demands reckoning with our collective history, both the good and the bad. Only if we accept this moral imperative can we work together to create a brighter, more equitable future for everyone.

Mississippi, historically, was a majority African American state, largely due to the legacy of plantation agriculture and slavery in its once fertile soil. However, its demographic composition drastically changed because of a mass exodus, often referred to as the Great Migration, that occurred in the 20th century. African Americans in Mississippi were pushed to their limits, not just by the lack of economic opportunities but more so due to the pervasive racial terrorism they faced daily.

Lynching and other forms of racial violence were rampant and were used strategically to maintain white supremacy. African Americans were systematically terrorized and brutalized, forcing them to live in a state of constant fear and insecurity. The socio-political environment was steeped in racism and discrimination, and the legal system offered little to no protection for those subjected to hate crimes. This widespread racial terrorism propelled many Mississippi African Americans to seek refuge elsewhere, primarily in northern and western cities, to escape the racially hostile environment and seek better employment opportunities.

Mississippi's history is a stark reflection of the painful and oppressive past that African- Americans endured. It showcases a narrative of survival, resilience, and the relentless pursuit of justice and equality that is central to the understanding of American eschatology. Amazingly, the exodus of African Americans from this state is a historical reminder of the extensive, lasting impacts of white domestic terrorism and oppression. This disruption and the destruction of black cities has biblical implications, and it is important to recognize the long-term legacy of European oppression and how this has come to shape current eschatological realities. Recognizing this history, empowers us to better understand our present state and collectively work towards a brighter future where justice, peace, and equality can be realized for all people.

If Mississippi had remained a predominantly black state, the dynamics of political power and opportunities would likely be significantly different. With a majority, African Americans would have been able to elect representatives who truly represented their interests, potentially altering policies to address systemic racism and socioeconomic disparities. A stronger political voice might have led to progressive reforms in education, healthcare, and economic infrastructure, turning the tide on centuries of disenfranchisement. The recognition and celebration of black culture, history, and achievements would have been more prevalent, challenging the deep-rooted narratives of racial inferiority. The ripple effect of such changes could have led to increased economic opportunities, breaking the cycle of poverty and systemic oppression. The power structures entrenched in Mississippi's history is a story about untapped potential that was stifled by racial prejudice and fear. This history underscores the critical role of representation and inclusivity in shaping a society's trajectory.

Hebrew prophets often referred to the destruction of cities and communities as metaphors for the Day of the Lord, a compelling narrative tool to deliver its eschatological teachings. For example, in the Old Testament, Isaiah 13:6 states, "Wail, for the day of the LORD is near; it will come like destruction from the Almighty." This verse is a part of a prophecy concerning Babylon, predicting its impending doom as a manifestation of God's divine judgment.

Similarly, Zephaniah 1:14-15 reads, "The great Day of the LORD is near, near and coming quickly. The cry on the day of the LORD is bitter; the Mighty Warrior shouts his battle cry. That day will be a day of wrath, a day of distress and anguish, a day of trouble and ruin, a day of darkness and gloom, a day of clouds and blackness." This passage uses the destruction of the city of Jerusalem as a metaphor for the Day of the Lord, linking the city's downfall to the larger theme of divine retribution.

Jerusalem's destruction, according to the prophet, was a cataclysmic event, seen as a manifestation of the Day of the Lord. This perspective was not merely limited to the biblical era but has been echoed throughout history, often interpreted as divine retribution against immorality and sin. The tragic downfall of

Jerusalem was seen as an end of an epoch, leading many to perceive this as an end of the world scenario, a common theme in eschatological teachings.

In the New Testament, there are passages that directly tie the destruction of Jerusalem to the end times. For instance, in the Gospel of Matthew 24:1-2, Jesus says, "Truly I tell you, not one stone here will be left on another; everyone will be thrown down." This prophecy of the destruction of the Jerusalem Temple, which came true in 70 AD, is often interpreted as symbolic of the end of the world.

Luke 21:20-24 offers another poignant example, "When you see Jerusalem being surrounded by armies, you will know that its desolation is near... This is the time of punishment in fulfillment of all that has been written." Here, the fall of Jerusalem is depicted as a cataclysmic event, a time of divine punishment, resonating with the concept of 'the end times'.

Finally, Revelation 11:1-2 reads, "I was given a reed like a measuring rod and was told, 'Go and measure the temple of God and the altar... But exclude the outer court; do not measure it, because it has been given to the Gentiles. They will trample on the holy city for 42 months.'" This passage, considered by many to be a prophetic depiction of Jerusalem's downfall, also hints at the grand scheme of the world's end and divine judgement.

While the ancient prophets may not directly reflect the experiences of colonized and oppressed populations, their underlying themes of destruction, punishment, loss, and despair echo the sentiments felt by these communities. When we consider the African diaspora's experiences of cities being razed and communities decimated due to the trans-Atlantic slave trade, we begin to see parallels with the biblical destruction of Jerusalem.

In the American theological imagination, the apocalypse is often forecast as a moment when the dominant world senses the erosion of its own power—a self-centered eschatology in which the "last days" are signaled not by justice denied, but by privilege disrupted. Yet, for Black communities, the apocalypse has already come—in fire, erasure, and forgotten glory. It came when Black

Wall Streets were bombed, when cities like Rosewood and Elaine were silenced, and when cultural centers were buried beneath concrete or memory. Chancellor Williams names this erasure with prophetic clarity: *"Who remembered Thebes, Napata, Memphis, Elephantine, Heracleopolis or Nekheb? Indeed, who remembered even Meroe, the most advanced center not only of the African age, but also of writing?"*[27] The question itself is a lament. It is the voice of the ancestor thundering through time: the true apocalypse is not merely in cataclysmic judgment—it is in the theft of memory, in the desecration of sacred Black geographies, in the systematic unremembering of African greatness. This is what the Day of the Lord looks like when told from the underside of history.

As they witnessed the obliteration of their societies, they might have interpreted these devastating events through a lens similar to that of eschatology. Just like the downfall of Jerusalem, the destruction of African American cities and the inhumane treatment of their people could have been perceived as an apocalyptic event - a catastrophic ending to their world as they knew it.

It's worth noting that, for these communities, the oppression didn't end with the destruction of their cities - it continued in the form of the military draft, police brutality, and economic trickery. This sustained period of suffering and endurance could be likened to the biblical prophecy of 'Gentiles trampling the holy city for 42 months.' In both cases, there's a sense of enduring tribulation and injustice.

Negro spirituals, a powerful form of African American folk music, add another layer to the discourse on eschatology and the enduring effects of trauma. These songs, born out of the depths of despair and suffering endured during slavery, are imbued with an eschatological vision that reflects the black experience of trauma.

Additionally, the blues music provides significant insight into the black experience of pain and trauma. These genres, steeped in

---

[27] Chancellor Williams, *The Destruction of Black Civilization: Great Issues of a Race from 4500 B.C. to 2000 A.D.* (Chicago: Third World Press, 1987)

the painful history of slavery and oppression, articulate the anguish of their creators. Through haunting melodies and poignant lyrics, these songs convey a deep sense of despair, sorrow, and a longing for liberation.

Moreover, the Negro spiritual, *Sometimes I Feel Like a Motherless Child*, resonates deeply within the context of African American history, eschatology, and the pervasive themes of despair and longing for freedom. The song speaks to a profound sense of abandonment, akin to that of a child bereft of their mother's love and protection. It is a metaphorical expression of the bone- deep loneliness and desolation felt by those subjected to slavery and oppression. The phrase *I wish I was never born* underscores the intensity of this despair, echoing the biblical lamentations of Job, and suggesting an existential yearning to escape the hardships of their world. Thus, this spiritual is a poignant cry for liberation and a testament to the indomitable spirit of a people who, in the face of relentless suffering, held onto hope and resilience.

Such spirituals often drew from biblical narratives of deliverance, mirroring the African American yearning for freedom. Songs like 'Swing Low, Sweet Chariot' and 'Wade in the Water' echo the Israelites' journey from bondage to the promised land, symbolizing the slaves' hope for release from their own bondage.

Similarly, blues music, born out of the hardships of the post-slavery era, encapsulates the black experience of pain in a raw, unsettling manner. The mournful tones and lyrics of blues songs reflect a spectrum of emotions - from deep sorrow to stoic endurance and a defiant spirit. For instance, B.B. King's 'Nobody Loves Me but My Mother' speaks of loneliness and rejection, while Robert Johnson's 'Cross Road Blues' explores themes of desperation and existential crisis.

In essence, negro spirituals and blues music serve as a poignant chronicle of black trauma and pain, offering a window into the African American experience of suffering and resilience under the weight of systemic racism and oppression. It's important to recognize the centuries-long legacy of racism and oppression experienced by African Americans as deeply connected to their interpretations of eschatology.

Contextually speaking, eschatology may serve not as a prophecy of end times, but as a revelation, another way to define apocalypse, or a framework for understanding and interpreting the profound suffering and upheaval experienced by oppressed populations over centuries. This perspective provides a basis for challenging the Eurocentric narratives that dominate eschatological teachings, and for incorporating the experiences of those who have been marginalized and oppressed into theological discourse.

Equating the biblical cities which were destroyed with the destruction of black cities offers a compelling, albeit tragic, parallel. From Tulsa in the USA, where a thriving black community was decimated during the infamous Tulsa Race Riot of 1921, to the violent pillaging of African civilizations during the colonial era, one can perceive a similar pattern of devastation and loss. Like Jerusalem, these cities and communities were prosperous centers of culture, commerce, and life—until they were unjustly razed, and their inhabitants subjected to unthinkable atrocities.

For the victims and survivors, the destruction of these communities was their end of the world, a Day of the Lord fraught with wrath and judgment. It's a chilling reminder of the systemic racism, oppression, and violence that have afflicted black communities for centuries—a reality that, much like Jerusalem's destruction, demands recognition and response.

These scriptures serve as a reminder that the Day of the Lord is often portrayed as a day of reckoning, where wrongs are righted, and justice is served. It is this search for divine justice that resonates with those who seek solace and redemption in the face of oppression and injustice. In the Old Testament perspective, the city of Jerusalem deserved their destruction, but none of our griots or prophets would agree we deserve our destruction. The eschatological promise of a day of reckoning provides hope for those who have been historically marginalized and oppressed.

Gentrification has emerged as another form of systemic oppression, devastating black communities in the modern era.

Originating under the guise of urban renewal, it effectively displaces marginalized communities, erasing their history, culture, and social fabric. This trend can be seen from Harlem in New York to Brixton in London—once vibrant black neighborhoods have now transformed into spaces catering to affluent, predominantly white demographics.

The process of gentrification goes far beyond the mere physical displacement of black communities. It's a form of cultural erasure that undermines the identity, heritage, and collective memory of these communities. Not unlike the pillaging of African civilizations during the colonial era, gentrification wipes clean the slate of history, leaving only the narrative of the privileged.

In the wake of this dislocation and cultural erasure, black communities suffer from increased inequality, economic instability, and social isolation. The loss of affordable housing and the uprooting of longstanding communities compound the existing socio-economic challenges. These realities echo the eschatological themes of destruction and disarray, raising new questions about justice, morality, and the promise of a better future. As such, gentrification becomes yet another chapter in the larger narrative of systemic oppression and racial injustice that has defined black history in the Eurocentric world.

The implications of gentrification on future generations cannot be understated. Unquestionably, displacing marginalized communities, gentrification diminishes the social capital of these communities, dismantling support systems and networks that have been built over generations. Moreover, it reinforces social and economic disparities, as rising property values and living costs often result in a cycle of poverty that continues into the next generation. Children and youth in gentrified neighborhoods find their family roots and cultural heritage gradually stripped away, replaced by unfamiliar customs and structures that cater to the privileged. This generational loss of identity can lead to feelings of alienation and disconnection, with potentially detrimental effects on mental health and social development.

In an economic sense, gentrification disrupts the potential for wealth accumulation in marginalized communities. Home ownership, a traditional method of building wealth, has become an unattainable dream for many displaced families due to skyrocketing property prices. This forms a barrier to the transference of wealth and security to subsequent generations, further exacerbating the socio-economic divide.

Contextually speaking, the apocalyptic impacts of gentrification resonate deeply with themes of displacement, destruction, and the struggle for redemption. It underlines the need for equitable urban development policies that respect and preserve cultural diversity, promote social inclusion, and provide opportunities for prosperity for all, irrespective of race or social standing.

One poignant example of the devastating impact of gentrification can be found in the historical African American neighborhood of Harlem, New York City. Once renowned as a vibrant hub of African American culture, Harlem has witnessed a disquieting pattern of displacement over the years. Rising property prices, driven by an influx of wealthier, predominantly white residents and businesses, have made it increasingly difficult for the original inhabitants to maintain their homes and livelihoods.

Throughout the 20th century, Harlem served as a beacon of black pride and creativity, birthing a cultural renaissance that deeply influenced American art, literature, and music. However, the unchecked gentrification of the late 20th and early 21st centuries has significantly diluted the neighborhood's cultural richness and legacy.

This displacement has had profound social implications for the African American community in Harlem. Families that had lived in the neighborhood for generations have been forced to relocate, their close-knit networks disrupted and their sense of community eroded. For many, the process has been symbolic of a broader pattern of systemic racism and social injustice, signifying the erasure of their heritage and identity.

The gentrification of Harlem began on a noticeable scale in the late 20th century, particularly in the 1980s and 1990s. This period saw an influx of wealthier outsiders attracted by lower property prices, triggering a cycle of rising rents and property values. It was a period marked by significant socioeconomic change, stimulated by urban regeneration projects and private investment that, while revitalizing the neighborhood, also inadvertently displaced long-term residents.

Manifold are the struggles faced by the displaced. The loss of their homes goes beyond a mere physical displacement; it signifies a disruption of their social fabric and an unsettling sense of alienation. Many have been forced to relocate to unfamiliar neighborhoods, often ones with inadequate social infrastructure and fewer opportunities. Displacement also fragments tight-knit community networks, further isolating individuals and families. Moreover, those displaced often grapple with the psychological impact of their erasure from a neighborhood intrinsically tied to their identities, leading to feelings of dislocation and loss. The gentrification of Harlem is a stark reminder of the overlooked casualties of urban progress, a narrative repeated in cities across the globe.

Numerous historic buildings destroyed due to the gentrification of Harlem are tangible reminders of the community's rich cultural history. Iconic structures like the Renaissance Ballroom and Casino, a hub for Black social life during the Harlem Renaissance, were demolished to make way for luxury condominiums. Similarly, the neo-Gothic style Mount Morris Bank Building, an architectural gem from the early 20th century, was replaced by a modern retail complex. The Lafayette Theatre, once a celebrated venue of Black arts and performances, too fell victim to the relentless march of gentrification. This loss of architectural heritage symbolizes not just the erasure of physical structures but the gradual disappearance of Harlem's vibrant cultural legacy, further exacerbating the sense of displacement felt by the community.

Harlem represented more than just a geographical location for the Black community; it was a beacon of cultural identity, hope, and resistance. A refuge for many African Americans fleeing the racial oppression of the South, Harlem became a vibrant hub of Black culture, creativity, and intellectualism, birthing the renowned Harlem Renaissance. It was here that luminaries such as Langston Hughes, Zora Neale Hurston, and Duke Ellington rose to prominence, their artistry echoing the triumphs and struggles of their people. Harlem gave voice to the silenced, power to the oppressed, and recognition to the overlooked. It was, and to many remains, a potent symbol of Black identity, resilience, and the will to rise against oppression. The gentrification of Harlem, then, signifies not merely the loss of homes and historical buildings, but the erasure of a vital piece of Black heritage and identity.

Sadly, the gentrification of Harlem has not just physically altered the neighborhood, but it has also profoundly affected the pride and community spirit that were once its defining features. As wealthier inhabitants move in, their influence overrules the historical and cultural significance of Harlem, essentially commodifying a legacy that is steeped in struggle, resilience, and triumph. This change in demographics prioritizes economic gain over preserving the rich tapestry of Harlem's heritage. Like Harlem, more recently Atlanta, also referred to by its Black citizens as "The ATL," is no longer the Black mecca, as it has lost its status as a majority black city due to gentrification.

From the post-Civil War era through the mid-20th century, it is estimated that over 200 Black towns and settlements were systematically destroyed, displaced, and gentrified. These communities, many of which were flourishing centers of Black culture and economic activity, were subjected to racial violence, unjust legal actions, and economic dispossession by white supremacists and structurally racist policies. Destruction or gentrification of these communities resulted in significant loss of Black wealth, displacement of families, and erasure of cultural heritage. This historical injustice continues to reverberate in contemporary patterns of racial and economic disparities in the United States.

In essence, gentrification has sent a clear message that money and privilege often wield greater influence than the value of people and their history. This trend undermines community pride, as the unique narrative of a place and its people are swept aside in favor of a more homogenized, commercially appealing identity. Not only does this erode the collective memory and identity of a community, but it also perpetuates systemic oppression, reinforcing the notion that prosperity and progress are exclusive to certain demographics. This phenomenon is a representation of the persistent injustices that still pervade society, particularly concerning race, wealth, and privilege. It serves as a call to action to rectify these imbalances and restore dignity to those marginalized in their own homes and communities.

Similarly, the destruction of Jerusalem, including its sacred temple and protective walls, was a catastrophic event for the people of Judah. The despair and desolation they felt is mirrored in the Psalms, in verses showing a profound sense of loss, grief, and desolation. They felt as if their world had ended, their spiritual and cultural heart ripped out. This sentiment is embodied in Psalm 137:1: "By the rivers of Babylon, there we sat down and wept, when we remembered Zion."

The Babylonians, under the reign of Nebuchadnezzar II, were oppressively brutal in their destruction of Jerusalem and treatment of its inhabitants. The city was besieged, its walls torn down, and the sacred Temple of Solomon was razed to the ground. This wanton destruction marked an attempt not only to assert political dominance but also to erase the spiritual and cultural identity of the Judeans.

Babylonian captivity of the people of Judah further demonstrated this oppressive force. The exiles were forcibly removed from their homeland and made to live in a strange and foreign land. They were stripped of their cultural and religious freedoms, and their forced assimilation into Babylonian society represented a denial of their unique identity. This oppression wasn't merely physical, but psychological and cultural, a form of violence that sought to erase their existence and history. The rivers of Babylon, therefore, came to symbolize a place of sorrow, a painful reminder of home, and a testament to the oppressive forces they were subjected to. To them it was an end of days apocalypse, a dark age from which there was no escape.

Their anguish was deepened by the desecration of their holy places. The temple, a tangible symbol of God's presence among them, was laid waste, leaving them feeling abandoned and without spiritual guidance. Similarly, their once-great city, the epitome of their cultural and national pride, was reduced to rubble. This mirrored their status as a nation - downtrodden, defeated, and dispersed.

The destruction of the Temple in Jerusalem and the burning of Black churches by white supremacists may be seen as parallel instances of violence aimed at erasing cultural and spiritual identity. Both acts reflect an attempt to dominate, subjugate, and erase the existence and history of a marginalized group. Black churches, like the Temple, served not just as places of worship, but also as symbols of community, places of education, and platforms for activism, particularly during the Civil Rights Movement. The burning of these churches was a blatant act of terror, designed to impose fear and exert control.

According to the National Fire Protection Association, an estimated 1,780 fires occur at religious and funeral properties in the U.S. per year. While not all of these are acts of arson or racially motivated, a significant number of Black churches have been targeted throughout history.

Between 1995 and 1996 alone, following a high-profile series of arsons at Black churches, the Center for Democratic Renewal identified around 300 suspicious church fires. These destructive acts were not just attacks on buildings, but targeted assaults on a community's faith, resilience, and sense of security. Much like the Babylonian destruction of the Temple in Jerusalem, these events served to oppress and attempt to erase the identity of a people, demonstrating the power dynamics of racism and white supremacy.

During the Civil Rights Movement of the 1960s, the bombing of Black churches was a widespread and horrifying phenomenon. According to historical accounts, at least 45 bombings occurred at

Black churches and locations associated with the civil rights fight between 1955 and 1965 alone. The most notorious of these was the 16th Street Baptist Church bombing in Birmingham, Alabama, on September 15, 1963, which claimed the lives of four young girls and injured many others. The names of the four girls, who were between 11 to 14 years old, were Addie Mae Collins, Denise McNair, Cynthia Wesley and Carole Robertson.

These terroristic acts represented a kind of community apocalypse for Black congregants and community members. The church, a place of worship, refuge, and community, was transformed into a site of violence and terror. These bombings were not just physical attacks, but psychological warfare aimed at suppressing the quest for civil rights, instilling fear, and enforcing white supremacy. The bombing of Black churches during this era exemplified the monstrous face of racism, illustrating its capacity to infiltrate even the most sacred communal spaces. It was a stark reminder of the collective trauma inflicted upon the Black community; a trauma echoed throughout eschatological narratives.

The same oppressive forces have been felt by many cultures throughout history. Indigenous people who were colonized and enslaved, African Americans who were lynched and discriminated against, Jews who were persecuted and murdered during the Holocaust—all these victims of oppression experienced their own rivers of Babylon. In each case, we can see a clear example of how power and privilege were used to oppress and erase the identities of those who were different. Black people who have been displaced from their historic communities can relate to these passages because they too have experienced a kind of exile from their own homes. This occurred during the destruction, displacement and gentrification of their historic locations, a very real form of oppression that has been ignored and overlooked for centuries.

This period was an 'end of days' for them, a brutal awakening to the depths of despair and desolation that they never thought they would experience. Yet, even in their darkest hour, the Psalms also carry a spark of hope - a longing for restoration and deliverance that eventually shapes their resilience and determination to rebuild what was lost.

The Book of Revelation in the Bible contains a prophecy often interpreted as predicting the demise of one third of the Roman Empire. In Revelation 9:15, it states: "And the four angels who had been kept ready for this very hour and day and month and year were released to kill a third of mankind." This verse is generally linked with the 'Trumpet Judgments' described in the preceding verses, where a series of cataclysmic events are unleashed on the world as seven angels sound their trumpets. The conditions that led to the demise of the Roman Empire, due its colonization of the world, which was met by this trumpet warning by the early Christians should speak a word to imperialism today. Indeed, history repeats itself.

From a Preterist perspective, Revelation 9:15 is viewed in a historical context, asserting that the prophecies in the Book of Revelation were fulfilled in the first century AD. This approach interprets the "third of mankind" as a reference to the Roman Empire, a dominant power during this time. This cataclysmic event described could be a metaphor for the political, social, and spiritual upheaval experienced during the downfall of the Roman Empire. The "four angels" are seen as symbolic of divine agents of judgment, their release indicating the culminating point of God's retribution on the oppressive Roman regime. This preterist understanding deems these prophetic visions not as foretelling the end of the world in a literal sense, but rather as coded messages of hope and liberation for early Christians enduring severe persecution under Roman rule.

The devastation wrought upon the innocent echoes through the ages, reverberating far beyond individual lives to touch entire nations. When societies are built on foundations of oppression, genocide, and erasure of identities, the destructive forces unleashed are not only physical but also profoundly spiritual and cultural. This is a stark testament to the interconnectedness of humanity; we are woven together in a garment of destiny, our fates interlinked in ways that transcend geographical boundaries and epochs.

Applying this understanding to the passage from Revelation 9:15, one might perceive the prophesied destruction of a third of mankind not merely as a literal cataclysm, but as a metaphorical reflection of the societal and spiritual decay resulting from pervasive injustice and oppression. It paints a grim picture of a society that, having turned a blind eye to the suffering of its most vulnerable members, now finds itself on the brink of self-destruction.

In this context, the inevitable repercussions of systemic evils such as racism, slavery, lynching, and economic disenfranchisement, which have left deep scars on the collective psyche of mankind are brought to view. This concept, deeply rooted in eschatology, serves as a sobering reminder that the injustices we allow to persist today can sow the seeds of our own future destruction.

Dr. Martin Luther King Jr.'s famously insightful warning that if we don't *learn to live together as brothers, we will perish together as fools,* strongly resonates within this a certain narrative. It echoes the core eschatological view that societal and spiritual decay, resulting from systemic injustices including racism, slavery, and lynching, could lead to our collective destruction. Dr. King's admonition is a call to unity, driving home the point that our survival hinges not only on the eradication of these deeply entrenched evils, but also on the establishment of a society founded on equality, respect, and mutual understanding. Thus, in the grand scheme of eschatology, his words can be seen as a prophetic warning against self-inflicted apocalyptic scenarios stemming from continued oppression and division.

Malcolm X made a statement that "chickens coming home to roost" after the assassination of President John F. Kennedy. This statement was deemed controversial at the time, but Malcolm X was drawing parallels to the law of causality - that every action has an effect. The phrase "chickens coming home to roost" is an idiom indicating that deeds or actions, particularly ill-intended, or sinful ones will inevitably return to impact the originator.

As Malcolm X suggested, these systemic evils have been

perpetrated for centuries by dominant powers, and the repercussions are inescapable. In the frame of eschatology, his words underscore the notion that the collective moral decay, manifested through incessant oppression and division, could lead to our collective destruction. The "chickens coming home to roost" implies that the continuous disregard for the value of human life and dignity by the oppressors will eventually result in the downfall of dominant powers.

We can see this principle in the gospels as well - Jesus repeatedly warned his followers of the consequences of their actions, emphasizing that they would reap what they sow. This sentiment is echoed by Malcolm X's words, and it serves as a reminder that justice will ultimately prevail against those who continue to oppress other human beings. As we look back on the long legacy of racism, oppression, and genocide, it is essential to remember that the chickens will indeed come home to roost. In this way, we can ensure that justice prevails, and history doesn't repeat itself. It is also worth noting that Malcolm X's words were a warning for those who perpetrate injustice and disregard Black life as disposable. His words remind us of the importance of eliminating harm and working together to bring about a more equitable world. This is ultimately what eschatology teaches us: that in order to create a better future, we must learn from our past mistakes and be mindful of the consequences of our actions. In this way, we can work towards creating a positive legacy for generations to come.

One of the most salient instances of the 'end of days' experience for black people can be found in the devastation caused by the prison industrial complex. This system, intrinsically linked with practices of systemic racism and injustice, has led to an alarmingly high proportion of black men being removed from their homes and communities. Consequently, the very fabric of these communities is left frayed and tattered, echoing the prophetic warnings of eschatology.

Cruelly, the prison industrial complex, a term coined to describe the overlapping interests of government and industry that use surveillance, policing, and imprisonment as solutions to economic, social, and political problems, disproportionately targets black men. As a result, fathers, sons, and brothers are taken from their homes, leaving behind a vacuum that reverberates through the lives of those left behind, destabilizing family structures and community cohesion.

Mass incarceration not only represents a physical removal but also an erasure of black men from society's narrative, akin to a form of social death. The repercussions are far-reaching and multi-dimensional, negatively affecting the socioeconomic status of these communities, their access to resources, and their overall well-being. This scenario illustrates an 'end of days' experience as it reflects an extensive and systematic form of oppression, which, in the context of eschatology, serves as a stark warning of the consequences of human actions, particularly those driven by prejudice and hatred.

The phenomenon of mass incarceration is not a historical relic confined to the 1990s but persists with alarming intensity in the present day. It has historically manifested in a variety of forms, from the school-to-prison pipeline that disproportionately affects students of color to the three-strikes laws, which mandate life sentences for individuals convicted of a felony after two prior convictions. The war on drugs, despite evidence of similar rates of drug use across diverse racial and ethnic groups, still disproportionately incarcerates black men, perpetuating a cycle of systemic racism.

While there have been minimal changes in policy aimed at reducing mass incarceration since the 1990s, the reality is that the system has largely remained the same, or in some cases, worsened. Initiatives intended to lessen the prison population, like the Fair Sentencing Act or the First Step Act, have been approved, but these laws only scratch the surface of the problem and fail to address the systemic racism deeply ingrained in the criminal justice system.

Moreover, the advent of private prisons has created an industry that profits from the incarceration of individuals, often with contracts stipulating that prisons must remain a certain percentage full. This profit-driven model exacerbates the problem by creating a demand for prisoners that bears no relation to actual crime rates or societal needs.

Furthermore, the use of technology, such as predictive policing and risk assessment algorithms, has introduced a new level of racial bias. These tools, which are supposed to predict criminal behavior, often reinforce existing prejudices and stereotypes, leading to a higher rate of surveillance and arrests in communities of color. Despite being cloaked in the guise of objective science; these systems perpetuate and amplify oppressive practices. Simultaneously, the rise of the immigration detention industry has expanded the reach of mass incarceration, targeting, and criminalizing non-native populations in a manner reminiscent of the war on drugs. This expansion has swept up black non-natives, regardless of documentation, without due process.

In essence, while some steps have been taken to mitigate the worst outcomes of mass incarceration, the problem has evolved and persisted, adapting to societal changes, and exploiting the most vulnerable in new and insidious ways.

Economic downturns often provide a convenient pretext for a surge in "tough on crime" rhetoric by politicians across the American political spectrum. In the face of financial insecurity and rising unemployment, punitive measures are intensified and presented as necessary to maintain order and safety. However, this approach disproportionately impacts poor communities and Black people, exacerbating existing racial and socio-economic disparities.

Despite the visceral appeal of hardline policies, there is scant evidence to suggest a correlation between increased incarceration and reduced crime rates. Instead, these measures often lead to a vicious cycle of poverty, crime, and recidivism, failing to address the root causes of criminal behavior such as socio-economic inequality, lack of educational opportunities, and systemic racism. Rather than fostering safer communities, this approach further entrenches structural inequities, penalizing the economically disadvantaged and perpetuating a cycle of oppression that echoes historical practices of slavery, lynching, and genocide.

In the context of eschatological interpretations, this recurring pattern of oppression and marginalization presents a poignant critique of the dominant Euro-American perspectives, challenging the premise that societal deterioration and immorality are signs of the 'end times.' For those communities that have been subjected to centuries of colonization, exploitation, and erasure, the 'worst' is a historical continuity rather than a prophesied future.

Disparities in sentencing laws also continue to contribute to the overrepresentation of black men in prisons. For instance, offenses related to crack cocaine, a substance more commonly used in black communities owing to socio-economic factors, carry harsher sentences compared to powdered cocaine, a drug more commonly used in white communities. This bias in the judicial system is a clear testament to the ongoing racial discrimination that fuels mass incarceration.

In essence, the diabolical and godless machinery of mass incarceration, fueled by systemic oppression and racism, continues to churn unabated, marking a grim 'end of days' reality for our "nation within a nation."

This is far from the apocalyptic prophecy often associated with eschatology, but it is an apocalyptic reality for those living through it.

The racial targeting within the prison industrial complex is deeply rooted in systemic racism, a historical legacy that has witnessed the criminalization of black men. It is slavery in another form. This bias is not an accidental occurrence, but a reflection of ingrained stereotypes that perceive black men as inherently more dangerous or criminal.

Statistical evidence substantiates this racial disparity. According to a report released by the NAACP, African Americans are incarcerated at more than five times the rate of white Americans.[28] In 2014, African Americans constituted 2.3 million,

---

[28] NAACP, "Criminal Justice Fact Sheet," accessed May 24, 2025,

or 34% of the total 6.8 million correctional population, despite only making up about 13% of the U.S population. This stark disproportionality points towards an underlying bias in the criminal justice system, where black men are especially targeted and overrepresented.

The 'War on Drugs', initiated in the 1970s, further illuminates this racial targeting. Although studies have consistently shown that illicit drug use among white and black Americans is roughly comparable, African Americans are six times more likely to be incarcerated for drug- related offenses than their white counterparts. This over-policing and harsh sentencing of black communities for drug offenses have had devastating consequences, contributing significantly to the mass incarceration of black men. In essence, the prison industrial complex serves as a modern-day mechanism for continued enslavement and cultural genocide, targeting black men and perpetuating a cycle of marginalization, disenfranchisement, and social inequality.

Abolitionists argue that the prison system exacerbates societal issues rather than resolving them. They posit that prisons do not effectively rehabilitate offenders but instead foster a cycle of criminality. This criticism stems from the belief that the punitive nature of prisons does not address the root causes of criminal behavior, such as socioeconomic inequality, lack of education, and systemic racism. Instead, it stigmatizes and marginalizes incarcerated individuals, making it more challenging for them to reintegrate into society post-imprisonment.

Furthermore, abolitionists advocate for the confinement of only those criminals who have committed violent offenses, seeing alternatives to incarceration as more effective for non- violent offenders. They suggest approaches such as restorative justice, community service, and drug rehabilitation programs, which focus on reparation and rehabilitating offenders. This perspective emphasizes that holistic, community-centered solutions can help

---

https://www.naacp.org/criminal-justice-fact-sheet/.

break the cycle of recidivism, reduce crime rates, and foster a more equitable justice system.

The evidence presented paints a vivid picture of a social apocalypse for black people, particularly black men. In this context, social apocalypse is characterized by the systematic erasure of a community's rights, dignity, and potential for progression. This form of social devastation is not marked by a singular catastrophic event, but instead, it steadily manifests over time, gradually eroding the fabric of the affected community.

Mass incarceration of black men, driven by systemic racism and racial targeting, is a clear exhibition of such a social apocalypse. It creates a vicious cycle where black men are thrust into the criminal justice system, often for minor offenses, which then limits their future opportunities, reinforces stereotypes, and perpetuates socioeconomic disparity. Amazingly, those who state that America is a Christian nation, wholeheartedly support the Carceral state, which is antithetical to the Christian gospel which "sets captives free."

This condition of chronic oppression and marginalization is akin to a social end of days, a continuous state of crisis for the black community. The slow, steady genocide seen in the prison industrial complex is a testament to this, perpetuating oppression and effectively erasing the potential for many black men to contribute to society. Thus, the alarming statistics and practices of the criminal justice system symbolize a black social apocalypse.

In the realm of eschatology, the Bible often utilizes the metaphors of imprisonment and chains. The apostle Paul, for instance, in 2 Timothy 2:9, refers to himself as a prisoner as he writes, "for which I am suffering, bound with chains as a criminal. But the word of God is not bound!" His literal incarceration illustrates a spiritual reality, the confinement of human potential under systemic oppression, and yet, the enduring power of the divine truth.

Within Revelation, chains have apocalyptic implications. Revelation 20:1-2 depicts an angel coming down from heaven, holding in his hand the key to the bottomless pit and a great chain.

He seized the dragon and bound him for a thousand years, symbolizing the eventual restraint of evil powers. This temporary binding of Satan is an eschatological prophecy, forecasting a period of relative peace before the final battle between good and evil. This prophecy shows how it is the diabolical forces of racism, white supremacy, colonialism, and economic exploitation that ought to be chained in the divine scheme of things and not God's beautiful Black children or those that have been historically colonized.

Ultimately, this dark age of history and legacy should be seen as a call to action; the suffering of one's fellow human cannot be ignored in favor of abstract theological interpretations. It is only through collective struggle against racial injustice that we can hope to create a just society where the last days can give way to a new age of "milk and honey" for everybody. Moreover, Isaiah 42:7 gives a prophecy about the role of the Messiah as one to open blind eyes, bring out the prisoners from the dungeon, and those who sit in darkness from the prison. This prophecy reveals the divine intention of liberation from all forms of oppression and captivity. Seen in a broader context, such passages from the Old Testament challenge the narrative of eschatology that focuses solely on European and American experiences, reminding us of God's concern for the oppressed and his promise of ultimate deliverance.

These scriptures, while they speak of physical chains and imprisonment, also carry a deeper, spiritual significance. They resonate with the experiences of African Americans who have been metaphorically 'chained' by systemic injustice and oppression. Yet the promise of liberation, inherent in these prophecies, brings hope for an impending deliverance from the chains of oppression.

Chapter 6

LEFT BEHIND AND THE ANTI-BLACK CHRIST

Due to ignorance and biblical illiteracy, the Eurocentric "Left Behind" movie has had a profound impact on the Evangelical community, which has largely embraced its narrative. This movie, rooted in the Euro-American worldview, presents an apocalyptic scenario where millions of Christians are suddenly raptured, leaving the world in chaos. It paints a picture of imminent tribulation and the rise of the Antichrist, reinforcing the belief in a literal interpretation of biblical end times prophecies.

This acceptance is indicative of the Euro-American dominance in interpreting eschatological narratives. The premise of the "Left Behind" series, with its emphasis on the Rapture and Tribulation, could only work within a Euro-American setting, as it reflects their experiences and fears, while marginalizing other historical and cultural contexts. It fails to address the tribulations that colonized and oppressed communities have been enduring for centuries, thus reinforcing both the overt and subtle racism ingrained in much of the American evangelical eschatological beliefs.

As a result, the series perpetuates an insular and Eurocentric interpretation of biblical prophecies, neglecting the diverse and multicultural nature of the global Christian community and the varied experiences of suffering and hope that each contributes to the broader understanding of eschatology.

The "Left Behind" series, upon which the movie was based, was co-authored by Tim LaHaye and Jerry B. Jenkins. LaHaye, a renowned evangelical minister, and Jenkins, an accomplished Christian fiction writer, brought to the series a distinct theological perspective deeply rooted in Dispensational Premillennialism. This branch of eschatological thought asserts that the rapture of Christian believers will occur prior to a seven-year tribulation period, following which Christ will return to establish a 1000-year reign on Earth. This interpretation forms the narrative backbone of the "Left Behind" series. However, it is important to note that while this perspective is prevalent among many Evangelicals, it is not a universally accepted interpretation of biblical end times prophecies and is often criticized.

Many scholars have voiced their criticism towards the "Left Behind" series, largely focusing on its American-centric world view. One key critique is that the series propagates a form of 'religious nationalism', in which the notion of Christian faith becomes inextricably linked with American identity, thereby marginalizing Christians of other cultural backgrounds. The series embeds a troubling geopolitical message, positing that the United States is God's chosen nation, thus perpetuating a narrative of American exceptionalism.

Another criticism lies in the series' handling of non-Christian characters, who are predominantly portrayed as antagonists. This narrative choice inadvertently promotes an 'us versus them' mentality, suggesting that only those who adhere to a specific American evangelical interpretation of Christianity are truly 'saved'. This promotes religious arrogance rather than unity, thereby contradicting the universal message of love and acceptance preached by Christianity.

Finally, the series' depiction of the tribulation period is seen by some scholars as an amplification of Western fears and anxieties, rather than being a representation of global suffering. Critics argue that major global tragedies and injustices, such as genocide, slavery, and systemic racism, are largely ignored, whilst the focus remains on a hypothetical future calamity, which is depicted as being primarily detrimental to the Western world.

According to critics, the "Left Behind" series amplifies Western fears and anxieties by focusing on a future period of tribulation which is essentially a projection of Western-centric concerns. For instance, the depicted collapse of economy and government, widespread chaos, and the rise of a totalitarian regime resonate with anxieties embedded in Western societies about their established order being disrupted.

For many white individuals, the concept of totalitarianism is commonly associated with a loss of power and a shift in societal norms, transforming from an ethnocentric perspective where they are the center to a more egalitarian setting. This shift constitutes a dismantling of systems where white individuals are no longer at the top but are equal members of society. It's a change from a society where whites define the normative standard to one where diverse experiences and perspectives are acknowledged and valued equally. They perceive this change in societal structure as the arrival of totalitarianism, an oppressive government system characterized by centralized power. However, it is crucial to note that this fear can be more accurately characterized as an unease about giving up deeply ingrained privileges rather than a genuine concern for the erosion of democratic ideals. Politically speaking, more recently, the Euro-Evangelical voting public has shown their acceptance of retribution-oriented authoritarian leadership in the White House should it promise to keep them in power while targeting those they don't agree with.

It is indeed remarkable to observe the fear within white evangelical communities of a prospective totalitarian regime stripping away their rights. This apprehension, often expressed in apocalyptic or eschatological terms, seems to overlook the historical and ongoing reality of systemic racism and anti-Black violence in the United States and beyond. Countless Black people have, for centuries, lived under the oppressive yoke of totalitarian white supremacy, with their basic human rights routinely violated. Every day, these individuals face the constant fear of being unjustly singled out, arrested, or subjected to even worse treatment, all because they happen to fit racially biased stereotypes. Black people in America find it difficult to imagine a totalitarian figure worse than what they endured during the Jim Crow era and the time of mass incarceration. The failure of the evangelical community to acknowledge this highlights a significant divide between those who have firsthand experience of systemic racism and those who do not. To bridge this gap, it is crucial to acknowledge the history of oppression faced by marginalized communities. This understanding will foster mutual respect and comprehension among individuals and groups with different backgrounds. Moreover, Christians should take the initiative to question and reflect upon these issues.

Moreover, it's striking to find in their eschatological framework an undercurrent of anxiety about the specter of communism. Meanwhile, the Black community has been living under a pervasive, violent anti-Black capitalistic system since the inception of American history. This system, in many ways, mirrors the oppressive aspects of totalitarian regimes that white evangelicals fear in their eschatological visions. Therefore, it is essential to realize the importance of reevaluating and broadening our perspective on eschatology to consider the lived experiences of oppressed communities.

Moreover, the series emphasizes the threat of a one-world government, often associated with fears of losing national sovereignty, a concern especially prevalent in American political discourse. The depiction of a one-world religion also plays into fears of religious syncretism and the erosion of Christian orthodoxy, concerns that echo particularly in the Western evangelical circles.

The concern over the loss of national sovereignty, as expressed predominantly by white evangelicals, stands in stark contrast to the ongoing struggle for individual sovereignty and self- determination by Black people. This worry about a one-world government eclipsing national autonomy appears inattentive to the fact that many Black communities are still striving for fundamental civil liberties and individual rights. In essence, the fear of losing national sovereignty often overshadows the reality that for the marginalized and oppressed, the quest for personal sovereignty remains an unachieved goal. It is vital to comprehend that while discussions around sovereignty for some are framed in the context of preserving existing privileges, for others it is a continuous battle for basic human dignity and freedom.

Jackson, Mississippi, among other majority-Black cities, offers a vivid case study of how systemic policies have repeatedly undermined their sovereignty and impeded their progress.

While many people remain oblivious to these systemic tactics, the state legislature's actions in Jackson, Mississippi demonstrate a glaring example of attempts to usurp control over a majority-Black city. Through manipulation of law enforcement and the judicial system, the state legislature has launched a silent offensive against the autonomy of the city. Deploying state police in disproportionate numbers and intensities in cities like Jackson is a tactic that symbolizes and reinforces the assertion of state power. This increased police presence often leads to escalated levels of arrests and convictions, perpetuating a cycle of systemic oppression.

The court system, too, has been weaponized as a tool for undermining the sovereignty of these majority-Black communities. Draconian laws, biased sentencing, and the denial of fair trials contribute to the perpetuation of a cycle where Black communities are disproportionately affected. This state-directed assault on Jackson's sovereignty is a stark reminder of the systemic and often insidious ways in which racism and oppression continue to operate.

State governments often intervene when Black mayors seek to implement policies for the betterment of their community. For example, the Alabama state legislature interfered with the vote for a living wage and has hampered attempts by local authorities about moving confederate statues.

In 2016, the city of Birmingham, Alabama, made a historic move to increase the minimum wage to $10.10 per hour. The decision was a victory for its predominantly Black workforce that had long been crippled by inflation and stagnating wages. However, the success was short-lived.

The Alabama state legislature swiftly passed a law banning individual cities from setting their own minimum wage, effectively blocking Birmingham's wage increase.

Subsequently, Black Birmingham mobilized, taking to the streets to protest this blatant act of overreach, demanding their rights to fair wages. This act of solidarity was more than just a fight for economic justice; it was a statement against the systemic oppression and racism deeply rooted in the state's actions.

The community's response was a powerful assertion of their right to self-determination, underscoring the ongoing struggle for equity and justice in the wake of colonialism and slavery. Their fight continues today, a testament to the indomitable spirit of those who have been marginalized and oppressed for centuries.

This situation presents a stark contradiction to the rhetoric often espoused by evangelical groups who champion local rights and decry governmental interference. These groups are frequently vocal about their belief in local sovereignty, yet their silence when state governments override local decisions that are beneficial to black communities is telling. This hypocritical stance is noteworthy because it exposes a selective application of their principles when the outcomes do not align with their entrenched beliefs or the status quo.

Jesus reserved his sharpest public rebukes not for sinners on the margins, but for the religious community who cloaked injustice in piety. His cry of "Woe to you, hypocrites" was not simply a theological disagreement; it was an indictment of those who manipulated divine truth to preserve power.[29] In today's political landscape, we see this spirit revived in the contradictions of voting Christians who champion federal overreach and authoritarianism when it secures their interests, but decry "big government" when it dares to enforce justice for the least of these.

When the city of Birmingham, Alabama, with deep historical wounds from racial and economic oppression—voted to raise its minimum wage to $10.10 an hour, the state government swiftly intervened to block the effort. Many of the same Christian voices that normally exalt "local control", and fear federal interference remained silent. Why? Because the status quo, not justice, was their true idol. They were comfortable with power from above—as long as it descended to protect wealth, not to lift the poor.

This selective theology reveals a spiritual crisis. It's not about the size of government—it's about the aim of government. When

---

[29] Matthew 23:23, *New Revised Standard Version Bible*, National Council of the Churches of Christ, 1989.

power is used to preserve inequity, and Christians cheer, we are watching an *apocalypse* unfold. Not the sensational kind with beasts and fire, but the biblical kind—a *revealing* of where the true allegiances lie. The hypocrisy is not benign; it erodes the soul of public witness. When Christians champion empire but resist equality, they betray the kingdom of God.

Jesus named this kind of duplicity clearly: neglecting the "weightier matters of the law—justice, mercy, and faith." It is these virtues, not partisan gain, that mark God's reign. The moral test of political theology is not whether it upholds personal comfort, but whether it embodies neighbor love and lifts the crushed.

In the case of Birmingham, the state's interference was not met with outrage or protest from these evangelical factions, revealing a cognitive dissonance between their preached values and their actions. This denial and refusal to honor local sovereignty when it comes to issues of racial and economic justice underscores a deep-seated bias that perpetuates the legacy of racism, oppression, and colonialism. It's a stark reminder of how these narratives of sovereignty and local rights are often weaponized to maintain systems of inequality, rather than to foster justice and equality as they claim.

Ironically, the narrative thread of evangelical eschatology often focuses on a prophesied future where autonomy and sovereignty are lost, a world in chaos, which they interpret as signs of the impending 'end times'. However, there is a glaring blind spot in this perspective, a profound disconnects with the lived experiences of the Black communities who have suffered under the weight of lost sovereignty for centuries due to oppressive systems rooted in racism and colonialism.

This blind spot, evident in the silence and inaction of these evangelical groups, exemplified in their response to the loss of local sovereignty in Birmingham is telling. Despite their fervent prophecies and sermons about the future loss of control, there was no outcry, no mobilization when the sovereignty of a predominantly Black community was blatantly usurped by state interference. This illustrates a jarring inconsistency between their eschatological teachings and their real- world reactions, revealing a deeply entrenched, systemic bias.

Tragically, blindness extends beyond the inability to see the existing loss of sovereignty among the oppressed. It includes a failure to relate their eschatological teachings to the historical and ongoing struggles of communities that have been subjected to the horrors of slavery, genocide and systemic racism. This lack of empathy and understanding is a stark example of the selective vision that perpetuates the cycle of oppression, obscuring the realities of the past and present while focusing on a distorted, Eurocentric interpretation of the future.

Finally, the portrayal of an Antichrist figure who arises from Europe, aligns with historical Western anxieties about the political power and influence of the European Union. Such narratives, critics argue, divert attention away from the real and present suffering experienced by marginalized communities worldwide due to systems of oppression instituted by Western powers themselves. Thus, the "Left Behind" series, in its focus on Western fears and anxieties, overlooks the broader global context of suffering and injustice, thereby skewing eschatological perspectives.

Unquestionably, the reality for America is the fact the African American community has been unjustly left behind as it relates to societal advancement. From the Transatlantic Slave Trade to Prison-for-Profit, African Americans have been continually marginalized in society. This is further seen in the number of African Americans who are incarcerated, as well as those living in poverty or lacking healthcare access and education opportunities. What's more, the modern threat of racial violence has led many in America to feel unsafe and unheard, a feeling that continues to be pervasive in communities of color across the United States.

Historically, the Compromise of 1877 marked a significant turning point, effectively ending the era of Reconstruction and leaving the recently emancipated African Americans to face the wrath of racial terror unfettered. It was an unwritten deal that resolved the intensely disputed 1876 presidential election and saw Republican Rutherford B. Hayes ascend to the presidency under the condition that federal troops be withdrawn from the South. This withdrawal cleared the way for the resurgence of white Southern Democratic rule, putting an abrupt end to the protections offered to African Americans during Reconstruction. With the federal troops gone, the South was free to enact a series of laws known as the Jim Crow laws, which mandated a comprehensive system of racial segregation. These laws not only disrupted the potential of the African American community but also denied them basic constitutional rights, reinforcing the racial hierarchy in the post-Civil War South. During this period, racial terror erupted unabated, with the establishment of the Ku Klux Klan and other white supremacist groups. Lynchings, racial violence, and mob riots became common occurrences, terrifying black communities and effectively disenfranchising them.

Beyond the physical terror, the Compromise of 1877 also had broader socio-economic implications. The lack of protection and rights for African Americans led to economic exploitation and deprivation, further deepening the racial divide. African Americans were largely left out of the economic growth and societal advancement of the late 19th and early 20th century, a legacy that continues to impact communities of color today. Thus, the Compromise of 1877 shows how racial terror, unleashed and unchecked, can lead to long-term marginalization and institutional oppression. The compromise with racist confederates in 1877 stands out as a real-world example of a left-behind tribulation. This enduring legacy of state-sanctioned racism continues to fuel the socio-economic disparities between whites and people of color in America today. It is crucial to recognize and address this historical injustice that has shaped our society.

One significant term, "Color Line," coined by W.E.B. Du Bois, aptly encapsulates the racial segregation and discrimination in America. Du Bois recognized the Color Line as a defining characteristic of the 20th century. Like the enduring legacy of the Compromise of 1877, the concept of the Color Line highlights how systemic racism has left an indelible mark on America's socio-economic fabric.

Color Line sociology, as defined by Du Bois, refers to the visible and invisible boundaries separating white and black communities. This racial barrier was fostered and perpetuated by the same power structures that enacted and enforced the Jim Crow laws, leaving a lasting impact on the lives and futures of African Americans. In essence, the Color Line and the legacy of the Compromise of 1877 are two sides of the same coin, both serving as stark reminders of America's historical and ongoing struggle with racism and inequality.

Du Bois' prediction of the "Color Line" as the problem of the 20th century was not only astute but also hauntingly prophetic. The escalating racial tensions and the stark wealth gap between white and black communities witnessed in the 20th century and beyond attest to the accuracy of his prediction. The systemic racism entrenched in the power structures implemented policies that systematically disadvantaged black communities, leaving them economically and socially marginalized.

W.E.B. Du Bois made his prediction about the "Color Line" being the problem of the 20th century in his widely admired book, "The Souls of Black Folk," published in 1903. This prophetically insightful statement was not a detached observation but a direct outgrowth of the Compromise of 1877. The compromise abruptly ended the Reconstruction era, leading to the withdrawal of federal troops from the South and abandoning the African American population to the mercy of white Southern leadership. The "Color Line," as outlined by Du Bois, was not only a reflection of this social segregation but also a grim prediction of the systemic racism that would pervade the 20th century and beyond.

This marginalization was evident in the housing and education disparities that were rampant throughout the century. Strict zoning laws and redlining practices significantly limited access to quality housing for black communities, leading to concentrated poverty and the creation of ghettos. The underfunding of schools in these areas further exacerbated the situation, providing subpar education and closing the door to upward mobility. Thus, Du Bois' "Color Line" has indeed left many behind, with the impact still resonating in the lives of countless individuals today. This persistent racial divide serves as a stark reminder that the tribulation is not an impending event, but rather a lived reality for those relegated to the wrong side of the "Color Line," which has been the experience of those colonized, oppressed and marginalized, not just over the last century, but for the past 400 years.

Just as the Compromise of 1877 facilitated the spread of racial terror and economic exploitation, the Color Line has perpetuated the deep-seated racial disparity in America. Both have contributed significantly to the socio-economic disparities between whites and people of color, maintaining an unjust system of privilege and oppression. Recognizing these historical injustices is the first step toward rectifying them and breaking down the lingering barriers of the Color Line.

Eric Betts

Chapter 7

FEAR OF A BLACK PLANET

Malcolm X, boldly prophesied about the persistent racism in America. He asserted that as long as the mindset of white superiority prevails, the struggle for racial equality will continue. He critiqued the anti-Black racism political and social structures in American life, which perpetuates inequality and oppression. He named those who perpetuate or normalize these systems as "devils." His words resonate today, echoing in the continued fight against racial disparities in education, employment, housing, and the justice system.

In truth, Malcolm X spoke extensively on the topic of Anti-Blackness and its impact on the African American community. He famously noted in one of his speeches, *If you stick a knife in my back nine inches and pull it out six inches, that's not progress. If you pull it all the way out, that's not progress. Progress is healing the wound that the blow made. They won't even admit the knife is there.* His pointed metaphor underlines the deep-rooted nature of systemic racism, and the way society often falls short in genuinely addressing these issues. He urged his listeners to recognize not just overt acts of racism, but also the subtle, systemic ways in which discrimination is perpetuated.

He was not only a vocal critic of America's anti-African social and political structure, but also a firm believer in the eventual end of white world supremacy.[30] Declaring this eventual end, he stated with unapologetic fervor, *So we of this present generation are also witnessing how the enslavement of millions of black people in this country is now bringing White America to her hour of judgment, to her downfall as a respected nation. And even those Americans who*

---

[30] Malcolm X, *The End of White World Supremacy: Four Speeches*, ed. Imam Benjamin Karim (New York: Arcade Publishing, 1989).

are blinded by childlike patriotism can see that it is only a matter of time before White America too will be utterly destroyed by her own sins, and all traces of her former glory will be removed from this planet forever. He argued that this predictive, and eventual paradigm shift would be a transformative event, drastically reshaping power structures and social systems globally. He once stated, *The day that the black man takes an uncompromising step and realizes that he's within his rights, when his own freedom is being jeopardized, to use any means necessary to bring about his freedom or put a halt to that injustice, I don't think he'll be by himself.* A potent prophet of black empowerment, he gave speeches addressing the end of white world supremacy. He passionately delivered his viewpoints on the shifting global dynamics and the impending decline of white dominance. In his fiery orations, he emphasized the rise of the black man and their rightful place in the world. However, it's crucial to note that his speeches were not an endorsement of black supremacy, but instead, a call for equality, justice, and recognition of African descended people's human rights.

He believed that the end of white world supremacy would mean a new era of social justice, where individuals of all races, religions, and backgrounds would be treated equitably. However, he understood that this change would not come easily or quickly. Malcolm X emphasized that it would require persistent struggle, vigilance, and the concerted effort of colonized people groups around the world. His predictions underline the importance of continuing the fight against systemic racism and all forms of oppression today, as the journey towards the end of the racially skewed world order is still ongoing.

With the predictive decline of white world dominance, fears of a new world order have emerged, particularly among those who hold power in the current system. This new world order is often portrayed as one where "America"—or more specifically, a monolithic, white vision of America—is no longer supreme and where voices of racial and ethnic minorities gain prominence. This shift in power dynamics symbolizes not only a change in who holds material resources or political control, but also in who shapes cultural narratives, defines societal norms, and dictates moral codes. This fear, however, often stems from a lack of understanding and an unwillingness to relinquish privilege, overlooking the possibility that this new order could usher in an era of true equality, justice, and human dignity. Truly, in Malcolm's vision, evangelicals are correct in their assessment of the end of days, but it is one where they are the antagonists on the wrong side of sacred history and not the victims in the prophetic drama they envision.

Released in 1990 by Public Enemy, the rap song "Fear of a Black Planet" echoes these anxieties about a shifting world order. The title itself is a direct commentary on the paranoia surrounding the decline of white supremacy and the corresponding rise of African and African American influence. In the lyrics, the group explores themes of systemic racism, oppression, and the fear of miscegenation. They debunk the fear of a black planet by exposing it as nothing more than an irrational fear of equality - a fear that the privileges and power dynamics associated with whiteness will be dismantled. Ultimately, the song serves as a powerful indictment of the racially skewed world order, underlining the urgency of confronting systemic racism and working towards social justice and equality.

The termination of white supremacy is inherently linked to the eschatological narrative of a forthcoming new world order, a system that they believe threatens their established position and assumed liberties. This fear stems from the notion that a world no longer dominated by white societal structures and cultural norms will jeopardize their entrenched privileges. This eschatological worldview is skewed, focusing on a doomsday scenario triggered by the loss of their privileged status, instead of acknowledging the inherent justice and equality in the dismantling of oppressive systems. Therefore, it becomes crucial to challenge this eschatology that is centered around maintaining oppressive power structures and promotes an understanding of eschatology that aligns with a vision of equitability and universal dignity.

Carter G. Woodson, often referred to as the "Father of Black History", also made significant prophecies about racism in America. Woodson observed that the erasure and distortion of Black history served as a tool for perpetuating racial oppression and subservience. He insisted that a true understanding of Black history, unfiltered by Eurocentric biases, was essential for overcoming racial prejudices and forging a path towards racial equality. His prophecy underscores the importance of Black History Month, a time for celebrating and acknowledging the significant contributions of Black individuals throughout history.

Woodson's words find a striking relevance in today's sociopolitical climate, especially as we witness concerted efforts to erase Black history from educational curricula. Organizations like Moms for Liberty, primarily composed of conservative Christian parents, are at the forefront of this cultural erasure. These groups advocate for the removal of teachings on systemic racism, slavery, lynching, and other historical atrocities inflicted upon the Black community, deeming them 'divisive' or 'unpatriotic'. They view their own children as being oppressed or made guilty for being white should a fuller picture of Black history be presented in the classrooms. Kendi famously asked, *Why don't those parents teach their children to identify with the great white abolitionist movements?* Could it be that in their historical imagination, they don't identify with that side of European American history?

The ideologies of the old White Citizens' Council echo ominously in the beliefs of contemporary conservative Christian groups like Moms for Liberty. Much like Moms for Liberty, the White Citizens' Councils of the Jim Crow era was composed primarily of conservative Christian individuals. They employed their faith not as a vehicle for love and tolerance, but as a shield to justify racial segregation and systemic oppression. Their philosophy was rooted in preserving a social order that privileged white Americans, advocating for 'separate but equal' policies that were anything but equal.

White Citizens' Councils, operating under the facade of respectability and Christian morality, were largely responsible for upholding the racially oppressive status quo in the South.

Their tactics included economic boycotts, social ostracism, and political lobbying to resist desegregation. Remarkably, these councils did not resort to overt violence; instead, they exercised their influence through economic and political power, contributing to the pervasive nature of systemic racism.

Under the guise of their perceived Christian righteousness, they firmly believed they were not promoting racism but rather carrying out what they saw as God's work. This distorted interpretation of divine purpose allowed them to distance themselves from the label of 'racist', instead considering themselves guardians of a divinely ordained social order.

Their belief system was rooted in a skewed theology, rationalizing segregation and systemic oppression as anticipated in their understanding of eschatology. This dangerous ideology, framed as the fulfillment of divine will, served as a potent tool for them to preserve their socio- political privilege, perpetuating a grievous cycle of racism and oppression.

They would often defend their actions, denying any accusations of racism, by using distorted religious and moral arguments. For instance, they claimed their support for segregation and discrimination was not based on racial hatred, but on the preservation of social harmony and divine ordination. They argued that races, like the threads in a tapestry, were meant to remain distinct and separate, each contributing to the overall beauty of the human race, but catastrophe would ensue if they were mixed. They presented their views as a necessary evil, a heavy burden they bore to maintain God's intended social order, rather than a manifestation of racial prejudice.

Moms for Liberty seem to mirror this philosophical alignment, albeit in a different context. Their mission to eliminate teachings on systemic racism, slavery, and lynching from school curricula is a modern form of historical erasure and oppression. While their methods might be nonviolent, the implications of their cause are equally harmful.

In an ironic twist of self-justification, organizations like Moms for Liberty often assert that their fight is not against racial equality, but against the purported threats of communism and socialism. They argue that encouraging discourse around systemic racism, slavery, and lynchings in educational curricula is a ploy to indoctrinate the youth with 'Marxist ideologies', ultimately leading to a socialist society. Portraying themselves as defenders of free thought and democracy, they vehemently oppose what they perceive as an attempt to subvert the American way of life. Framing their opposition to historical truth as a defense against communism and socialism, they deflect attention from the underlying racial prejudices driving their cause, thereby perpetuating a cycle of denial and racism.

Unfortunately, organizations like Moms for Liberty fail to recognize the profound irony in their stance. They battle the phantom of communism, blind to the reality that, for many Black people, racism itself has become a form of communism. Systemic racism, with its pervasive oppression and persistent suppression of Black voices, echoes the very totalitarianism these organizations claim to resist. It is a form of social and economic control that restricts opportunities, limits upward mobility, and perpetuates wealth and power disparities. This modern-day communism is not enforced by foreign ideologies but by homegrown prejudices that are deeply ingrained within our society. Ignoring this reality is a further testament to the lopsided narrative these organizations promote, and it underscores the importance of inclusive historical education in dismantling systemic racism.

Undertone of racial exclusion becomes evident when analyzing the objectives of Moms for Liberty. The very name of the organization subtly implies a focus on the liberties of white mothers, given their lack of concern for the needs and perspectives of black mothers. While they campaign for the control and 'liberty' to shape their children's education, they appear to overlook the rights of black mothers who wish their children to be educated about their rich, albeit painful, history. This selective focus on a liberty which minimizes slavery, conveniently ignoring the educational desires of black mothers, serves as a stark reminder of the racial disparities that exist in America. The dismissal of black mothers' concerns regarding the teaching of black history reflects a disconcerting level of indifference, which only reinforces racial disparities and contributes to the ongoing cycle of systemic oppression and racism.

Sadly, the actions of organizations like Moms for Liberty speak volumes about the deep-seated fear that black equality represents a threat to white liberty. Their attempts to erase important aspects of black history from school curricula tend to reinforce the narrative that equality for black individuals somehow infringes upon the liberties of white citizens. This fear, largely rooted in a perceived loss of privilege and power, continues to fuel racial disparities and systemic oppression. In striving to preserve a skewed version of 'liberty', they unknowingly (or perhaps knowingly) perpetuate a cycle of ignorance - an ignorance that fosters discrimination, stifles progress towards human equality and undermines the very essence of a democratic society that values the rights and freedoms of all its citizens, irrespective of their continental origins or ethnic backgrounds.

Unfortunately, members of organizations like Moms for Liberty, would vehemently deny that their actions are motivated by racism. Viral clips of these mother's stating with tears, "god-dammit, I am not a racist," spread like wildfire on social media. They argue that their endeavor is merely to protect their children from what they deem as inappropriate or harmful content in the education system. However, unbeknownst to them, their thinking has been significantly influenced by the historical and ongoing propaganda that perpetuates racial biases and stereotypes. The narrative they've been fed over generations has subtly yet effectively conditioned them to view the world through a lens tainted by racial prejudice, even if they are not consciously aware of it. This unconscious bias, born out of a deeply entrenched legacy of racism, shapes their perception of what constitutes 'liberty' and 'equality,' causing them to act in ways that inadvertently uphold systemic racism and oppression.

Ironically, these so-called "Christian" mothers, who claim to act in the best interest of their children, starkly differ from the mothers of the movement led by Sabrina Fulton and others. These courageous mothers, who have experienced the heartbreaking loss of their children to racial violence, work tirelessly to combat anti-Black state sponsored violence and promote social justice, embodying the true Christian values of love, compassion, and equity. In contrast, the Christian mothers opposing critical race theory and advocating for a whitewashed version of history are inadvertently perpetuating the very injustice the gospel of Christ condemned. Their actions, driven by unconscious biases and a distorted perspective of liberty, paradoxically contradict the teachings of Christ, who championed for the oppressed and stood against all forms of injustice.

The Mothers of the Movement represent an inspiring group of women who have turned their personal tragedies into a relentless fight for social justice. Born out of the devastating loss of their children to racial violence, these mothers aim to bring about reform in the law enforcement and justice system and combat systemic racism at all levels of society. Their advocacy stems from a profound understanding of the human cost of racial injustice, and their efforts are rooted in the fundamental Christian values of love, tolerance, and fairness.

This movement comprises several bereaved women who have utilized their grief to galvanize social change. Some of these prominent figures include Sybrina Fulton, the mother of Trayvon Martin; Lesley McSpadden, the mother of Michael Brown; Gwen Carr, the mother of Eric Garner; and Lezley McSpadden, the mother of Michael Brown. These women, among others, are the driving force behind the Movement, leveraging their personal tragedies to advocate for a world free from racial injustice and systemic oppression.

In their fight for justice and equality, these grieving mothers embody the spirit of Christ's teachings, which emphasize compassion for the oppressed and marginalized. Their activism is a testament to Christ's message of love and justice, a stark contrast to the stance taken by the Moms of Liberty.

Ironically, this group, despite their professed Christian values, fail to recognize the violent policing structures and injustice that the Mothers of the Movement are combating. Their opposition to critical race theory and their push for a sanitized version of history blinds them to the harsh realities of anti-Black prejudice, injustice, and violence that persist in society.

This movement, often disguised as protecting children from 'indoctrination', clearly demonstrates the link between the erasure of black history and the perpetuation of white superiority. They have been unconcerned with Black children being indoctrinated in Eurocentric saviorism embedded in American and World history classes in schools. Downplaying or even eliminating the critical examination of racial injustices in history, these initiatives effectively support the systemic racism that Woodson warned against. They rob students of the opportunity to engage with an unfiltered, factual representation of Black history, thereby reinforcing Eurocentric biases and impeding progress towards Black advancement. The fight against this form of educational censorship underscores the urgency and significance of Woodson's legacy in shaping an enlightened and just society. The following is a pertinent reflection from Carter G. Woodson that underlines the dire consequences of not knowing one's history:

If a race has no history, if it has no worthwhile tradition, it becomes a negligible factor in the thought of the world, and it stands in danger of being exterminated.

The erasure of the history and heritage of Black people can indeed be seen as a form of apocalypse, not in the traditional concept of end-of-world scenarios often depicted in popular culture, but an apocalypse of identity, culture, and self-worth. It represents an apocalypse that doesn't involve fiery cataclysms or celestial wrath, but rather, silent subjugation and quiet extinction. It's an apocalypse where the rich mosaic of diverse histories, experiences, values, and wisdom are wiped out, replaced by a singular, monolithic narrative that serves the interests of the privileged. This ongoing cultural, historical, and racial 'Armageddon' is every bit as devastating as any physical catastrophe could be.

The fear of totalitarianism, touted by groups like Moms for Liberty, is ironically being manifested in the very structures they prop up. This fear, often expressed as an apprehension of an overarching authority dictating the norms and rules of society, is paradoxically being inflicted by those at the top of the social hierarchy upon those at the bottom. Marginalized communities, systematically placed at the bottom rungs of this ladder due to the lasting impacts of racism, oppression, genocide, slavery, and lynching, are the ones experiencing the brunt of this totalitarian spirit.

Moms for Liberty, along with a significant segment of evangelical students of eschatology, present an intriguing paradox in their vehement opposition to perceived threats of totalitarianism from the left wing. These groups, in their advocacy for liberty and their fear of an all-encompassing, overreaching authority, seem to overlook their own support of authoritarian figures that they believe represent their interests.

This manifestation is sometimes unconscious, stemming from unexamined biases, yet it contributes to an insidious cycle of institutionalized racism. These groups unknowingly become agents of this same totalitarianism they fear. They enforce a monolithic narrative that erases the painful histories of oppressed communities and silences their voices, thus imposing a type of intellectual and cultural totalitarianism. This is a stark reminder that true freedom lies not in ignorance, but in the broadening of perspectives and the dismantling of systemic biases.

Religious support for Donald Trump among these groups, despite his unapologetic authoritarianism, provides a striking example of this paradox. Many evangelicals and conservative groups, despite professing a commitment to freedom and liberty, were willing to overlook or even outright support policies and actions that undermined these same values. From attempts to curtail legal immigration to the implementation of aggressive law and order policies, Trump's tenure was and in his second term marked by an iron-fisted approach. Intriguingly, many of these supporters saw these actions not as detrimental to their freedom, but as steps necessary to preserve it. They regard it as simply the state using its divine privilege to punish evil doers, and we must trust that those whom Trump punishes are indeed evil doers. This is likely due to the perception that their cultural and religious identity is under threat, and that an authoritative figure is needed to safeguard their innocent way of life. The connection to eschatology here is stark, as it highlights how apocalyptic fears can be exploited politically to gain support, even when the methods used contradict the very values these groups profess to hold dear.

Donald Trump's presidency was and is in his second term rife with instances of him endorsing white domestic political violence. In 2025, he pardoned the domestic terrorists who invaded the capital to overthrow the will of the people in the 2020 election, even though police were killed or injured in the process. One of the terrorists, who lost her life attempting to break into a location where congresspersons were secured, received millions in reparations. His rhetoric often seemed to embolden his followers and incite them against those who opposed his narrative. A prime example of this was his reaction towards protesters at his rallies. Rather than encouraging peaceful dialogue or expressing respect for the constitutional right to protest, Trump's speeches often contained thinly veiled provocations. He would speak nostalgically about the "good old days" when protesters would be "carried out on stretchers," or suggest that his followers should "knock the crap out of" protesters. His words, arguably, acted as a catalyst for aggression, emboldening his followers to take the law into their own hands.

Trump ran his 2024 presidential election on this very platform of standing up for the January 6, Benedict Arnold's who violently raided the capitol to overturn the 2020 election results and were consequently jailed. He was re-elected with the majority of support from the Evangelical voting bloc. His political tribe often focuses upon law and order, but the political reality showed that "law and order," is not for those at the top or the status quo.

Both the first and second term of the presidency of Donald

Trump, was and does reflect the egregious use of authoritarian tactics aimed at capturing and imprisoning both the documented and undocumented residents and thought policing in academia. As cities across America erupted in widespread demonstrations, during his first term, calling for justice reform, the Trump administration responded by deploying federal marshals. These forces were sent into cities under the guise of maintaining law and order. However, their true objective was to incite conflict and suppress the voices demanding change. The marshals, often unidentified and heavily armed, used aggressive tactics, including the indiscriminate use of tear gas and rubber bullets. This was not a move to protect citizens or preserve peace but a blatant effort to create chaos, discredit the legitimate protests, and further perpetuate a narrative of fear and disorder. This tactic, reminiscent of authoritarian regimes, underscored the administration's willingness to employ oppressive measures to resist reform and maintain the status quo of systemic racism and inequality.

The authoritarian bent of President Trump, in his first term and likely in his second has extended and will extend into the world of sports. In his first administration, he attempted to intervene in the NFL's handling of players who peacefully protested police brutality by kneeling during the national anthem. Trump publicly criticized these players, calling for them to be dismissed from their teams - a move that was clearly aimed at stifling their freedom of expression and using their livelihoods as leverage. This was another stark example of the former President's unwillingness to respect, engage, or even acknowledge the legitimate concerns of the black community. Instead of addressing the issue of police brutality, which was at the heart of these protests, Trump chose to weaponize patriotism and twist the narrative to portray these players as unpatriotic, thereby diverting attention from the systemic racism and police brutality issues they were protesting. This tactic served to further polarize the nation and amplified the voices of those who refused to acknowledge the reality of racial inequality in America. Once again, we see how authoritarianism was employed to maintain oppressive systems, suppress dissent, and uphold the status quo.

Facing mounting pressure from various quarters, including the then-President, NFL owners began to feel the heat, and in response, started to institute rules to restrict these acts of peaceful protest. A policy was proposed in May 2018, mandating players to stand during the national anthem if they were on the field, while giving them the option to remain in the locker room if they chose not to stand. This move was largely seen as a capitulation to President Trump's demands and an attempt to appease the section of the fan base that viewed these protests as offensive. The policy effectively sought to restrict the players' right to express their dissent on the field, thereby limiting their platform for raising awareness about the systemic injustices they were protesting against. In effect, the NFL owners traded the voices of their players for a semblance of peace, choosing to ignore the deep-seated issues of racism and oppression echoed in their protest. During the 2025 Superbowl, Trump decided to attend in person. However, before his arrival, it was reported that he demanded that the NFL officials remove the tag line "End Racism" from the end zones. At half time, he appeared in a video stating that his new administration was the beginning of America's golden age. This present writer could not help but think of what we refer to in the Black church tradition of "Ole' King Nebuchadnezzar" and his golden image on the plains of Dura, in defiance of his dream concerning his predicted end.

It is truly ironic how a certain segment of society can rally behind leaders who openly champion a form of totalitarianism that promotes white cultural Christianity. The palpable irony lies in their fear of an alternative form of totalitarianism, which blinds them to their own support for a version that aligns with their cultural, religious, and racial biases.

This cognitive dissonance, where one's actions contradict their professed beliefs, highlights the deep-rooted racial and cultural prejudices that continue to afflict American society.

Authoritarian rhetoric and actions, reflected in Trump's politics was never more evident than in his staunch refusal to accept the results of the 2020 election. His repeated assertions of voter fraud, particularly in predominantly Black cities like Detroit, Philadelphia, Atlanta, and Milwaukee, recall the tactics used to disenfranchise Black voters in the Jim Crow era. This shows how racism is routinely weaponized for political gain - a reality only exacerbated by Trump's inflammatory rhetoric and willingness to stoke racial tensions for electoral advantage.

The post-election targeting of Ruby Freeman and her daughter Shaye Moss—two Black poll workers in Fulton County, Georgia—reveals the creeping normalization of authoritarianism in American civic life. Vilified by conspiracy theorists, harassed by mobs, and slandered by powerful voices including the former president, these women became scapegoats in a fabricated narrative of electoral fraud. Their only "crime" was doing their job in a predominantly Black district during a democratic election.

That this abuse has not drawn mass condemnation from large segments of the white evangelical community—communities that have long declared themselves the guardians against tyranny—is itself apocalyptic. The very group that claims to fear the rise of a totalitarian government targeting Christian values has, in this case, cheered on a soft autocracy when it aligns with their cultural preferences. Their fear is not of authoritarianism—it is of egalitarianism. They are not worried about government overreach when it undermines Black political power; they only cry "freedom" when their own privilege feels exposed.

In this context, Freeman and Moss stand as signs—not just of democratic vulnerability—but of theological hypocrisy. They were faithful stewards of the vote yet treated as enemies of the state by those who idolize order over justice. This is what the Book of Revelation might call a "beast system": a power structure that dresses itself in religious language but devours truth and the vulnerable.

When Black labor is deemed fraudulent and Black bodies are targeted for simply being seen, we are not witnessing the rise of tyranny—we are seeing its acceptance. Not in silence, but in song, from pulpits and rallies that have confused cultural dominance with divine mandate.

This reality laid bare the violent implications of a Eurocentric eschatology that equates societal change with an impending apocalypse. It underscores the disturbing willingness of this segment to resort to violence when the structures that uphold their privilege are threatened. This is a stark departure from the teachings of love, peace, and acceptance that are central to Christian doctrine, illuminating the chasm between professed beliefs and actions when racial and cultural biases are at play.

Paradoxically, the ironic twist of this authoritarian display is that it mirrors the very dystopian future they dread - a future marked by a loss of control, infringement of rights, and oppressive rule. In their quest to resist an imagined totalitarian regime, they've adopted the authoritarian tactics they purport to fear. Manifestations of their supposed nightmares are evident in their actions - a blatant disregard for democratic principles, a readiness to suppress opposition, and a willingness to use force to maintain their perceived superiority. This self-fulfilling prophecy, driven by their distorted eschatology, unveils a paradoxical reality. Their attempt to prevent a dreaded future is, in fact, hastening its arrival, underscoring the profound disconnect between their fears and their actions.

The refusal of the Governor of Alabama to comply with a Supreme Court directive to redraw a predominantly Black district serves as another glaring indication of the authoritarian strain that those with a distorted eschatology claim to fear. This stark display of disregard for democratic norms and procedures mirrors the very totalitarian tendencies they dread - the control of power by a select few, the subversion of the judicial process, and the systematic stifling of diverse representation. This behavior represents an attempt to maintain a status quo anchored in racial and political dominance. Ironically, in their efforts to resist an oppressive regime, they are perpetuating the oppressive structures they purport to stand against. This act further underscores a deep-seated fear of losing control and an unwillingness to share power, revealing once again the profound disconnect between their professed fears and their actions.

It was on the 9th of March 2023, the Supreme Court ordered the Governor of Alabama to redraw the predominantly Black district. However, instead of complying with this directive that aimed at ensuring fair representation, the government in Alabama blatantly resisted. They opted for a course of action that further entrenched the imbalance in representation, maintaining the existing boundaries that disproportionately favored the white majority. This move was a stark illustration of a colonizer's mentality, prioritizing their dominance and control over the principle of equal representation, thereby perpetuating systems of oppression and racial disparities.

In this context, the role of the evangelical community was not only disappointing but deeply troubling. Rather than advocating for justice and standing against this clear violation of the law that disadvantaged Black people, they displayed a disturbing alignment with these unjust practices. Shockingly and not so shockingly, many evangelical leaders and followers openly supported the Alabama government's defiance. They chose to turn a blind eye to the blatant racial disparities and instead focused on preserving their interests, masked under the banner of religious freedom and moral superiority. It is a chilling reminder that religious institutions can often serve as a stronghold for prejudice and oppression, rather than a beacon of hope and equality. Their silence and complicity served to further entrench systemic racism and served as a stark reminder of the church's historical role in legitimizing and perpetuating racial inequality.

Ultimately, the ongoing battle between authoritarianism and democracy in America serves as urgent testament of how fearmongering and xenophobia remain integral components of the nation's political culture. The legacy of dark times lingers, as people continue to be oppressed in the name of a form of cultural Christianity that has yet to be truly challenged or uprooted. To make progress on this issue, it is important to recognize how deeply embedded these ideologies are in our society and work towards dismantling them through education, dialogue, and meaningful action. Only then will we be able to truly move forward in the pursuit of freedom and justice for all.

Statistical data illuminates the systemic disparities faced by the African American community, which illustrated a real life "left behind" scenario. All of this paints a much darker picture than the one depicted by popular eschatological narratives and reveals just how far America is from achieving true justice and equity. To truly understand eschatology, we must consider both its theological context as well as the historical legacy of racial injustice that continues to exist in American society today. Only then can we begin to have meaningful conversations about the future of our world and envision a more equitable, just society. In terms of wealth, the racial wealth gap in America is alarming. As of 2016, the median wealth for non-retiree black households 25-55 was less than $13,460, while for white households in the same age category, it was 10 times that, at $142,180.[31]

Ultimately, the legacy of racism and oppression in American during the past 400 years must be taken into account; these stories cannot continue to be ignored or overlooked. As we look ahead towards an uncertain future, we must recognize that real justice can only come when all people are afforded equal rights and respect.

Reformed ex-felons, particularly those of minoritized communities, face an uphill battle in America's socio-economic landscape. The consequences of a criminal record often stretch far beyond the duration of a prison sentence, creating a perpetual cycle of disenfranchisement. For instance, individuals with a criminal history are frequently met with discrimination in employment opportunities, irrespective of the gravity of their offenses or the time elapsed since their convictions. This lack of access to gainful employment hinders their efforts to rebuild their lives post-incarceration. This is a real left behind scenario for ex-felons who

---

[31] Danyelle Solomon, Connor Maxwell, and Abril Castro, *Systematic Inequality: How America's Structural Racism Helped Create the Black-White Wealth Gap* (Washington, DC: Center for American Progress, February 21, 2019), https://www.americanprogress.org/article/systematic-inequality/.

perhaps were unfairly targeted by the criminal justice system in the first place.

Furthermore, the social stigma associated with a criminal record follows the formerly incarcerated, exacerbating their difficulties in renting housing or pursuing higher education. This societal marginalization further cements their status as second-class citizens, even after serving their time and demonstrating reform. Thus, the narrative of post-prison reform is fraught with systemic barriers that continue the cycle of oppression and inequity. Such circumstances prompt a serious reconsideration of the prevailing eschatological views, emphasizing the necessity to address the racial and social disparities that plague contemporary American society.

When it comes to education, as of 2018, the high school graduation rate for white students was 89%, while for black students, it was only 79%.[32] Moreover, African Americans are more likely to attend high-poverty schools, with 45% of black students attending such schools compared to just 8% of white students.[33] According to the respected authority on education, Dr. Jawanza Kunjufu, black children and youth are left behind in the following ways:

- Low expectations in the school system
- Lack of access to highly qualified teachers
- Poorly funded classrooms with outdated textbooks
- Limited access to art, music and physical education classes

These disparities in educational opportunities make it difficult for African Americans to fully participate in society. The legacy of

---

[32] National Center for Education Statistics, "Public High School Graduation Rates," *Condition of Education*, U.S. Department of Education, accessed May 24, 2025, https://nces.ed.gov/programs/coe/indicator/coi.

[33] National Center for Education Statistics, "Concentration of Public School Students Eligible for Free or Reduced-Price Lunch," *Condition of Education*, U.S. Department of Education, accessed May 24, 2025, https://nces.ed.gov/programs/coe/indicator/clb.

oppression continues, resultantly affecting a large portion of the American population.

It is essential that we take action to confront centuries of racism and oppression, and work towards a more equitable society. We must look beyond our own experiences and recognize how others have been treated throughout history in order to ensure equal rights for all persons in the present and future. While much progress has been made, there remain stark disparities between racial groups in the US and around the world. Therefore, it is our duty as citizens of a global society to be aware of history's legacy—particularly the horrors of racism and oppression—and strive towards eradicating these ills from our world. Only then can we truly move forward into a better future.

Kunjufu's groundbreaking research on the achievement gap and the effective strategies to uplift African American students have made him a sought-after figure in academic and policy circles. The author of several influential books—like "Countering the Conspiracy to Destroy Black Boys"—he has worked tirelessly to challenge systemic bias and advocate for an equitable education system.

Dr. Kunjufu's unique insights in the realm of education and social justice center around his conviction that systemic transformation is required to truly address the disparities faced by African American students. He believes that a curriculum that acknowledges and respects the cultural heritage of these students is critical. This includes teaching history from an African- American perspective, thereby instilling a sense of pride and self-worth in these students. His insights also extend to the classroom environment, where he emphasizes the need for more teachers of color and a pedagogical approach that caters to diverse learning styles. When it comes to social justice, Dr. Kunjufu emphasizes the crucial role of education in combating racism and inequality. He believes that an equitable education system goes beyond just providing access; it should also deliver quality education that fosters the full potential of students, regardless of their race or socio-economic background. Civic leaders would greatly benefit from reading his writings and implementing his strategies to ensure that no one is left behind.

The policy of redlining and the phenomenon of white flight have played significant roles in perpetuating racial disparities and economic inequality. Redlining, a discriminatory practice by federal government agencies in the mid-20th century, involved the color-coding of neighborhoods based on their racial and socioeconomic composition. Predominantly African- American neighborhoods were often marked in red, indicating a high risk for mortgage lenders. This resulted in black families being systematically denied loans, hindering their ability to purchase homes and accrue wealth.

Simultaneously, the post-World War II era saw mass migration of white populations from urban centers to suburban communities, in a trend known as white flight. This left behind predominantly black urban neighborhoods starved of valuable resources, as tax bases eroded, and public services dwindled. The lack of investment implied by redlining, coupled with the economic drain of white flight, entrenched black communities in a cycle of poverty and disinvestment, creating racially segregated neighborhoods characterized by economic hardship. These practices have had a long-term impact, with the effects still being felt today in the form of racial wealth gaps, educational disparities, and other forms of systemic inequality.

Apocalyptic implications of these discriminatory practices are often overlooked, reinforcing a Eurocentric eschatology that downplays the profound distress experienced by oppressed communities. The impacts of redlining and white flight can be seen as a form of societal apocalypse for black communities. When resources are drained from already marginalized communities, the fabric of society begins to unravel. Schools are declining, healthcare is inaccessible, and poverty becomes entrenched. These conditions can be likened to the predicted 'end times' scenarios, with the significant difference being that they are not universally experienced but disproportionately affect those who have been systematically oppressed.

Chapter 8

DISASTERS IN DIVERS BLACK PLACES

The catastrophe of Hurricane Katrina in 2005 revealed the stark racial divide in the United States and the terrifying vulnerability of marginalized communities in the face of disaster. As the storm devastated the Gulf Coast, it was the predominantly black and impoverished neighborhoods in New Orleans that bore the brunt of the destruction. The city's Ninth Ward, a majority-black community, was virtually erased as the levees failed, and the government's response was woefully inadequate and delayed, exacerbating the suffering of these already marginalized citizens.

The toll of Hurricane Katrina was catastrophic. It claimed the lives of an estimated 1,200 people, making it one of the deadliest hurricanes in the history of the United States.

Additionally, it resulted in the displacement of more than one million people in the Gulf Coast region. Particularly in New Orleans, majority of the displaced were African Americans, further exacerbating the racial disparities in the city.

President George W. Bush, a figure of reverence among white Christian evangelicals, drew significant criticism for his administration's lackluster response to Hurricane Katrina. The perceived delay and inadequacy of his administration's handling of the disaster underscored the deep racial disparities in America, leading many to question the priorities of his government. The criticism was not merely about the slow response, but also the lack of preparedness and the apparent disregard for the disproportionately affected African American communities. Critics suggested that this failure reflected a broader indifference to the sufferings of Black America, a mindset that had been historically nurtured by the doctrines of white supremacy and privilege within the evangelical Christian community. Despite his standing among the white Christian evangelicals, Bush's handling of Katrina was seen by many as a stark illustration of how racial and socioeconomic disparities can influence governmental response to crisis.

The image of President Bush surveying the devastation of Hurricane Katrina from the comfort of Air Force One became an enduring symbol of his administration's detached and inadequate response. Rather than being on the ground, engaging directly with the people affected, Bush chose to view the catastrophe from a far-off and elevated perspective. This reinforced perceptions of a disconnect between the political elite and the everyday black Americans grappling with the aftermath of the disaster. For many, this act amplified a sense of alienation, particularly among the predominantly African American victims, further underscoring the institutionalized racism and systemic oppression prevalent in American society. The president's aerial overview seemed to embody the broader indifference and disregard towards the hardships and struggles endured by those who had been colonized, oppressed, and stigmatized over centuries.

Prominent African American leaders sharply criticized President Bush for his detached response to the crisis. Reverend Al Sharpton, among others, expressed deep disappointment and frustration, equating the flyover to a glaring example of the continuing implicit bias and institutionalized racism. Sharpton argued that the President's distant overview of the disaster mirrored the government's historical neglect of African American communities, which have been persistently subjected to systemic oppression and marginalization. Other critics, like NAACP Chairman Julian Bond, pointed out the stark contrast between the swift governmental response to disasters affecting predominantly white communities and the delayed, inadequate attention given to the predominantly black victims of Hurricane Katrina. They contended that the flyover symbolized the racial disparity in crisis management, reinforcing the long-standing narrative of inequality and racial bias in America.

Reverend Jeremiah Wright, the influential pastor from Chicago, also weighed in on the tragedy of Hurricane Katrina. He sparked controversy with his provocative statements, asserting that the catastrophe was not merely a natural disaster, but also a manifestation of America's systemic racism and institutionalized oppression. Wright viewed the government's inadequate response to the predominantly African American victims as a reflection of America's historical pattern of neglect towards marginalized communities. His comments, while contentious, underscored the deep-seated racial disparities underlying the Katrina catastrophe. Wright's perspective echoed a sentiment felt by many within the African American community: that the true disaster lay not only in the storm itself, but also in the longstanding racial injustices that it had brought to the surface.

The Hurricane Katrina catastrophe served as a stark embodiment of a real-world "left behind" scenario, a term often used in eschatological discussions. The phrase typically refers to those who remain after a chosen group has been removed, often in the context of a divine intervention or rapture. In the case of Katrina, the "left behind" were disproportionately from marginalized, African American communities, who were both physically left to grapple with the devastation and symbolically left out of the societal safety nets meant to protect citizens in such calamities. The inadequate and delayed response from the government, coupled with the pre-existing socio-economic disparities, only served to underscore the grim reality of societal abandonment. The scenario starkly mirrored the grim predictions of eschatological teachings, yet it was all too real for those in the aftermath of Hurricane Katrina. This exposes the myopic perspective of Euro-centric eschatology, where calamities like Katrina and the systemic oppression it revealed, are often overlooked in discerning the 'signs of the times'.

The legacy of Hurricane Katrina continues to this day. It exposed and magnified the existing racial and socioeconomic disparities in the region. The hurricane left an indelible mark on the psyche of the nation, revealing the stark inadequacies in disaster preparedness, response, and recovery. Moreover, it laid bare the inextricable link between systemic racism and environmental vulnerability, highlighting how African-descended communities often bear the brunt of climate disasters. As we scrutinize issues of racial justice and move towards a more equitable society, the lessons learned from Katrina continue to be relevant and instructive.

The aftermath of Katrina was nothing less than an apocalypse for the African American community. With homes destroyed, livelihoods lost, and a death toll disproportionately high among black residents, the storm's effects were devastatingly racialized. The natural disaster, coupled with systemic negligence, highlighted the cruel reality: for the oppressed and marginalized, the apocalypse isn't a distant event predicted in eschatology—it is a lived experience, a vivid illustration of the ongoing effects of systemic racism, economic inequality, and social neglect.

The real catastrophe is the normalization of this suffering, the acceptance that it's a part of everyday life for these communities. This is where eschatology intersects with social justice. The traditional Eurocentric view of eschatology anticipates a worsening world as a sign of impending apocalypse, yet fails to acknowledge that for many, the apocalypse is already here. This narrow view can blind people to the suffering of others, obscuring the urgent need for change.

Healthcare disparities are equally stark. According to a report by the Centers for Disease Control and Prevention, African Americans in the age bracket of 18-49 are twice as likely to die from heart disease than whites.[34] Furthermore, the infant mortality rate is 2.3 times higher among black infants compared to white infants.[35] The realm of healthcare is marred by a disturbing racial disparity that is especially pronounced within the African

---

[34] Centers for Disease Control and Prevention, "Vital Signs: Racial Disparities in Age-Specific Mortality Among Blacks or African Americans—United States

[35] Centers for Disease Control and Prevention, "Infant Mortality Statistics from the 1995 Period Linked Birth/Infant Death Data Set," *Monthly Vital Statistics Report* 46, no. 6, supplement 2 (1998): 1–24.

American community. Not only are African Americans 30% more likely to die from cancers than white Americans, but they also suffer from diabetes at a 77% higher rate.[36]

The prevalence of hypertension among African Americans in the United States is among the highest in the world, with more than 40% of non-Hispanic African American men and women having high blood pressure.[37] These disparities are even more alarming in the context of mental health. For instance, while African Americans are 20% more likely to experience serious mental health problems than the general population, they are also less likely to seek mental health treatment due to stigma and lack of resources.[38] This stark reality of racial healthcare disparity illustrates a profound social injustice that needs to be urgently addressed.

There is a growing body of evidence suggesting a correlation between the unique stresses faced by African Americans and the disproportionately high rates of heart disease within this community. The chronic stressors of racism, social inequality, and economic disparity have been found to contribute significantly to the development of heart disease. These societal pressures trigger a stress response that, over time, can lead to high blood pressure and inflammation that damage the heart. Furthermore, the lack of accessible and affordable health care exacerbates these conditions and prevents early detection or effective treatment. This connection underscores the fact that health disparities are not

---

[36] Centers for Disease Control and Prevention, "An Update on Cancer Deaths in the United States," CDC, November 2022,

https://www.cdc.gov/cancer/dcpc/research/update-on-cancer-deaths/index.htm.

[37] Centers for Disease Control and Prevention. "QuickStats: Age-Adjusted Percentage of Adults Aged ≥18 Years with Hypertension, by Sex and Race and Ethnicity — United States, August 2021–August 2023.

[38] U.S. Department of Health and Human Services Office of Minority Health. "Mental and Behavioral Health - African Americans." Accessed May 24, 2025. https://minorityhealth.hhs.gov/mental-and-behavioral-health-african-americans.

merely the result of individual behaviors or genetics, but also a manifestation of systemic oppression and inequality.

The escalating costs of healthcare present a daunting challenge, particularly within the black community. The lack of affordability of medical services and medications means that many African Americans are unable to access the care they need, exacerbating health disparities. The high costs deter individuals from seeking preventative care, leading to delayed diagnoses and treatment that ultimately result in worse health outcomes. Moreover, the financial burden of healthcare expenses can push families into a cycle of debt, creating further social and economic disadvantages. This is yet another manifestation of the ongoing societal apocalypse that disproportionately affects marginalized communities. It underscores the urgent need for societal reform, to ensure equitable access to affordable, quality healthcare for all.

Reflecting upon these statistics, will underscore the harsh reality of racialized inequality in America, a testament to the systemic racism and oppression that continues to disproportionately affect the African American community. Likewise, Native Americans experienced a period of colonization and genocide that left behind their communities to face immense levels of poverty, illness, and systemic oppression. From the Indian Wars to the forced displacement of indigenous populations, and the Trail of Tears, many Indigenous communities continue to struggle for sovereignty and recognition today.

These examples serve as a reminder that the worst that Europeans and Americans fear for themselves, pales in comparison to what many non-Westerners have experienced since colonization. In this way, much of modern eschatology fails to address the urgent issues faced by those who were left behind long before Europe started worrying about its own end times.

The 1994 Rwandan genocide serves as a potent example of the indifference of Western powers to the apocalyptic experiences of colonized people. The international community, primarily European and American, had ample warning of the impending catastrophe. Yet, shockingly, the primary concern became the safety of their own nationals. In a calculated operation, white expatriates were swiftly airlifted out of Rwanda, leaving behind a Black nation on the brink of a horrifying genocide. This exodus of Westerners symbolized a chilling assertion: their lives were deemed more valuable than the lives of the Rwandans about to be caught in the crossfire of mass murder. The left-behind apocalypse that ensued—hundreds of thousands of Tutsis ruthlessly slaughtered within a span of 100 days—stands as a stark reminder of how Western- centric eschatology often blinds us to the apocalyptic experiences of non-Western communities.

Horrors that unfolded during the 1994 Rwandan genocide are incomprehensible, with the highest estimates suggesting that as many as 1 million people may have lost their lives in a span of merely 100 days. The scale and intensity of the violence was such that it stunned the world into a chilling silence. Men, women, and children were systematically hunted down and eradicated, based on their ethnic affiliations. The Tutsis and moderate Hutus were subjected to unspeakable acts of violence, their lives snuffed out in their homes, churches, and even hospitals. The rivers flowed with blood, while the land was littered with bodies, unveiling a macabre landscape that bore testimony to humanity's capacity for barbarity.

Yet, despite the magnitude of this atrocity, the response from the former colonizers and the international community was notably passive. The indifference largely stemmed from a complex interplay of political, economic, and racial biases. The post-Cold War political landscape and the economic insignificance of Rwanda in global markets played a significant role in the reluctance of Western powers to intervene. Moreover, deeply ingrained anti-African bigotry and a Eurocentric worldview, which devalues non-European lives, further contributed to their apathy. This indifference to the Rwandan genocide illuminates a bitter truth about our world - where one's geographical location and Human identity can determine the value placed upon one's life and suffering.

Deeply entrenched European views which paint Africans, and by extension Black people, as inherently violent and perpetually at war, significantly influences the political perspectives of white evangelicals. This narrative, borne out of longstanding anti-African stereotypes, often leads to a lack of empathy for the trials that these communities face. Perpetuating the notion that violence and unrest are intrinsic elements of African culture; these white evangelical communities can conveniently absolve themselves of any responsibility or need to intervene.

This, in turn, fuels their political apathy towards the suffering of those who have been colonized and oppressed. Furthermore, such damaging stereotypes serve to obscure the historical and systemic causes that have contributed to geopolitical instability in various African regions, such as artificially drawn national borders, economic exploitation, and the enduring effects of colonial rule. Attributing turmoil to the supposed 'nature' of Black people, rather than recognizing the devastating impact of colonialism and imperialism, white evangelicals are able to maintain a comfortable distance from the harsh realities of anti-African oppression and injustice. This indifference is not only morally problematic but also contributes to the perpetuation of ideologies and policies that continue to inflict harm upon colonized communities.

The indifference displayed by white evangelical politicians to the Rwandan genocide juxtaposes starkly with their concern for crises in Europe, such as in Ukraine. This contrast can be traced back to deeply entrenched racial and geographic biases. When conflict erupted in Ukraine, a predominantly white and Christian nation, the response from these politicians was immediate and pronounced. They were quick to advocate for sanctions against the aggressors, financial aid for Ukraine, and diplomatic interventions to resolve the crisis. The plight of the Ukrainian people was given a platform, their stories amplified, their struggles acknowledged.

Additionally, when the atrocities under the reign of Slobodan Milosevic in the former Yugoslavia came to light, the response from America was swift and decisive. The regime of Milosevic, accused of ethnic cleansing and genocide, drew immediate international condemnation, spearheaded by American politicians and media. The American government, with its allies, intervened militarily, imposed economic sanctions, and played a crucial role in bringing Milosevic to justice in the international court.

The suffering under Milosevic was portrayed vividly in American media, and the victims were humanized, their stories eliciting empathy and calls for justice from the public. This robust response, while necessary and commendable, reveals an uncomfortable disparity. The geographical proximity to Europe, the racial identity of the victims, and the strategic interests in the region influenced this rapid action. It highlights the inconsistency in the American response to international crises, which seems to hinge on the racial and geographical markers of the victims.

In contrast, during the Rwandan genocide, their response was markedly absent. Despite the brutal extermination of an estimated 1 million Tutsis and moderate Hutus, no major initiatives were made by these politicians to halt the bloodshed or provide aid. The cries for help from Rwanda were largely ignored, their stories suppressed, their existence negated. This stark disparity in response exposes an uncomfortable reality of racial and geographic preference within the global political landscape. It underlines a Eurocentric view where crises in Europe elicit immediate action, while those in Africa, more so among black Africans, are often overlooked, feeding into a narrative of structural racism and bias in international relations.

In the current white nationalist imagination, the "Great Replacement" theory and the myth of white genocide have become central apocalyptic scripts. Once confined to the margins— espoused by figures like David Duke, skinheads, and neo-Nazis— this racial panic has now entered mainstream evangelical political rhetoric, camouflaged in language about "demographic anxiety," "heritage," and "border control." What was once fringe is now fused with eschatological fervor, casting diversity not as divine beauty but as existential threat.

This fear has manifested in absurd but politically potent ways—most notably in the prioritization of white South African asylum seekers. Fast-tracked by Donald Trump into the United States under the pretense of a white genocide—despite the fact that there is absolutely no systemic extermination—these applicants have been welcomed with urgency, while Black and brown migrants fleeing actual warzones, famine, and persecution are met with walls, cages, and expulsions. There was no such outcry for the Tutsis in Rwanda, no theological mobilization for the women of Congo or Darfur, no evangelical altar calls during the Sudanese civil wars. The same political leaders who now weep over faux "white genocide" were silent when the Interahamwe wielded machetes with chilling efficiency, when neighbors turned on neighbors, and rivers filled with bodies. Nor have they sounded the alarm over human rights abuses in Saudi Arabia or Syria. Their antennae are selectively tuned—to whiteness, not justice.

Amid the manufactured panic of white genocide in South Africa—cynically weaponized—Christian leaders within South Africa itself offered a striking rebuke. In a formal statement signed by theologian Cobus van Wyngaard and other white South African Christian leaders, they condemned the U.S. narrative as "founded on fabrications, distortions, and outright lies," adding that such claims "serve to heighten existing tensions in South Africa."[39] These leaders recognized what American white cultural Christianity refused to confront: that this was not about justice or safety, but about preserving whiteness as a dominant moral category. While brown and Black asylum seekers from war-torn nations were met with detention and deportation, white South Africans were presented as martyrs of a fictive apocalypse—fueling the fear, as Wyngaard state, that if white Christians lose demographic control in the West, they too will face extermination. But the true catastrophe is not theoretical. It has already unfolded—in Rwanda, in Congo, in Darfur—while those same prophets of white grievance offered no lament. Their silence in the face of real genocide unmasks the idolatry at the heart of their eschatology: a gospel not of liberation, but of possession. These

---

[39] Cobus van Wyngaard et al., "Statement from White South African Christian Leaders on Recent Actions by the United States Government," INFEMIT, February 28, 2025, https://infemit.org/south-africa-statement-feb2025/.

ideas were behind the motivations of anti-Black domestic terrorist and mass murderer Dylan Roof.

This make-believe "white genocide" in South Africa and the United States, as media personality Tucker Carlson would suggest, is only a script to preserve power. It echoes through pulpits and policies, inverting the gospel of liberation into a gospel of hatred and self-preservation. But in Rwanda, the world saw what real apocalypse looks like when hate becomes systematized and dehumanization turns communal. The true horror of biblical judgment is not demographic decline—it is silence in the face of blood crying from the ground. And in that silence, the sin is collective.

Horrifically, the establishment of settlements, destruction of homes, bombings and displacement of Palestinians paint a chilling picture of an ongoing, left-behind apocalypse scenario. This crisis often goes unnoticed or is explicitly supported by a significant segment of evangelical Americans, who view the state of Israel through a strictly Biblical lens, often dismissive of the Palestinian plight. Their unwavering support for the Netanyahu regime, often rooted in a narrow interpretation of eschatology, overlooks the human rights abuses and expropriation of Palestinian lands.

Such endorsements, often paired with wholesale condemnation of Palestinians, create an unbalanced narrative that dehumanizes the victims, erases their suffering, and justifies their oppression. This bias mirrors the historical pattern of selective empathy and action that we have observed in international crises. The pernicious effects of racism, colonization, and oppression are evident in this scenario, where geopolitical and religious interests eclipse fundamental human rights and justice, perpetuating suffering, and devastation for the marginalized and the oppressed.

The evangelical community's disregard for Palestinian human rights is not an isolated phenomenon but extends into their attitudes towards the human rights of African Americans as well. The same narrow interpretation of eschatology that obscures the plight of Palestinians also fosters indifference towards the systemic injustices faced by African Americans. This indifference, at times even hostility, is manifest in a lack of response to police brutality, mass incarceration, and economic oppression targeted at black communities. The racialized lens through which they view global events often results in a mischaracterization of black Americans as responsible for their own disenfranchisement, much like the Palestinians. This systemic bias, deeply rooted in a Eurocentric worldview, essentially devalues the lives of those who do not fit their narrative, thus perpetuating cycles of racism and oppression.

A profound yet often overlooked aspect of eschatology lies in the contrasting experiences of those at opposite ends of the social hierarchy, particularly in Western societies. The Anglo community, typically positioned at the top, enjoys a metaphorical "rapture" - a state of relative peace, prosperity, and privilege, shielded from the harsher realities of life that many others face. This "rapturous" state is characterized by an abundance of opportunities and resources, access to quality education and healthcare, and a largely unhindered exercise of basic human rights. The perceived tribulation that Eurocentric scholars envision following the rapture has been an enduring phenomenon for African.

In stark contrast, the African American community continues to endure a harsh reality reminiscent of the "left behind" - those deemed unworthy of the rapture in the traditional eschatological narrative. This painful analogy bears witness to the systematic racism, oppression, and systemic barriers ingrained in the social fabric, which have long hindered the community's progress. The echoes of slavery and lynching continue to reverberate in the form of mass incarceration, educational disparities, and racial violence.

In essence, while the Anglo community flourishes in its metaphorical "rapture," the African American community, cruelly "left behind," grapples with the enduring legacy of centuries of injustice. This dichotomy underlines the need to reevaluate and broaden our eschatological narratives, acknowledging and addressing the disparities and injustices that persist in our societies. Although the topic of eschatology may seem abstract, it is essential to remember the history of colonialism and oppression that has shaped current conditions for many around the world. Without acknowledging this context, much of eschatology remains disconnected from its real- world implications.

In conclusion, the criticisms leveled at the "Left Behind" series largely stem from its portrayal of Christianity and end-time events through a narrow, American-centric lens, which often overlooks the diverse and complex realities of the global Christian community. For too long, eschatological teaching has been exclusive to white Europeans and Americans. In order to be truly inclusive and accessible to all communities around the world, it must incorporate perspectives from other cultures. It's essential to remember and reflect on our history since it allows us to find insight and hope in the darkness. Together, we can push forward towards a brighter future that is free from oppression, racism, and injustice. We have endured centuries and now it's time to confront our history together so that we may build a better world for all of us.

Eric Betts

Chapter 9

THE FOUR HORSEMAN OF THE BLACK APOCALYPSE

Steven Charleston asserts that the word "apocalypse" is often misinterpreted. He says, *The word apocalypse is now used to describe disasters of all kinds, including the Hollywood vision of a zombie apocalypse...it is a popular shorthand term for total destruction... [but while this is true] apocalypse is what we are living through. It is the coming true of our worst fears, which in turn generates more visions, either of salvation or destruction...*[40]

He also makes mention of how so many in the mainstream society are fearful of a nuclear Armageddon, and how in the past they trained students to hide under their desk in the event of such an apocalypse and adds that *This situation is nothing new for me as a Native American. My ancestors already lived through an apocalypse. For us, the end of the world is 'been there, done that.' In 1831, the world came to an end for my family--and for all the families that were part of Chanta Yakni, the Choctaw Nation. That year, we were forced off our ancestral homeland and made to walk on a death march we called the Trail of Tears. Thousands of our people died. We lost our homes, our way of life, even our graveyards. We lost everything-- everything, that is, except the one thing they could not take from us: hope.*

He says that while the word apocalypse is associated with catastrophe, war and the end of the world, that it also means to uncover or reveal a vision for the future and what was to come. *It can be used to describe both a vision of what is to come and a description of what is already happening,* says Professor Charleston.

---

[40] Charleston, Steven. *We Survived the End of the World: Lessons from Native America on Apocalypse and Hope.* Minneapolis: Broadleaf Books, 2023.

He further adds that *Conquest, war, famine and death: the four horsemen of the apocalypse are still with us, both as fear and experience...It was the experience of apocalypse, not just the fear of it, that my ancestors faced. On Turtle Island, the name many Indigenous nations gave to North America, the apocalypse began its inexorable consuming of our Indigenous way of life from the moment European settlers reached our shores. Our people died from a host of diseases for which they had no immunity or cure. The Mayflower was a plague ship. It and the countless others like it, brought smallpox, measles, and influenza-diseases we had never known before that wiped out whole communities to the last person. European colonialism... brought war and destruction upon us no matter how many peace treaties we signed...We were left in poverty and isolation, with the expectation that our genocide would soon be complete...If apocalypse means cataclysmic destruction--in essence, and end of the world--my ancestors went through it.[41]*

Drawing parallels with Professor Charleston's narrative, the African American experience, too, carries the weight of an apocalyptic journey. It began with our capture in Africa, a land of diverse cultures and profound spirituality. Stripped of our identities, our traditions, and our tongues, we were tied with chains of subjugation and ushered aboard slave ships. This 'Middle Passage' - an understated term for such a horrific journey - was the first glimpse into our impending apocalypse.

We were crammed into those ships like sardines, the stench of despair filling the air. Struggling to breathe, lying next to others who would not see the dawn, we journeyed across vast, unforgiving waters. Survival was the only prayer our parched lips could utter. This was our first war against death and the beginning of our understanding of apocalypse.

Arriving on foreign shores, we were forced into bondage, our bodies bruised, our spirits often broken. This was our famine - the

---

[41] Ibid.

hunger for freedom, for dignity, for respect. This was our daily war, our continuous struggle against the harsh realities of slavery. Colonialism for us, much like it was for the Indigenous people, was a cataclysmic event that brought about a severe rupture in our ways of life, making us question the very essence of our existence.

Despite enduring such profound suffering and turmoil, our spirit, like that of the indigenous people, remained unbroken. Amidst all the darkness, we held onto hope, the light that continues to guide us on our path towards healing and liberation. If apocalypse is to reveal a vision for the future, then ours is that of continued resilience and unyielding pursuit of justice and equality.

It is quite fitting that Professor Charleston would apply the four horses of the apocalypse of Revelation 6 to the experience of the original nations. Quite appropriately, when analyzing the language of the text, one cannot help but find similarities in the African and African American experience also.

- **The first horse,** the white one, symbolizes Conquest, representing the oppressive force of enslavement and white supremacy. This force rode through our lives, subjugating us and erasing our identities, forcing us to grapple with the foreign culture that was violently imposed upon us. Our arrival on foreign shores represented the conquest. Stripped of our identities, traditions, and tongues, we were chained and ushered onto slave ships, crammed together in the unbearable conditions of the 'Middle Passage.' This horrific journey was our first glimpse into our impending apocalypse and the conquest of our freedom and dignity.

In mainstream prophecy books, the first white horse is often depicted in a manner that sidelines other narratives and experiences. These works frequently portray this horse as a harbinger of divine providence, inevitably reinforcing the dominant narrative of conquest and colonization. The symbol of the white horse, under the guise of righteousness, is used to justify the forceful imposition of a singular worldview, implying a divine endorsement of such actions. However, such depictions overlook the significant and systemic trauma that this 'conquest' inflicted on African and Indigenous peoples - the erasure of cultures, languages, and identities, and the enduring hardship of displacement and disenfranchisement. In the grand narrative of the white horse, the experiences of the oppressed are often marginalized or entirely omitted, thus perpetuating a mono-cultural understanding of history and prophecy.

- **The second horse**, the fiery red, stands for War, embodying the unending struggles and bloody battles we had to wage to claim our freedom, our dignity, and our very existence in the face of brutal subjugation. The daily struggle against the brutal realities of slavery represented the war. Forced into bondage, our bodies were bruised and spirits often broken. Yet, this continuous combat against dehumanization bred a stout resistance and unyielding spirit within us.

The narrative of the second horse, the fiery red, is often slanted towards the European plight, painting a picture of their struggles and conflicts without considering the experiences of enslaved Africans and their descendants in the Americas.

Applying the symbolism of the second horse, the fiery red one, to the Crusades or religious conflicts in Europe indeed centers the experiences of those of European descent. This interpretation, while valid, sidelines the experiences and perspectives of the African diaspora. As the fiery red horse symbolizes War – the unending struggles and battles – it's crucial to remember that the wars weren't confined to the European landscape. The battleground extended to the shores of Africa, where millions were taken away, their lives irrevocably altered by the horrors of slavery. The struggle for freedom, dignity, and existence waged by enslaved Africans and their descendants parallels the intensity of any war experienced by those of European descent. By focusing solely on the European context, we inadvertently eclipse the African narrative, rendering their harrowing experiences and indomitable resistance invisible in the annals of history.

This Eurocentric interpretation of the red horse overlooks the brutality and bloodshed that marked the African and African American experience. European historians privilege their continent's wars and revolutions, while the relentless fight of enslaved Africans for dignity and survival is a mere footnote. This war was not a battle fought on distant lands with soldiers in uniform; it was a silent war, fought every day, in every corner where oppression thrived, by individuals who were stripped of their basic human rights. This struggle, this ceaseless war against dehumanization and subjugation, remains unacknowledged in the conventional application of the second horse of the apocalypse.

- **The third horse**, a black one, signifies famine, pointing to our spiritual hunger - a yearning for our lost traditions, our erased histories, and the respect and recognition that was persistently denied to us. The famine we experienced was not just physical, but a deep, gnawing hunger for freedom, respect, and dignity. The Transatlantic enslavement apocalypse brought about a severe rupture in our ways of life, and we found ourselves famished for the life we once knew.

The third horse, the black one, is also a chilling representation of America's economic exploitation of African Americans, particularly in the deeply entrenched system of plantation economics. This cruel system, designed to ensure that the rich grow richer while the poor continue to languish in poverty, mirrors the unsettling vision of the rider on the black horse holding a pair of scales.

These scales, a symbol of economic imbalance, reflect the grotesque economic disparity that has persisted for centuries in American society.

This economic disparity was particularly evident during the era of slavery, where African Americans were forced to labor under brutal conditions on plantations, generating immense wealth for their white masters. Yet, despite their hard work and the wealth they created, they were left with nothing but pittance. This mirrors the voice proclaiming, "A measure of wheat for a penny, and three measures of barley for a penny," signifying the meager wages African Americans received for their labor post-emancipation.

The symbolic scales of economic imbalance held by the rider on the black horse in the biblical narrative persist into our present day, manifesting in the form of childhood poverty and food deserts within the African American community. Our children, the very future of our community, are born into a system rigged against them, a system that perpetuates poverty and denies them the basic rights to nutritious food and a healthy life.

Food deserts, areas where fresh, healthy food is not readily or affordably available, are alarmingly common in African American neighborhoods. This reflects the economic deprivation faced by our community, where the scales of balance are tipped against us. The dire lack of fresh food outlets exacerbates health issues and feeds into the vicious cycle of poverty, mirroring the famine symbolized by the first horse. The rider on the black horse of yesteryear has evolved into the modern structures of capitalism that continue to exploit and sideline our community. This is a testament to the antichrist-like nature of these actions, actions that starkly contrast the Christian values of fairness and love thy neighbor.

Meanwhile, the command "see thou hurt not the oil and the wine" is indicative of the wealth and luxury maintained by the elite at the expense of the laboring poor. In the context of plantation economics, it represents the extravagant lifestyles of the plantation owners, financed by the sweat and toil of enslaved African Americans. Thus, this biblical passage succinctly captures the appalling economic exploitation of African Americans, reflecting the harsh realities of racial capitalism and systemic inequality in America.

The phrase "hurt not the oil and the wine" echoes the profound disparity and economic injustice ingrained in our society. The "oil and the wine," symbols of unbridled luxury and wealth, are often hoarded by the top 1 percent who are ensnared in the mirage that providing a livable wage to the laboring masses would somehow dilute their affluence. Their groundless fear of diminished luxuries blinds them to economic deprivation and struggle endured by the majority. This skewed perception, which upholds their excessive luxuries at the cost of systemic deprivation, manifests the antichrist-like disregard for the welfare of their fellow beings.

Those who dare to voice against the prison-industrial and military-industrial complexes are portrayed as a threat to the "oil and the wine." Their call for justice, equity, and a fairer distribution of resources is often manipulated as an attack on the richness of the few. This attempted silencing of dissent merely underscores the profound fear of the privileged that their unbounded luxury may be questioned. The outcry against institutionalized exploitation and militarism, therefore, is not a threat to individual riches, but a challenge to a system that perpetuates inequality and injustice.

The billionaire class, masters of the oil and wine, continue to weave their webs of influence by backing politicians who align with their self-serving agenda. Such is the machination of their power that they often use their wealth as a tool for political persuasion. They fill the campaign coffers of politicians, ensuring their votes on policies and regulations are in favor of sustaining the status quo, preserving the metaphorical oil and the wine, and perpetuating the systemic oppression of those at the bottom.

These wealthy barons, under the guise of donations, essentially buy political influence, ensuring lawmakers remain beholden to their interests rather than the constituents they swore to serve. This capitalistic manipulation of democracy serves not the public good but the vested interests of the billionaire class. Their priorities skew towards policies that protect their wealth, their oil and wine, while turning a blind eye to the plight of those at the bottom, the laboring masses who bear the brunt of economic inequality.

In this way, the aristocracy of wealth, through political patronage, manages to maintain their luxurious status at the expense of both poor "whites" and Black people. Their actions, contrary to the spirit of familyhood and common good professed in the principles of Christianity, mirrors more the antichrist, spreading not love and equity but disparity and hardship. They, therefore, become oppressors, enriching themselves on the back of the struggle and suffering of the less fortunate.

The scales of justice, alas, have fallen prey to the apotheosis of greed and self-interest. They tip shamelessly in favor of those who clutch the oil and the wine, leaving the rest of us grappling with the rising, unaffordable costs of basic sustenance such as food. It's a silent, insidious war on the poor, the marginalized, the forgotten— the Gullah people and countless others—who are forced to scrape by while the masters of wealth feast on their abundant loaves and fishes. The cost of living skyrockets, yet wages remain stagnant, tightening the noose of economic inequality. This is the unholy dance of capitalism, a far cry from the teachings of Christ. It's a system that feeds the rich and starves the poor, a perverse inversion of the biblical call to "feed my sheep".

The scripture from Revelation 18:3 is a prophetic snapshot that mirrors our present situation, where corruption and greed are the orders of the day. The nations drunk with the maddening wine of her adulteries represent societies intoxicated by the allure of excessive wealth and power. The kings of the earth committing adultery with her are the political and economic elites who, in their lust for more wealth, have forsaken their moral and ethical duties, plunging their societies into a state of perpetual inequality and suffering. The merchants growing rich from her excessive luxuries are the billionaire class and corporations, fattening themselves from the exploitation of the poor. This is the Babylon of our time, an economic system that thrives on inequality and the suffering of the masses. Its downfall, as foreseen in the scriptures, will be a result of its own excesses and moral bankruptcy.

- **The fourth horse,** the pale one, is the emblem of Death. This horse rode through our communities, leaving a trail of destruction and despair. Yet, in its wake, we found strength - the resilience to rise from the ashes, the will to rebuild, and the spirit to resist and reclaim our lost glory. The 'Middle Passage' was our initial encounter with death.

154

Forced to lie next to those who would not see the dawn, survival was the only prayer our parched lips could mutter. Yet, despite the omnipresence of death, we held onto hope, an enduring light that guides us on our path towards healing and liberation.

Often, when the narrative of the pale horse of death is discussed, it is almost exclusively associated with the European experience – particularly in the context of epidemics such as the Bubonic Plague or the Spanish Flu. This Eurocentric interpretation overlooks the similar, if not more devastating, instances of mass death experienced by other communities, most notably the African diaspora. The Atlantic slave trade, for instance, was a death-dealing enterprise of unparalleled proportions. The Middle Passage, the journey across the Atlantic, was a nightmarish voyage where countless African lives were extinguished due to inhumane conditions, malnutrition, and disease. Yet, this pale horse of death is seldom invoked in these contexts. The Eurocentric understanding of the symbolic black horse often fails to consider the pervasive and enduring effects of such epidemics on communities like ours, and how they continue to shape our collective memory and experiences.

In the Biblical revelations, the fourth horseman of the Apocalypse rides upon a pale horse, carrying with him Death and Hell. This chilling imagery resonates with the experiences of African descendants, particularly during the era of captivity and the subsequent period of lynching. For these individuals, the pale horse served as a constant companion, an omnipresent specter of death and hell that persisted beyond the Middle Passage. The pale horse was not a mere metaphor but a lived experience, a personification of the almost inconceivable horror and dehumanization they suffered. This Hell figure on the pale horse is symbolically the state of being referenced by Malcolm X who famously said *We've been catching hell in this country for 400 years.*

The lynching era, a horrific period of racial terror, served to further solidify the presence of this pale horse among the African diasporas. Lynching, an act of terror designed to instill fear and maintain social control, resulted in the deaths of thousands of Black men, women, and children. This reign of terror was a manifestation of the hell brought by the pale horse, a brutal reminder of the systemic racism and violence that African descendants had to navigate. Thus, for the African descendants, the pale horse of the Apocalypse was not a distant, abstract symbol; instead, it was a cruel reality embedded in their collective experience. The endurance of our communities, despite these macabre odds, testifies to our resilience and unyielding will to survive.

Ida B. Wells, a courageous woman of African descent, emerged from the shadows of the pale horse as a beacon of hope and resistance. Born into the chains of slavery, Wells rose to prominence as a journalist, abolitionist, and a fierce advocate for racial and gender equality. She used her pen as her sword, piercing through the veil of silence that shrouded the brutal lynchings that ravaged African American communities. An indomitable force, she wielded her words to expose these atrocities, unmasking the pale horse's true, terrifying form. She once profoundly remarked, *The way to right wrongs is to turn the light of truth upon them.* This quote encapsulates Wells' commitment to illuminate the ghastly reality of lynching, to confront the horror directly, and to ignite the spark of justice in the hearts of her audience.

One of Wells' most chilling statements on the evil of lynching is: *Our country's national crime is lynching... It is not the creature of an hour, the sudden outburst of uncontrolled fury, or the unspeakable brutality of an insane mob. It represents the cool, calculating deliberation of intelligent people who openly avow that there is an 'unwritten law' that justifies them in putting human beings to death without complaint under oath, without trial by jury, without opportunity to make defense, and without right of appeal.*[42]

---

[42] Ida B. Wells-Barnett, "Lynch Law in America," speech delivered at the National Negro Conference, Chicago, 1900, in *The American Yawp Reader.*

This quote underscores the horrifying reality of lynching - not a spontaneous act of uncontrolled rage, but a systematic, premeditated crime against humanity, condoned and carried out by those considered 'intelligent' and 'law-abiding.'

Ida B. Wells' assertion that Black people are the victims of sin rather than the purveyors of it reverberates with profound implications for our understanding of the Apocalypse. She pierced through the fog of delusion, illuminating the stark truth - Black folks were not the sinners; they were being sinned against. This reframing is a critical disruption in the narrative, a seismic shift that challenges the deeply ingrained belief systems that justified such heinous acts of violence.

In the apocalyptic scriptures, the world's end is signified by rampant evil and sin overwhelming the earth. If we comprehend the systematic lynching of Black people and the erasure of entire communities like the Gullah people or other Black towns as a manifestation of this evil, then we can begin to perceive the apocalyptic proportions of this racial terror. This is not about individual sin, but a systemic and organized destruction of a people, a sin of biblical proportions.

The ordeal faced by these communities parallels the tribulations prophesied in the Apocalypse, where the righteous suffer at the hands of the wicked. Just as the Apocalypse signifies a moment of judgment and a call for divine justice, Wells' exposure of the lynching epidemic invoked a demand for human justice. She held up a mirror to the face of America, revealing the monstrosity of racism reflected therein, a revelation that echoes the unveiling of truth in apocalyptic texts.

The lynching era, a dark, brutal period in American history, spanned from the end of the Civil War in 1865 to the height of the civil rights movement in the 1960s. Throughout these gruesome 100 years, it's estimated that nearly 5,000 African Americans were terrorized, tortured, and murdered by lynch mobs. These numbers, however, only reflect recorded incidents. The true total, veiled in the shadows of silence and fear, is believed to be significantly higher. This time frame and the horrific number of deaths is a chilling testament to the systemic racism that permeated throughout every fiber of American society, plaguing it with violence and hatred.

In the harrowing annals of America's lynching era, the scripture, *And power was given unto them over the fourth part of the earth, to kill with sword, and with hunger, and with death, and with the beasts of the earth*[43] strikes a chilling resonance. White America's malfeasance during this period can be interpreted through the lens of this scripture. The 'sword' can symbolize the brutal violence inflicted upon African Americans, often executed with terrifying efficiency and chilling regularity. 'Hunger' can reflect the systemic oppression that starved African Americans of their basic rights and opportunities, relegating them to a life of poverty and hardship. 'Death' stands as a stark symbol for the countless lives stolen, often in gruesome public spectacles designed to instill fear and uphold white supremacy. Lastly, the 'beasts of the earth' allude to the monstrous, dehumanizing behavior exhibited by the perpetrators of these atrocities. This scripture, evoking such horrific imagery, underscores the depth of moral abomination that characterized White America's actions during the lynching era.

---

[43] Revelation 6:8, *Holy Bible, New Revised Standard Version* (New York: National Council of the Churches of Christ, 1989).

Chapter 10

THE END OF THE WORLD: GULLAH LANDS AND FLOODED TOWNS

Within the dominant white evangelical narrative in America, the sanctity of plantation capitalism often intertwines with their cultural Christianity, creating a conflation of faith and economics that is viewed as sacrosanct. However, for the Gullah community, who had long been rooted in the history and culture of the South Sea Islands of the United States, this economic system has not been a blessing but a bane. To them, it's an Antichrist force, a wolf clothed in a shepherd's garb, that has unleashed apocalyptic devastation on their homes, their heritage, and their very existence. The narrative of capitalism, painted as divine by some, stands in stark opposition to the lived experiences of these people. They found not prosperity, but displacement, not elevation, but erasure. The relentless march of greedy capitalism, far from embodying Christian compassion and charity, has been a harbinger of cultural annihilation and historical oblivion for the Gullah people.

The name "Gullah" holds deep roots, tracing its lineage back to the rich tapestry of African cultures that were brought to the South Sea Islands during the transatlantic slave trade. It is believed that the term "Gullah" possibly derives from "Gola" or "Gora", names of tribes located in Liberia and Sierra Leone. The Gullah people have preserved their unique African linguistic and cultural heritage more than any other African American community in the United States, a testament to their resilience and unbroken tie to their ancestral homeland.

The emancipation of slavery unfolded a new chapter in the narrative of the Gullah people. Many of the islands were abandoned by the white planters during the Civil War, leaving behind a population of freed slaves who had been forced to work on rice, cotton, and indigo plantations. This absence of white control allowed the Gullah people to hold onto their lands and continue their way of life with minimal interference.

In the aftermath of the Civil War, the Federal Government initiated the Southern Homestead Act of 1866, which transferred ownership of confiscated Confederate lands to the freedmen. The Gullah people, now free, seized this opportunity and legally claimed ownership of the land they had been tending for generations. They purchased their homes, the land surrounding them, and the marshlands that were once the site of plantations. In this way, the Gullah people transitioned from the status of enslaved laborers to landowners in their ancestral homeland.

Hilton Head, South Carolina, an island of rich history, was once a vibrant manifestation of Gullah culture. The Gullah people, descendants of enslaved Africans brought here to cultivate rice and cotton, imbued the island with a unique blend of African traditions, language, and arts. For generations, they lived in harmony with the landscape, their lives intimately intertwined with the ebbs and flows of the sea and the rhythms of the land.

However, the advent of the capitalist engine brought a tempest of destruction and displacement to this island paradise. The post-World War II economic boom saw the island being aggressively marketed as a prime tourist and retirement destination. Rapid infrastructural development followed, birthing golf courses, resorts, and gated communities where once there were marshlands, forests, and small-scale farms.

This growth, fueled by vulture capitalism, has come at a tremendous cost. The Gullah people, unable to compete with the soaring real estate prices, found themselves gradually pushed out of their ancestral lands. The economic displacement was soon followed by cultural erosion as schools, churches, and community spaces - the lifeblood of the Gullah culture - succumbed to the relentless onslaught of commercialization.

The implications of this displacement are far-reaching. The loss of the Gullah homeland signifies not just the erasure of a community, but also the obliteration of a living repository of African American history and culture. It's a stark reminder of the ruthless nature of parasitic capitalism, that in its pursuit of profit, it can endanger the very essence of human diversity and heritage.

In the wake of the brutal enslavement era, Hilton Head Island emerged as a sanctuary for many African Americans seeking solace and refuge. This island, teeming with life and resplendent with natural beauty, promised a chance at freedom and self-sufficiency. It was here that the formerly enslaved Africans, drawn by its fertile soil and abundant resources, began to build a life of their own. Enshrining their African heritage in every aspect of their lives, they cultivated the land, fished the sea, and infused the island with their cultural richness. This blossoming era saw the emergence of the Gullah community - a vibrant testament to African American resilience, survival, and ingenuity in the face of adversity. The Gullah people transformed Hilton Head into a living testament of their strength and spirit, a beacon of African American history that stood, until recent times, defiant and proud in the face of relentless societal change.

The construction of a bridge linking the mainland to Hilton Head Island was hailed as a symbol of progress and prosperity. Sadly, the reality was far from this romantic ideal for the local Gullah community. This bridge, rather than bringing benefits, signaled the beginning of a heart- wrenching era of displacement, loss, and cultural erasure. It became a conduit for outside developers, tourists, and wealthier migrants to flood into the island, leading to escalated property prices, making it unaffordable for many locals.

In this tide of so-called 'progress', the Gullah people, original stewards of the land, found themselves marginalized and pushed to the periphery. Their once-thriving community slowly began to dissolve, their voices drowned out by the clamor of relentless development. The land that held the memory of their ancestors and the promise of their future was snatched away from them, parcel by parcel.

Heartbreakingly, the bridge that promised connectivity instead brought about division, turning the Gullah's ancestral land into a playground for the affluent. This profound injustice underscores the stark contrast between the tenets of capitalism - which often prioritizes profit over people - and those of Christianity, with its emphasis on love, equality, and justice. The displacement of the Gullah people raises a profound question about the nature of progress: at what cost should it come, and who should bear the burden?

The parallels between the displacement of the Gullah people and the Palestinian settlements are striking and serve as a dark reminder of the destructive consequences of unchecked capitalism and expansion. Just as the bridge to Hilton Head Island heralded the beginning of the Gullah people's displacement, so too have the Israeli settlements in Palestinian territories symbolized an encroachment on the homes, livelihoods, and lives of the Palestinian people.

Just as Evangelical Christian leaders have remained largely indifferent, or even complicit, to the plight of the Gullah people, they have similarly failed to apply the principles of Christianity to the Palestinian crisis. The emphasis on love, equality, and justice, so central to Christian doctrine, seems to be conveniently forgotten when it comes to these communities. Instead, these leaders often side with the oppressor, conflating capitalism and colonialism with progress, and showing a profound misunderstanding of what true progress entails.

The indifference or complicity of Evangelical leaders in these instances highlights a deep-seated problem. By endorsing such injustices, they contribute to the continued marginalization of these communities. They become part of the problem, rather than the solution, reinforcing oppressive systems instead of challenging them. This is not progress, but a travesty against humanity that begs the question: Who benefits from this so-called 'progress', and at what cost?

Prominent social justice advocate, Benjamin Crump, also known as the *Attorney General of Black America*, has spoken vociferously against this travesty of justice. Crump joins his voice with others as he cries out against the displacement of the Gullah people, which is not just an attack on their land but an assault on their heritage and identity, which isn't progress, but cultural erasure, and a gross violation of human rights. It's high time we confront these greedy capitalistic tendencies that masquerade as progress while robbing entire communities of their homes and histories.

The case of 93-year-old Josephine Wright, a native islander of Hilton Head, starkly illuminates the struggles faced by the Gullah people. In a bitter twist of fate, Wright found herself slapped with a lawsuit by a developer, who claimed she was encroaching on the land next to hers, where he was constructing a new neighborhood. Wright, whose family has lived on their parcel of land for generations, is now surrounded on all sides by the dust and noise of this new construction project. Alarmingly, there are suspicions that this lawsuit is nothing more than a ploy to coerce Wright and her family into relinquishing their land. It is instances like this that underscore the exploitative practices employed by those who disguise their greed under the guise of progress and development. The fight of Josephine Wright is not just her own but symbolizes the broader struggle of the Gullah people against erasure and displacement.[44]

Former state legislator Bakari Sellers was chief among the legal experts who rallied to Josephine Wright's aid, recognizing the broader implications of her struggle. Sellers, well-known for his advocacy for marginalized communities, saw that this was not just a fight against a developer's lawsuit, but a battle for the survival of the Gullah people and their cultural heritage. The Gullah community, as an essential part of Southern heritage, and a living testament to the resilience of African Americans in the face of adversity, stands threatened by rampant capitalist exploitation masquerading as development. If unchecked, these practices will lead not only to the displacement of the Gullah people but also to the erasure of their rich history and contribution to American

---

[44] Aallyah Wright, "Developers Sue 93-Year-Old Woman Over Her Land. She's Fighting Back," Capital B News, June 27, 2023, https://capitalbnews.org/hilton-head-gullah-land/.

culture. The brave stance of Josephine Wright and the fervent advocacy of Bakari Sellers and his team illuminate the core issue – the fight for dignity, rights, and cultural preservation in the face of racialized capitalism.

Wright's situation mirrors a grim series of historical injustices, as Black landowners have often been strong-armed into selling their precious land, a pattern that rings all too familiar in the narrative of Gullah landowners. Sellers pointed out that the original inhabitants of Hilton Head, the Gullah people, who settled here in the aftermath of the Civil War, have experienced a steady erosion of their land ownership. Once the dominant landowners, they now hold just a meager fraction of private ownership on Hilton Head Island. Over the decades, the Gullah people have seen their share of the island's limited land dwindle, as capitalist forces encroach upon their ancestral lands. The relentless pressure on these landowners to sell their properties is not just an attack on their economic stability, but a brazen affront to their cultural heritage and historical roots.

Bakari Sellers spoke candidly and with passion about the challenges faced by the Gullah community. In the words of Bakari Sellers, we see a stark representation of the ongoing struggle against systemic oppression of Black communities. His assertion of a "concerted effort to take property from Black folk" is a pointed commentary on practices that disproportionately target Black landowners, particularly in the Gullah community. Seller's perspective illuminates the multi-layered challenge faced by the Gullah people, where land ownership is not just a means of economic stability, but also a conduit for preserving cultural identity and heritage against the encroachment of capitalist exploitation.

Commercial development and land confiscation, often sugarcoated as 'acquisition', starkly contradict the Christian principles of justice, fairness, and love of neighbor. They are akin to the diabolical forces depicted in Revelation, which thrive on chaos, exploitation, and the oppression of the powerless. The Book of Revelation underscores a struggle between good and evil where wealth and power are often used to subjugate the vulnerable, much like the land confiscation endured by the Gullah community.

Sadly, many in the predominant society, seduced by convenience and prosperity, remain blind to this reality. Wrapped in the comfort of their privileged lives, they overlook the suffering that underpins their lifestyle. This blindness symbolizes the spiritual myopia that Revelation warns against – a state of being where one is so consumed by worldly wealth and convenience that they ignore the cries of the oppressed. The Gullah people, whose land and heritage are being steadily eroded by capitalist greed, stand as a living testament to this biblical warning. The need to awaken to this reality, to challenge the systems of power, and to uphold the true Christian principles of justice and equality is more pressing than ever.

Modern translations of Revelation 14:8 and Revelation 17:4 read thus: "Then another angel followed him through the sky, shouting, 'Babylon is fallen—that great city is fallen!—because she made all the nations of the world drink the poisonous wine of her immorality.'" (Rev 14:8)

"The woman wore purple and scarlet clothing and beautiful jewelry made of gold and precious gems and pearls. In her hand she held a golden cup full of abominations and the impurities of her sexual immorality." (Rev 17:4)

These verses highlight the deceptive allure of Babylon, symbolized by the golden cup filled with abominations. It's tempting, much like the allure of vulture economics – a system that promises prosperity but essentially feeds on the vulnerabilities of the underprivileged. The 'wine of her immorality' and the 'golden cup' reflect the intoxicating illusion of wealth and power that ultimately leads to moral and spiritual downfall. Just as Babylon seduced nations into moral decay, vulture economics lure societies into perpetuating injustice and inequality, cloaked under the guise of progress and development. The fallout, as seen in the plight of the Gullah people, echoes the biblical warning: a system that thrives on exploitation and unfairness will eventually face a fall.

Just as the wine of Babylon mentioned in Revelation

intoxicated the nations, so too does capitalism seduce the masses with the illusion of prosperity and growth. This intoxication blurs the vision of those comfortably positioned within its structures, enabling them to partake in the exploitation of the vulnerable without awareness or guilt. Even more critical is the analogy with the golden cup full of abominations. The cup, radiant and alluring outside, symbolizes the veneer of prosperity that capitalism presents. Inside, however, it is filled with abominations, representing the oppression, injustice, and destruction that are the real costs of unchecked capitalist growth. The aggregation of the Gullah peoples' land is akin to these abominations: it is an ugly injustice concealed within the golden cup of what many perceive as economic progress and development.

Owners of multi-million-dollar properties, often seen as symbols of success in capitalistic societies, are afforded privileges that eclipse the rights of native communities like the Gullah people. These elite few, draped in their wealth and influence, are prioritized, their desires catered to at the expense of those who have called these lands their homes for generations. This is in stark contradiction to the teachings of Jesus, who in the Sermon on the Mount professed, "Blessed are the meek, for they shall inherit the earth" (Matthew 5:5). The plantation capitalist system, with its unquenchable thirst for expansion and profit, has turned its back on these words, choosing instead to uplift the wealthy while disregarding the poor and the meek.

This behavior is not just unchristian but goes against the very essence of Christ's teachings. Jesus spoke of love, compassion, and the shared familyhood of all people. He admonished his followers to care for the less fortunate and to defend the defenseless. Yet, what we see in the treatment of the Gullah people is the diametrical opposite - a relentless pursuit of wealth that tramples upon the meek, exploiting the vulnerable for material gains. It is important to distinguish between the teachings of Christ and the actions carried out in His name. An economic system that perpetuates such injustices is not just unchristian but is fundamentally against the words of Jesus.

In current scenarios, with a 90 percent white wealthy population dominating the landscape, effectively translates to an apocalyptic end for the historically thriving Gullah people. It's akin to a slow-moving tsunami of wealth that washes away the rich cultural heritage and displaces the original inhabitants of these sea islands. Relentless tides of gentrification and capitalistic expansion, under the mask of progress, systematically erodes the Gullah's ancestral lands and dilutes their deeply rooted culture. Their world, as they know it, is being reshaped, disregarding the sacred connection they hold with their land. Just as in any apocalyptic scenario, what once was familiar and safe is being decimated, leaving the Gullah people to grapple with a reality that's foreign and hostile. The destruction of their homeland and the obliteration of their cultural identity is a real-world apocalypse for the Gullah community. It shines a light on the dire consequences of unchecked capitalism and a call to action for those who believe in the teachings of Christ, to stand up against such injustices.

When one dreams of vacationing on the Gullah Islands, soaking in its pristine beauty and savoring its unique culture, they may not realize the harsh implications of their seemingly innocent aspiration. This dream, when fueled by a capitalist tourism industry, can perpetuate damaging cycles of gentrification, ultimately contributing to the erasure and displacement of the Gullah people. Each new hotel or resort built on the islands to accommodate vacationers means more land snatched away from the Gullah, their ancestral homes replaced with luxury villas and beachfront properties. Each touristic commodification of Gullah culture, may it be in the form of packaged tours or exoticized cultural experiences, results in the dilution and distortion of their heritage. By seeking comfort and enjoyment in a land that's silently suffering under the weight of economic exploitation, one unknowingly becomes an enabler of this antithetical version of Christianity. While the vacationer returns home with souvenirs and memories, the Gullah people are left grappling with the loss of their land and identity, an ever- growing chasm between their past and their future.

This situation, the forceful taking of the Gullah people's land and heritage, is nothing short of theft. The essence of theft lies in the unjust taking of what rightly belongs to another, and this is precisely what is transpiring on the Gullah Islands. In biblical scriptures, the thief is often associated with corrupt leaders, who are described as "the thief [who] comes only to steal and kill and destroy" (John 10:10). This depiction aligns alarmingly well with the actions of those perpetuating the erasure of the Gullah people. Just as Satan seeks to rob individuals of their salvation, the unchecked forces of capitalism are robbing the Gullah people of their land, culture, and identity. This association with thievery, destruction, and deceit - the hallmarks of the Antichrist in Christian teachings - underscores the moral crisis posed by the gentrification of the Gullah Islands. It's a stark departure from the principles of compassion, justice, and love that form the bedrock of true Christianity.

Construction of golf courses on the sacred burial grounds of the Gullah people is not only an act of desecration, but also an affront to the historical and spiritual significance these sites hold. These hallowed grounds, wherein lie the remains of African descendants, are not just burial sites - they are symbolic monuments embodying the collective memory of a people whose ancestors were taken from their motherland, Africa. The burial practice of laying the deceased to rest along the shoreline is a poignant tribute to this historical longing, a silent prayer for the departed soul's return to Africa.

Yet, these sacred spaces are being violated, their spiritual resonance drowned out by the noise of golf clubs striking balls, the laughter of leisure-seekers oblivious to the sacrilege they're partaking in. This act of irreverence not only denies the Gullah people their right to preserve their cultural heritage but also tramples upon the spirit of respect and understanding that should characterize interactions with other cultures and histories. The building of golf courses on these sacred grounds is a chilling testament to the ways in which capitalism, masquerading as progress, can perpetuate cultural erasure and spiritual violence.

In the context of the evangelical eschatology, there is a reference to a future tribulation period following the rapture, in which an Antichrist figure will desecrate a rebuilt temple. This vision speaks to a time of deep spiritual crisis, marked by desecration of holy spaces and a blatant defiance of divine principles. But we need not look into a distant, apocalyptic future to witness such desecration. For the Gullah people, this tribulation is not a prophecy but a living reality. Their sacred spaces have been and continue to be desecrated not by a mythical Antichrist, but by an economic Antichrist, manifested through the relentless machinery of capitalism.

In the holy texts, the abomination of desolation signifies the defilement of sacred spaces, an affront of sacrilegious magnitude that leaves an indelible scar on the cultural and spiritual fabric of a community. The desecration inflicted upon the Gullah people's sacred spaces mirrors this biblical imagery in a harrowing manner. Their ancestral lands, seen as spaces of communal bonding, shared history, and cultural preservation, have been violated, their sanctity desecrated by capitalist greed.

Sacred corners of the Gullah Geechee Sea islands, once vibrant with the echo of ancestral songs, the sway of spiritual dances, and the hum of communal narratives, have been trampled upon. These spaces, where generations of Gullah Geechee people have prayed, celebrated, and mourned, are now marred by capitalist structures that epitomize desolation. The bulldozing of ancestral homes to make way for luxury resorts, the silencing of traditional music for the din of tourist attractions, and the replacement of centuries-old landmarks with new-age capitalist symbols, reflect a contemptuous disregard for their sacred cultural spaces.

The echoes of this desecration ring loud, a chilling reminder of the biblical abomination of desolation, as the sanctity of the Gullah Geechee cultural essence is replaced by the cold, sterile hand of capitalism. Such actions are a stark contradiction to the values of love, respect, and community, revered in Christ, revealing a disheartening divergence between professed faith and practiced reality.

This economic Antichrist, hiding behind a veneer of Christian idealism, has furthered its agenda under the guise of progress and development. The historical sites of the Gullah, their spiritual temples, are being replaced with golf courses, their sacred traditions lost in the pursuit of profit. This is a clear contradiction of the Christian principles of love, respect, and preservation of history. The ongoing tribulation of the Gullah people, the desecration of their sacred spaces, mirrors the prophesied tribulation in evangelical eschatology, serving as a grave reminder of the spiritual violence that blind pursuit of economic gain can wreak.

Hebrew prophets delivered stern warnings about exploiting the vulnerable, displacing the destitute, and engaging in destructive practices. They maintained that such actions were not only morally reprehensible but also in direct violation of the divine law. They spoke of God's judgment against those who oppress the poor and the consequences that would befall them. The prophet Amos, for instance, vividly depicted the impending divine wrath upon the oppressors: "Therefore because you trample on the poor and take from them levies of grain, you have built houses of hewn stone, but you shall not live in them; you have planted pleasant vineyards, but you shall not drink their wine" (Amos 5:11).

Jeremiah's prophetic ministry also echoed these sentiments, raising a profound woe against those who build their houses through unrighteousness and their chambers through injustice. Jeremiah delivers a clear message, saying, "Woe to him who builds his house by unrighteousness, and his upper rooms by injustice, who makes his neighbor serve him for nothing and does not give him his wages" (Jeremiah 22:13). Jeremiah's vehement indictment of greed-driven construction remains a powerful indictment against systems that prioritize profit over people, exploiting the vulnerable and erasing their histories.

Stories surrounding historical devastation of island communities in the United States extends beyond the South Sea

Islands, taking root in other corners of the nation as well. Take, for example, the tragic case of American Island in Florida. This vibrant community, once brimming with the rich cultural tapestry of its inhabitants, has been systematically stripped of its identity in the name of capitalist development. The island's original residents, descendants of indigenous tribes and African slaves, lived harmoniously with the land, creating a unique culture that was a beautiful blend of their ancestors' traditions. However, the insatiable drive for economic growth led to the displacement of these residents, a modern-day repeat of the historical atrocities committed against their ancestors. Their homes were demolished, their lands seized, and their culture nearly erased to make way for luxurious resorts and vacation homes. This blatant disregard for the dignity and rights of these communities starkly contrasts with the Christian tenets of love, justice, and respect for all God's creation. The biblical prophets' warnings against such exploitative practices resonate loudly in these scenarios, serving as a critical reminder for us to examine and rectify the injustices committed in the name of progress.

At the heart of the 20th century, between the 1930s and 1960s, American Island was at its peak, resonating with the fervent hum of life and community. It represented more than just a geographical location; it was a testament to the enduring spirit of the Gullah people, a cultural crossroads where indigenous traditions intertwined with African roots, crafting a rich tapestry of unique customs, language, and art. This vibrant locale was a beacon of resilience, a testament to people who had endured much yet continued to thrive amidst adversity.

However, the onset of the 1970s marked the beginning of this community's disheartening transformation. The advent of unbridled capitalism began to overshadow the island's rich cultural heritage, heralding an era of destruction that can only be likened to an end-of-the- world devastation. As developers began to eye the island for its potential as a luxury tourist destination, the steady drumbeat of the community began to falter, echoing the prophetic warnings of biblical times.

Sapelo island is another tragic example of a Gullah community devastated by encroaching capitalist interests. Once vibrant with cultural richness, Sapelo has seen its indigenous population dwindle as property taxes skyrocket and developers swoop in. Similarly, St. Simons Island, formerly teeming with Gullah Geechee heritage, has been overtaken by resorts and vacation homes, leaving few traces of its original community. Cumberland Island, as well, is being threatened, its serene landscapes and historical significance are at risk due to continual pressure from capitalist expansion.

In the biblical narrative, there existed a man named Naboth, the Jezreelite, who owned a vineyard that adjacent to the palace of King Ahab in Samaria. The king coveted Naboth's vineyard, seeing its potential for a vegetable garden, and he proposed to buy it or provide him with a better vineyard in exchange. However, Naboth refused, citing the Lord's command to not part with the land of his ancestors. Enraged and sulking, Ahab returned to his palace, where his wife, Jezebel, noticed his low spirits. Upon hearing about Naboth's refusal, she hatched a malicious plan. Jezebel had Naboth unjustly accused and executed for blasphemy and treason, thus paving the way for Ahab to seize the vineyard. However, this sin did not go unnoticed by God, who sent the prophet Elijah to declare his divine judgment — Ahab's lineage would be obliterated, and dogs would devour Jezebel by the city wall, signifying a horrific end. This story underscores the sacredness of ancestral land, the moral implications of greed, and the consequences of committing injustices for personal gain.

The seizure and destruction of Gullah communities, in many ways, mirrors the biblical account of King Ahab's unjust acquisition of Naboth's vineyard. Just as Ahab coveted and seized Naboth's land, a cherished inheritance passed down through generations, so too are developers encroaching upon the Gullah islands, disregarding the cultural and historical significance these lands hold for their rightful owners. Ahab's actions, driven by selfish desire and a grotesque distortion of his kingly authority, are an ancient reflection of the insatiable greed that fuels capitalism.

The Gullah communities, much like Naboth, are victims of an injustice that seeks to strip them of their heritage and roots. These stark parallel underlines the perverse contradiction between capitalism and true Christian values, drawing a clear line between the pursuit of wealth and the respect for communal rights, heritage, and dignity.

Evangelicals, influenced by propagated fears and biased perspectives, often project an apocalyptic future driven by an Antichrist imagined in the form of a Muslim takeover or a socialist revolution that eradicates private ownership and instills atheism. This myopic view, entrenched in Islamophobia, anti-socialism, and a fear of atheism, is largely shaped by their comfort zones, devoid of the struggles faced by marginalized communities.

However, what they fail to see is the current manifestation of the Antichrist not in religious or ideological shifts, but in the ruthless machinery of economic Darwinism. This economic Antichrist, functioning under the guise of capitalism, thrives on survival of the economically fittest, often at the expense of the vulnerable, the marginalized, and those at the bottom. They overlook the devastation wrought on communities like the Gullah people, where unchecked economic expansionism has led to displacement, cultural erosion, and an adverse alteration of their world. This failure to perceive the Antichrist in present-day economic structures reveals not just a blindness to the experiences of the less privileged, but also a glaring disconnects between their prophetic fears and the realities of those suffering under the weight of capitalist exploitation.

Revelation 13 paints a vivid picture of a grotesque beast with the mouth of a lion, feet of a bear, the body of a leopard, and the voice of a dragon. Each animal, a hunter in its own right, aptly represents the predatory nature of this beast - a clear symbol of pervasive evil. Now, consider the implications of these animalistic traits present in modern society. The lion's mouth, known for its ferocious roar, emblematic of powerful and intimidating voices that silence the weak and marginalized. The bear's feet, a symbol of crushing force applied without remorse or hesitation, reflect the relentless march of gentrification and displacement of vulnerable communities like the Gullah people. The leopard's body, agile and stealthy, represents the cunning manipulation and exploitation of resources and people for personal and corporate gain.

The beast rising from the sea, as illustrated in Revelation 13, can be seen as a poignant allegory for the rise of European power and prosperity that was built on the harrowing transatlantic slave trade. The sea, representing the vast, tumultuous, and often treacherous Atlantic Ocean, was the unforgiving passage for millions of our African ancestors. They were forcefully taken from their land, their cultures, and their families, and tossed into the belly of the beast - the slave ships - under the harshest of conditions.

This beast, with its terrifying roar, crushing feet, and cunning agility, symbolizes the European nations that capitalized on the slave trade. Their economic might, much like the lion's ferocious roar, was amplified on the global stage, silencing the cries and struggles of the enslaved. The bear's feet, much like the relentless forces of capitalism, stomped forward without any remorse or concern for the cultures and communities it trampled underfoot. The leopard's stealth reflects the deceitful way in which they exploited these enslaved Africans, plundering their labor, and resources to fuel their economic engines.

This predatory beast, emerging from the Atlantic, is a stark representation of the European powers that rose to dominance on the backs of enslaved Africans. The transatlantic slave trade was their sea, their platform on which they built their prosperity, much like the beast rising from the sea. This exploitation has had lasting, devastating effects on African diaspora communities, with the displacement and erasure of communities like the Gullah people serving as a clear and painful reminder of this historical beast.

While the average Evangelical may struggle to view eschatology through this lens, African descendants who center their experiences may draw such conclusions with unnerving ease. Just as the Book of Revelation depicts beasts emerging from the sea, many African diaspora communities perceive the beast as white supremacy and plantation capitalism - destructive forces rising from the sea of past and present injustices. To them, the end times are not a distant, future occurrence, but a continuous, living reality shaped by historical and ongoing displacements, erasures, and oppression. This eschatological view, painful as it is, helps to make sense of the apocalyptic proportions of injustice they've experienced. The desolation of the Gullah community and the numerous black towns lost to racism becomes less of a historical event and more of a revelation of the true nature of the beast – a systematic, capitalistic, and racially motivated force that constantly seeks to destroy and displace.

It's no coincidence that those at the apex of our societal hierarchy, those wearing crowns of authority as depicted in Revelation 13 and wielding king-like power, often find their mandates not grounded in the divine providence of God, but from this dragon spirit.

Drawing upon biblical narratives, Revelation 13:2 reveals, *and the dragon gave him his power, and his seat, and great authority.* This passage is eerily reminiscent of the systemic injustices we face today. Those in power, those who oppress and displace communities like the Gullah people, are not acting on divine instruction, but rather, they are empowered by the proverbial dragon of white supremacy and plantation capitalism.

Their authority, rather than being an instrument of service, justice, and protection for all, becomes a tool for fostering narratives that validate their greed, sustain their lies, and sanction their exploitative practices. The dragon spirit does not just feed off the weak and oppressed, it thrives on sowing discord, promoting division, and maintaining a status quo that benefits only a select few. The Gullah people, along with countless other marginalized communities, bear the brunt of this dragon's fiery breath, reminding us of the urgent need to resist and challenge these oppressive power structures.

The beast with the lamb-like horns, as depicted in Revelation 13, serves as a potent symbol of deceptive tranquility, embodying leaders who wear a facade of gentleness and righteousness yet harbor predatory, dragon-like tendencies. This beast rising out of the earth not only signifies the immoral conquest of land but also symbolizes the insatiable appetite for wealth and power, a theme that continues to resonate in modern society. The historical trauma inflicted on the Gullah people, and other colonized communities, is a testament to this beastly ambition. Land, once viewed as a shared resource, nurturing all its inhabitants, was ravaged, its sanctity violated for the construction of towering edifices - physical manifestations of the beast's dominance. These high-rising skyscrapers, jutting out of the earth, stand as monuments to the displacement and disenfranchisement of indigenous peoples. They are stark reminders of how the beast's greed uprooted communities, desecrated cultural heritage, and scarred the landscape, transforming fertile land into concrete jungles. As we gaze upon these towering structures, we are reminded of the cost of their existence - a cost paid in the currency of human dignity and respect for our shared heritage.

Chapter 11

THE BEAST

In this twisted, beast-driven world, the worship of the beast is an unwitting tribute, an emulation that veers dangerously close to adoration. It epitomizes the saying, "imitation is the highest form of flattery," where the less affluent, swayed by the illusion of opulence, strive to mimic these avaricious principles. This perverse mirroring reveals an insidious, often overlooked facet of oppression: the subtle indoctrination of the beast's ideology into the minds of its victims. They are seduced by the allure of wealth and power, blinded by the glittering facade, and led to believe that the path to betterment lies in emulating the beast. This imitation, however, only serves to entrench the beast's dominance, fueling its destructive appetite and perpetuating the cycle of exploitation and displacement. The tragedy of this reality is heightened by the fact that the victims, in their quest for survival and betterment, inadvertently become enablers of the very system that oppresses them.

This beast, seemingly harmless with its lamb-like horns, nevertheless speaks as a dragon, representing leaders who project an image of benevolence and just action while their words and actions reflect the exact opposite. Their speech, like that of the dragon, is potent and incendiary, fueling division, invoking fear, and championing oppressive practices. They exploit the trust of the unsuspecting, ensnaring vulnerable communities like the Gullah people in a cycle of disadvantages and displacement. This deceptive beast symbolizes the hazardous reality of the world where appearance often defies the harsh reality, a stark reminder to remain vigilant against those who seek to exploit the less privileged under a guise of righteousness and prosperity. Finally, the dragon's voice, a chilling sound that echoes through the chambers of power, represents the twisted narratives and falsehoods disseminated to support and perpetuate exploitation and injustice. The dragon, a creature of deception, greed, and treachery, comes into play here.

In the notorious 1857 Dred Scott v. Sanford case, the dragon-like voice of white supremacy was at its most audible and destructive. Dred Scott, an enslaved African American man, had resided in free states with his captor, Dr. John Emerson. After the death of Emerson, Scott sought to gain his freedom through legal means, sparking a bitterly contested lawsuit. The ultimate decision of the U.S. Supreme Court, led by Chief Justice Roger Taney, held that Scott, by virtue of his race, was not a citizen and therefore lacked standing to sue in federal court. This decision, a chilling demonstration of the dragon's voice, marked one of the darkest chapters in American jurisprudence, fueling the flames of division and setting the stage for the American Civil War.

This malignant beast, wrapped in the cloak of judicial authority, bared its fangs and declared without any qualms that a *black man had no rights that a white man was bound to respect.* The echoes of this brutal pronouncement reverberated across the land, leaving a chilling legacy of injustice that continues to resonate to this day. The suggestion that one human being could be regarded as so inferior as to render him a mere commodity reflects the treacherous heart of the beast, a heart that is impervious to the principles of equality, justice, and human dignity.

Serving as a stark reminder, the case of the atrocities committed under the banner of white supremacy, allows the world to see the need to remain vigilant and combat such oppressive forces. This episode in our history underlines the fact that the beast's voice, no matter how disguised or ingratiating, invariably betrays its true intentions, which are to dominate, exploit, and dehumanize. The Dred Scott case is a painful reminder that we must constantly interrogate the narratives we encounter, question the motivations of those in power, and challenge the norms and practices that perpetuate inequality and injustice.

As we further expose the beastly character, we draw upon Chief Justice Taney's own chilling words: *They (the African peoples) had for more than a century before been regarded as beings of an inferior order and altogether unfit to associate with the white race, either in social or political relations; and so far inferior, that they had no rights which the white man was bound to respect.* This explicitly inhuman, barbaric and anti-African statement, delivered from the highest judicial platform in the land, crystalizes the beast's true nature and intent. The Black man, in the perverse worldview of the beast, was seen as nothing more than a commodity, an ordinary article of merchandise and traffic. As Taney chillingly stated, *He was bought and sold and treated as an ordinary article of merchandise and traffic, whenever a profit could be made by it.* This heart-wrenching account of commodification and dehumanization serves as a stark testament to the deeply entrenched anti-Africanness within the system, exposing the beast's insatiable greed and utter disregard for basic human dignity.

The malevolent nature of American white supremacy reveals its monstrous character in the conception of the Constitution, which designated black individuals as three-fifths of a human being. This insidious provision, known as the Three-Fifths Compromise, exposes the beast's draconian ethos. It served as a mechanism to strengthen the political power of slave-holding states, thereby reinforcing and perpetuating the beast's dominion. The Black man, in the beast's eyes, was not a full human being but a diminished entity, an affirmation of the beast's vile and perverse ideology. In the words of the Constitution itself, *Representatives and direct Taxes shall be apportioned among the several States which may be included within this Union, according to their respective Numbers, which shall be determined by adding to the whole number of free persons, including those bound to Service for a Term of Years, and excluding Indians not taxed, three fifths of all other Persons.* This chilling clause serves as an eternal testament to the dragon character of American white supremacy and a stark reminder of the beast's enduring presence.

In 1787, the abominable decree of the Three-Fifths Compromise was embedded into the United States Constitution. This heinous proclamation identified our Black kin as being three-fifths of a human in the eyes of the law, further underlining the monstrous nature of the systemic beast, the white supremacy. This declaration, a clear testament to the deep-seated racism, stood as law, further expanding the chasm of inequality. It was a dark chapter in the annals of American history, one that continues to cast a long shadow over the struggle for equality and justice.

The beast, in all of its grotesque forms, further revealed its monstrous visage in the passage of the Fugitive Slave Law of 1850. This abhorrent legislation, driven by the engine of American white supremacy, empowered any white man to accuse a Black man or woman of being a runaway slave. Without the right to testify in their defense, were forcibly returned to the shackles of servitude, sometimes pulled from the free northern states back into the hellish landscapes of the south. This law was the epitome of racial oppression, reflecting the unscrupulous nature of the beast. It embodied the beast's tenacity in preserving its power and control, while trampling on the basic human rights of the Black community. This law, much like the scars it left behind, serves as a stark reminder of the beast's relentless capacity for evil and its insatiable appetite for dominion.

The lamb-like horns symbolize a façade of innocence and righteousness, while the dragon's voice represents the true, horrifying nature of the beast - a beast that is white supremacy. It's a contradiction inherent in the system that espouses equality and justice on the surface but perpetuates racial oppression and inequality.

Scripture paints a grim picture: *And he had power to give life unto the image of the beast, that the image of the beast should both speak, and cause that as many as would not worship the image of the beast should be killed.* This passage is a chilling metaphor for our society, where not bowing down to the god of white supremacy could lead to social, economic, or even physical death.

The next lines state, *And he causeth all, both small and great, rich and poor, free and bond, to receive a mark in their right hand, or in their foreheads: And that no man might buy or sell, save he that had the mark, or the name of the beast, or the number of his name...* further underscore this sentiment. In our context, the 'mark' can be interpreted as complicity in systemic racism. Without it, one might face economic ostracism - losing jobs, businesses, and the ability to participate in the economy. This is a stark illustration of how the beast of white supremacy reinforces itself, compelling participation through fear and threat of exclusion. When Trump entered the White House, the second time, he bullied companies to bow to white supremacy and reverse their diversity initiatives. Target is one example of compliance, which was met by boycotts in the Black community.

Our history books are brimming with tales of Black heroes and who lost their livelihoods, their peace, and sometimes their lives, fighting for freedom and equality. One such story is that of Fannie Lou Hamer, a sharecropper who became a civil rights and voting rights activist. Hamer fought bravely against racial segregation and for black voting rights in Mississippi. Her activism cost her dearly. She was not just fired from her job but also suffered physical attacks and was arrested. Still, she continued to fight, undeterred by the white supremacy that sought to silence her.

Just as black people struggled and battled against this beast of pseudo-supremacy, there were white individuals who stood up and joined the fight. They too faced the wrath of the white value system that sought to quash any form of dissent against the status quo. They were ostracized, labeled traitors to their race, and faced the same economic and social penalties as their black counterparts. They were marked not by the color of their skin, but by their refusal to conform to the norm of racial segregation. These individuals showed that the fight against bigotry and prejudice is not a black fight or a white fight. It's a human fight, a fight for the soul of humanity. They showed us that brave hearts and brave acts transcend racial borders.

Post-reconstruction in America can be seen as a healing phase for the deadly wound inflicted on the South, particularly its white supremacist confederacy, by the defeat in the Civil War and the emancipation of black people. The rise of black individuals to positions of power, such as governorships and senate seats, signified a significant shift in the sociopolitical landscape of the time. This phase, however, was transient and came to an abrupt end in 1877 with the Hayes compromise. This compromise with confederacy to remove the federal troops, in order to approve Hayes presidency, which effectively marked the end of Reconstruction, allowed the South to restore white supremacy and establish a new racial hierarchy under Jim Crow laws. The Ku Klux Klan played a significant role in this process, ensuring the subjugation, displacement, and dehumanization of African Americans.

Pervasive longings of a select many to resuscitate the deadly wound is powerfully illustrated in their insistent preservation of Confederate emblems. The Confederate flag, names, and shrines at county courthouses are zealously maintained as false idols, an homage to a distorted narrative of American history. These symbols, deeply steeped in the blood-soaked soil of slavery and oppression, are twisted into emblems of a fabricated American greatness. The rallying cry to "Make America Great Again" is often a thinly veiled call to revert to a time when systemic racism went largely unchallenged, a time when black lives were marginalized, and black empowerment was an implausible dream. The prioritization of this deceptive narrative of greatness over the recognition of black lives and the necessity for black empowerment further exacerbates the racial wound, creating a chasm in our society rather than fostering healing and unity.

These demeaning statutes, akin to the beastly legacy of the dragon-like language, stripped African Americans of their inherent human dignity and equality.

Lastly, the Plessy v. Ferguson case in 1896 reinforced the dehumanizing concept of "separate but equal," effectively legitimizing systemic racism and segregation.

All these actions are in direct contradiction to the Christian principles of love, compassion, and equality, hence qualifying as Antichrist actions. They have created an ongoing socio-political apocalypse for those affected and an apocalypse characterized by racial inequality, systemic oppression, and social injustice. The aftershocks of these historical injustices continue to reverberate in today's society, manifesting in racial profiling, police brutality, and the socio- economic disparity between racialized groups. A critical examination of these realities is pivotal in our collective journey towards healing, reconciliation, and progress. And the dragon's voice, that of a beast known for its destructive capabilities, mirrors the harsh, dehumanizing rhetoric used by those in positions of power, both in government and corporate America. These 'dragon-like' conversations and decisions often prey upon Black people, stripping them of their cultural heritage, livelihoods, and dignity. Like the monstrous beast of Revelation, these predatory systems and practices embody a kind of evil that is antithetical to Christian values of love, justice, and communal harmony.

In Revelation 13:5, the prophetic Scripture tells of the beast continuing for 42 months. From a preterist perspective, this timeline aligns precisely with the duration of the brutal Neuronic persecution, which began in AD 64 and concluded with Nero's demise in June AD 68. This span of three and a half years, or 42 months, was a time of severe trial and tribulation for the early Christian church.

Similarly, the African descendants have endured centuries of systemic subjugation, a struggle that far surpasses the 42-month time frame. Yet, the essence of the biblical reference resonates more deeply within the African diaspora. The beast signifies the oppressive systems – slavery, segregation, and now socio-economic marginalization – that have sought to dehumanize and displace black communities, comparable to the brutal persecution in Nero's time. Despite the disparity in the time frame, the enduring spirit of resilience and resistance among African descendants reflects the steadfast faith of the early Christians who held on to hope amidst the terrifying reign of the beast. The dragon's voice may continue to reverberate, but like those early Christians, the African diaspora perseveres, holding on to their rich heritage and inherent dignity.

In parallels between ancient Rome and modern American capitalism can be seen in their shared propensity for destruction in the name of greed and power. Just as the occupiers of Wall Street and the corporate world have displaced communities and caused irreparable damage to black towns, so did the Romans in their time. They conquered and decimated villages, eradicating cultures, and imposing their own to achieve economic and political dominance. This relentless pursuit of wealth and power, heedless of the human cost, is an enduring trait of empires, past and present. The beast of Revelation, therefore, is a symbol of oppressive systems that spans across epochs, manifesting in different forms but always driven by the same insidious spirit of greed and dehumanization.

The devastation of the old Africatown's, once vibrant communities' home to freedmen, is a poignant example of this economic Antichrist in action. These historic towns, rich in heritage and cultural resonance, have been systematically erased from the landscape, their proud legacy and history overwritten by the indiscriminate sprawl of capitalistic expansionism. A once flourishing community, full of life, song, and stories, is now reduced to a distant memory, lost amidst the towering edifices of modernity and progress. Millennia-old traditions and communal bonds, the very essence of these Africatown's, have been ruthlessly dismantled, leaving behind a void that is palpable and heart-rending. The displacement and erasure of these communities under the banner of economic progress starkly underlines the true cost of unbridled capitalism, a cost too often paid by those least able to bear it. The destruction of these Africatown's is an indictment of our collective societal failure, and a sobering reminder of the dehumanizing power of unchecked capitalism.

Africatown's once thrived across the southern United States, notably in Alabama, Louisiana, and Florida. One such community was Africatown in Mobile, Alabama, founded by the last known group of Africans transported to America through the Atlantic slave trade. Nestled amidst the natural beauty of the Mobile River, the town was a testament to resilience and cultural fortitude. Similarly, vibrant Africatowns flourished in Louisiana, where they were a living testament to a unique blend of African and Creole cultures.

However, the rise of interstates and urban development in the mid-20th century began a relentless march of erasure. In Alabama, the construction of Interstate 165 plowed through the heart of Africatown, decimating homes, splitting the community, and leaving a scar that would never truly heal. The establishment of paper and chemical industries peripheral to the community further accelerated its disintegration. In Louisiana, communities were fragmented and uprooted to make way for new housing developments and expanding city centers. The vibrancy and cultural heritage of these Africatowns were gradually lost amidst the concrete sprawl, their lands eaten up by the ceaseless jaws of 'progress' and 'modernization'. The African diaspora, once firmly rooted in these lands, was displaced, their communal bonds and shared histories cruelly wiped from the landscape.

Developers zoned in on Africatown and similar communities due to a twisted calculus of socio-economic factors. These African diaspora communities, already marginalized and economically neglected, were seen as easy targets for urban development projects. Their lands, teeming with cultural history and communal bonds, were erroneously perceived as 'under-utilized' or 'degraded', prime for reclamation and reinvention. Moreover, their communities lacked political power and resources to resist or divert these invasive infrastructural developments.

This systemic bias and institutionalized prejudice, cloaked under the guise of urban renewal and progress, laid the groundwork for the decimation and displacement of Africatown and its kindred communities. Indeed, the destruction and displacement weren't limited to Africatown. Across the United States, numerous black towns and cities experienced similar fates, particularly during the expansion of the interstate highway system in the mid-20th century. Neighborhoods like Rondo in Saint Paul, Minnesota, and Jackson Ward in Richmond, Virginia, were torn asunder by the construction of highways. These vibrant, self-sustaining black communities were targeted precisely because they were seen as 'easy targets', with limited socio-economic and political power to resist the bulldozers of 'progress'. The construction of these highways dislocated thousands of African American families, rupturing the social fabric and accelerating economic decline. This pattern was replicated in cities across the country, from Syracuse, New York, to Miami, Florida, where the Overtown neighborhood was bisected by the construction of I-95. In many cases, these communities are still grappling with the aftermath, as the highways that once promised connectivity instead delivered division and economic hardship.

Dislocation of these communities resulted in more than just the loss of homes and neighborhoods. It was a cataclysm, a tearing apart of the social, cultural, and economic fabric that had been carefully woven over generations. Communities that once thrived, filled with families, businesses, and cultural institutions, were fragmented and scattered, their residents forced to start anew in unfamiliar and often hostile environments. The psychological impact was immense, with individuals and families grappling with a profound sense of loss, displacement, and dislocation. Not to mention, the economic hardship that came with losing businesses, jobs, and the network of community support that once existed. This displacement made it challenging for individuals to accumulate wealth or achieve economic stability, further entrenching systemic racial and economic disparities. In the end, the dislocated were left grappling with the deep-seated effects of this upheaval, struggling to reclaim their identities and rebuild their communities in the face of continued adversity and systemic neglect.

The assertion made by Public Enemy in their potent anthem "Fight the Power," that Central Park was once a flourishing Black town, holds historical weight. Indeed, before its transformation into one of the world's most famed urban parks, the area was home to Seneca Village, a predominantly African American community. Established in the mid-19th century, it was a beacon of Black home ownership and burgeoning prosperity. However, as New York City grew and Central Park was envisaged, the powers that be used eminent domain to displace Seneca Village's inhabitants, obliterating the community in the process.

This episode, much like the erasure of Gullah people, is a stark illustration of how progress and capitalism, camouflaged in the garb of social betterment, can perpetrate injustices and disruptions on marginalized communities. This historical instance thus amplifies the necessity for honest reckoning with such past actions and a commitment to equitable development, respect for existing communities, and reparative justice moving forward.

Public Enemy, in their trailblazing track "Fight the Power," wasn't just creating a rally cry for the masses, but also embedding a powerful history lesson within their lyrics. When they mentioned Seneca Village, they were unearthing a forgotten narrative, drawing attention to a thriving African American community that was bulldozed in the name of urban development and 'progress.' By referencing Seneca Village, they were laying bare the stark realities of systemic racism and displacement — a social and economic brutality that remains largely invisible in mainstream discourse. They were stressing that the powers that be, under the pretense of progress, have often disregarded the rights and needs of marginalized communities. In essence, *Public Enemy* was charging us to confront these buried truths, to 'fight the power' that perpetuates such injustices, and to strive for a more equitable world where progress doesn't come at the expense of vulnerable communities.

"Fight the Power" is not just a song, it's a call to arms against systemic oppression and iniquities championed by a beast of capitalism, seen in the Book of Revelation as the Dragon who gives power to the Beast. This Dragon, a symbol of supreme authority and control, empowers the Beast, representing exploitative systems and structures, not unlike the socio-economic engines that have driven the erasure of marginalized communities like the Gullah people and others. Public Enemy's music challenges this Dragon, this Beast, and calls for a resistance that mirrors the spiritual warfare detailed in biblical apocalyptic literature. Just as the forces of good battle, the Dragon and the Beast in Revelation, so too are we, through the lyrics of Public Enemy, implored to rise, resist, and 'fight the power' that continues to marginalize, displace, and erase integral parts of our shared community. This is the call to arms, this is the call to action — to stand against the Dragon, to defy the Beast, and to strive for justice and equity in a world that frequently falls short.

Here are a few other notable towns akin to Seneca Village, referenced by Public Enemy, that were destroyed in the name of 'urban progress':

1. **'Black Bottom' and 'Paradise Valley', Detroit:** These vibrant African American neighborhoods were demolished in the 1960s to make way for a freeway and the Detroit Medical Center.

2. **'The Hill District', Pittsburgh:** This culturally rich African American neighborhood was razed in the 1950s to construct a civic arena, displacing thousands.

3. **'Rosewood', Florida:** In an appalling act of racial violence in 1923, this prosperous Black town was destroyed, and its residents were murdered or driven out.

4. **'Central Avenue', Los Angeles:** This lively cultural hub of the African American community faced decline after the construction of freeways in the 1950s and 60s.

5. **'Greenwood', Tulsa, Oklahoma:** Known as the 'Black Wall Street', Greenwood was burned down by a white mob in the 1921 Tulsa Race Massacre.

6. **'Albina', Portland, Oregon:** A thriving Black community was displaced in the mid-20th century due to urban renewal programs and freeway construction.

The common thread that runs through these tales of displacement and erasure is the systemic vulnerability of these communities, stemming largely from a lack of wealth, political power, and the pervasive poison of racism. These communities, rich in culture and spirit, were often seen as 'disposable' in the eyes of those wielding power, an unfortunate side effect of their socioeconomic status and racial identity. The absence of economic wealth made them easy targets for predatory urban renewal programs. Simultaneously, the lack of political power meant their voices were sidelined, their protests muffled in the larger discourse of 'progress'. Racism, an enduring scourge, further amplified their vulnerability. It created an environment where their lives and communities were deemed less valuable, their existence seen as an impediment to urban growth and modernization. This combination of systemic disadvantages allowed for these gross injustices to occur, their histories buried under the weight of 'progress' and 'capitalism'.

Indeed, Revelation, the last book of the Christian Bible, speaks of a scourge - a divine whipping or punishment. It forecasts apocalyptic events as a punishment for mankind's sins, sometimes interpreted as a cleansing of the Earth. The suffering of the Gullah people, and many other marginalized communities, could be likened to such a scourge from a spiritual perspective. However, rather than being a divine act, this 'scourge' is a man-made disaster, a consequence of unjust systems and ideologies. This raises profound questions on the nature of wealth, power, and righteousness in our society. Are these actions, borne out of Darwinian plantation capitalism and disrespect for fellow humans, not antithetical to the teachings of Christ?

In Revelation 9:3, there is a powerful depiction of scorpions being unleashed upon the earth as part of the divine judgment. These venomous creatures are not sent to cause mere physical harm, but to torment, much like the torment endured by the Gullah people under the suffocating grip of capitalism. While the scorpions of Revelation were meant for divine judgment, the scorpions unleashed upon African descendants served diabolical purposes, driven by greed rather than punishment. These scorpions may be the same, but their intent differs significantly. The scorpions in Revelation are not merely creatures, but symbols of oppressive systems that inflict pain and suffering on the most vulnerable among us. Just as the Gullah people have been stung repeatedly by the scorpions of greed, racialized capitalism, and blatant disregard for their humanity, the biblical scorpions remind us of the torments that are inflicted when power is wielded without justice, love, and respect for God's creation. As followers of Christ, it is incumbent upon us to recognize these 'scorpions' in our midst and actively work to counter their harmful effects.

We must not forget the plight of our sisters and brothers whose wealth was stolen, whose homes were destroyed, and whose spirit was broken by these powerful forces. We will never be able to fully understand the depths of their suffering - it is too vast for us to fathom. But we can acknowledge that a great injustice has been done to them in the name of 'progress' and 'development'.

Amber Ruffin, an esteemed African American comedian and writer, has gained renown for her cutting-edge commentary on the Late Night with Seth Meyers and The Amber Ruffin Show. She uses humor as a tool to bring critical social issues to the forefront, including the erasure of black history.[45]

Ruffin highlighted the lesser-known history of prosperous black towns drowned for the sake of 'progress' in one of her powerful segments. These towns, once thriving hubs of African American culture, were forcibly submerged under water to make way for reservoirs and lakes catering to the interests of nearby white communities. This historical narrative, brought to light by Ruffin, serves as a stark reminder of how African American prosperity has often been sacrificed on the altar of so-called 'progress', further highlighting the systemic racism ingrained in American society.

Black comedians like Amber Ruffin are often more well-received for their commentary on racial issues because they skillfully leverage humor as a gateway to spark dialogues around these sensitive topics. They employ comedy to present the harsh realities of systemic racism, cloaking hard truths in a veil of laughter that makes the conversation more approachable and less confrontational. This humorous approach disarms the audience, allowing critical and often uncomfortable truths to penetrate their defenses. The laughter doesn't trivialize the message; instead, it amplifies it, making the bitter pill of societal critique easier to

---

[45] Amber Ruffin, "How Did We Get Here: Drowned Towns," *The Amber Ruffin Show*, Season 1, Episode 30, aired June 25, 2021, on Peacock.

swallow.

The necessity for marginalized voices to resort to humor to convey serious messages speaks volumes about the societal structures that prevail. It is a reflection of the systemic bias and prejudice entrenched within our communities, which tend to invalidate or dismiss the experiences and perspectives of these groups. This dynamic is indicative of a society that often prefers to engage with challenging topics through the safe and comfortable lens of humor, rather than confronting them head on. It is a critique of the collective discomfort around conversations that expose harsh realities, which are often deemed too 'heavy' or 'uncomfortable' to be undertaken in everyday discourse. While humor serves as a powerful tool to communicate these issues, its necessity underscores a societal shortcoming: the lack of willingness to engage sincerely and empathetically with the struggles of marginalized communities.

In a segment titled "How Did We Get Here?", featured on her Peacock show, Ruffin delves into the grim history of drowned Black towns in America, aimed at shedding light on the often-overlooked historical atrocities committed against African American communities. Her critique was sharp and uncompromising, questioning the blatant acts of systemic racism that led to the erasure of these towns in the name of 'progress'. She condemned the fact that this 'progress' was typically skewed towards white communities, leaving a trail of drowned Black prosperity in its wake. Her presentation was a response to the widespread ignorance of these events. Ruffin believed that by bringing this dark chapter of history to light, she could provoke thought and instigate much-needed dialogue about racial inequality and systemic racism, furthering the cause for racial justice.

There have been numerous Black towns, brimming with history and culture, that are now submerged underwater due to dam constructions and urban development. These towns include the vibrant African American community of Oscarville in Georgia and the historic Black town of Centralia in Florida. They were sacrificed for the creation of Lake Lanier and Lake Okeechobee respectively, eradicating evidence of a rich socio-cultural heritage and displacing entire communities.

Settled in the heart of Alabama, Kowaliga was a beacon of Black success, a thriving community that was a testament to the resilience and perseverance of its residents. Its citizens were dynamic, hardworking, and proud, building a town that celebrated African American culture, history, and achievements. Dotted with prosperous businesses, bustling schools, vibrant churches, a town where dreams flourished, and opportunities were abundant.

Kowaliga was not just a symbol of prosperity; it was a testament to the power of self- determination and Black entrepreneurship. The town was home to the first Black-owned railroad, a remarkable feat accomplished by the visionary William E. Benson. He saw an opportunity where others saw impossibility, turning the tide in a time where Black ownership was nearly unheard of. His railroad not only served as a vital conduit for commerce and communication but became a beacon of hope for his community, signaling progress in the face of adversity.

Adjacent to this testament of entrepreneurial spirit stood the Kowaligia Academic & Industrial Institute, a beacon of enlightenment in the heart of the South. Equipped with the staunch belief in the transformative power of education, the institute was a stronghold of wisdom. It fostered an environment of inquisitiveness and intellectual exploration, equipping its students with the tools and knowledge necessary to face the world.

Yet, in the midst of such vibrant Black success, the ominous shadow of displacement loomed large. Developers, blinded by prospective profit and a distorted sense of progress, cast their sight on the town. Their eyes didn't see the thriving community; they saw the potential for Lake Martin; a reservoir they believed could generate significant revenue and serve as an emblem of modernity. They argued that the creation of the lake would stimulate economic growth, provide recreational opportunities, and show off the prowess of human engineering. But these purported benefits belied the destructive undercurrents of their plans. The creation of Lake Martin would necessitate the erasure of Kowaliga, an obliteration of its rich legacy and a displacement of its resilient people. Their dreams, their businesses, their homes, and their history were all overlooked in the pursuit of this new development.

John Benson, a visionary and a stalwart in his community, laid the foundation stone for the development of the town in 1899, initiating an era of prosperity and growth. His blueprint of community development and advancement was a testament to Black success and resilience. Then, nearly a half-century later, in 1940, the specter of Lake Martin emerged. The creation of this reservoir signaled the onset of a period of destruction and displacement that would brutally disrupt the community Benson had so painstakingly built.

However, the blooming rose that was Kowaliga did not escape the destructive scythe of 'progress'. It was deliberately drowned under the waters of Lake Martin, a reservoir constructed by the Alabama Power Company in the 1920s. The residents who had built their lives and dreams on the land of their ancestors, were displaced, their homes and livelihoods swallowed by the rising waters. The arduous struggle and triumph of it's residents, their vibrant culture and prosperous businesses, now lie silent and obscured beneath the surface of Lake Martin. As we recount this tale of loss, let us remember Kowaliga not as a submerged town, but as a symbol of resilience, a testament to the indomitable spirit of the African American community.

Like Kowaliga, Susannah—or Sousana as it was endearingly referred to by its inhabitants—was not spared the devastation brought on by the creation of Lake Martin. Sousana, a tight knit, predominantly Black community, was a place where generations of families had been born, raised, and laid to rest. But as the waters of Lake Martin began to rise, the heart of Sousana— their cemetery, the final resting place of nearly a thousand souls—had to be uprooted. These grave sites were more than just markers of death; they were records of life, symbols of the unbreakable bonds of family, community, and heritage. Yet, they were brutally exhumed under the guise of progress and economic growth. The removal of the cemetery from Sousana was not just a physical displacement of bodies; it was an erasure of history, an affront to the memory of the ancestors, and a stark reminder of the cruel price they had to pay for capitalism's relentless march.

"Drowned towns" is not just a phrase, it's a stark illustration of the drowning of history, culture, and life by the surging waves of capitalism. The label signifies the ruthless submergence of our ancestors' works, their toils, their dreams, and their existence. These were vibrant communities filled with laughter, joy, sorrow, and life. But now, they exist merely as underwater shadows, drowned and silenced. The name "drowned towns" is a chilling reminder of how the thirst for progress and economic gain can mercilessly drown the voices and histories of those standing in its path.

Vanport, Oregon, once the second largest city in the state, stands as a case study of the devastating impacts of both human negligence and natural disasters. Constructed during the Second World War to house shipyard workers, this hastily built city was never meant to be permanent and therein lay its vulnerability. On Memorial Day in 1948, this impermanence took on a cruel reality as the waters of the Columbia River broke through a railway embankment serving as a makeshift levee. The flood waters rushed in, and within hours, Vanport was submerged, erased from the landscape.

The flood was not just a natural disaster; it was a human one. Despite the looming threat, the residents of Vanport, many of whom were African American, were given no warning to evacuate. The disaster claimed numerous lives, rendered thousands homeless, and obliterated a community.

In the wake of Vanport's destruction, Delta Park was created. Today, where once the city stood, there are stretches of green fields, sports facilities, and a raceway. While it serves as a recreational space, Delta Park is also a silent testament to Vanport. It stands on a history drowned, not by floodwaters, but by a system that prioritized economic gain over human lives. The creation of Delta Park is emblematic of how, too often, the narratives of capitalism seek to erase the past, replacing it with facades of progress and development. Yet, those who know its history understand that beneath the green veneer of Delta Park, the echoes of Vanport still resonate, a submerged reminder of a drowned city.

This systematic erasure of Black history is alarmingly similar to the destruction of Nubian history with the creation of Lake Nasser. The construction of the Aswan High Dam in Egypt during the 1960s resulted in the flooding of vast sections of Lower Nubia. More than 45 Nubian villages, along with countless historical monuments and archeological sites, were submerged under Lake Nasser's waters. Entire communities were displaced, their ancestral homes lost forever. This colossal loss of Nubian cultural heritage serves as a chilling testament to how 'progress' can sometimes masquerade as a scorpion stinging the most vulnerable, annihilating their history and their identity. Let us acknowledge these submerged histories, understand the pain embedded in their narratives, and learn from these acts of injustice. Only then can we truly commit to a path of restitution and reconciliation.

An overwhelming 90% of ancient Nubia was submerged as a result of the creation of Lake Nasser, an act that obliterated a significant part of Nubian history. This event marked a catastrophic event in our collective global heritage, burying centuries of civilization, culture, and stories beneath its implacable waters. The result was not just a physical submersion, but also a symbolic one, as a considerable part of Nubian identity was forever lost to the depths.

This displacement, this erasure, feels akin to an apocalypse, a cataclysm of cultural and ancestral identity. It's as if a flood of biblical proportions has swept through, not in literal terms of water and rain, but through the damning waters of capitalism and so-called 'progress'. Their world was submerged, their histories drowned, their voices silenced under the relentless tidal wave of erasure. This was no act of God; this was an act of man, a capitalist cataclysm that led to the cultural apocalypse of entire communities.

Indeed, the sins of racialized capitalism have not spared Black towns when it comes to the construction of bridges and other infrastructural projects. The construction of the Innerbelt Bridge in

Cleveland, Ohio during the late 1950s serves as a haunting testament to this. The Central Vine neighborhood, a thriving Black community, was obliterated to make way for this bridge. The area was a vibrant mix of homes, businesses, and churches, an emblem of Black resilience and community. The construction of the bridge not only destroyed physical structures but also a sense of community, scattering the residents and erasing a rich tapestry of African American history and culture. This was more than an act of displacement; it was a testament to how racism, masked under the guise of progress and capitalism, can decimate communities.

Indeed, it is no small irony that the predominant Evangelical community, so quick to raise the specter of an imagined socialist antichrist, clings steadfastly to a vision of vulture capitalism that is veiled in a cloak of divinity. They laud this system as godly, even as it leaves in its wake a trail of devastation, the ruins of Black communities and histories. Yet, they remain blissfully ignorant or, perhaps more accurately, purposely blind to the damage wrought by their so-called righteous model. They fail to question, to look deeper beyond the veneer of economic prosperity and to see the broken lives, the shattered communities, the drowned histories. It is a convenient blindness, one that allows them to profit while avoiding the unsettling reality of their actions. The true Antichrist, it seems, may not be the one they so fear but the one they so fiercely uphold.

Situated in the heart of Charleston, South Carolina, Central Vine was home to a thriving black community, a beacon of African American culture and enterprise during a time of deep-seated racial discrimination. A jewel of African American resilience and unity, it was located in the bustling heart of the city. This neighborhood began its story in the early 1900s and flourished until its untimely disintegration in the late 1960s. A casualty of so-called "urban renewal," its vibrant voices were silenced, and its rich history was paved over in the name of progress and prosperity. The erasure and displacement of our black communities and histories, represented in the destruction of neighborhoods like Central Vine, is not just a tragedy – it's an apocalyptic annihilation, akin to the end-time prophecies foretold in scriptures. The obliteration brings to mind images of the biblical flood, a cataclysm that leaves no trace of what once was, a deluge driven not by divine wrath but by the insatiable maw of capitalism. The Evangelical's vision of plantation capitalism, masquerading as a divine entity, stands as a false prophet, leading not to salvation but to the desolation of vibrant cultures and histories. This is an apocalypse of culture, a systematic eradication of black resilience and identity, hidden beneath the guise of progress and prosperity. This parasitic-capitalist beast, praised and protected by those who benefit, is the real Antichrist, the harbinger of cultural demise. Yet, amidst the destruction, it is the spirit of the black community, like a phoenix, that continually rises, refusing to be extinguished.

In the thick of this unfolding cultural Armageddon, these so-called Evangelicals attribute their prosperity to their Christian identity, painting an image of blessed abundance. They dance in the masquerade of righteousness, claiming their overflowing coffers as proof of divine approval, all the while turning a blind eye to the deep scars inflicted on the oppressed for the accumulation of that wealth. Their prosperity, though cloaked in the guise of faithfulness, is but a by-product of the relentless decimation of others. It's wealth built upon the ruins of vibrant cultures, torn apart by systemic discrimination and marginalization. Yet they stand in their pulpits, preaching a gospel of prosperity, oblivious to the dire contradiction in the heart of their doctrine. They conflate capitalism with Christianity, and in doing so, betray the very essence of the teachings they profess to uphold.

These self-acclaimed Evangelicals, parading in a cloak of piety, rationalize their prosperity further, correlating it with their militant support for the state of Israel against the vulnerable Palestinians. In their distorted interpretation of scripture, they convince themselves that they are chosen, thus justifying their affluence and reinforcing their complicity in the oppression of the Palestinians. They stand, hands outstretched in prayer for peace, while their actions contribute to the very chaos they decry. They revel in their delusion of being the righteous defenders of the Holy Land, all the while turning a blind eye to their own role in perpetuating poverty, displacement, violence and apartheid. In essence, their prosperity is a direct result of their exploitation of the poor, yet they choose to attribute it to their stance on international politics, thus conveniently absolving themselves of any moral responsibility.

The Black towns that were razed to the ground, too, were holy lands. But their sanctity was not derived from the soil beneath their feet, rather it emanated from the hopes, dreams, and prayers that nourished their foundations. These were communities built on the backs of former slaves, individuals who had only known suffering under the yoke of oppression, but whose spirits could not be broken. They dreamed of a future where they could live free and prosperously. Each brick laid, each home built, each school established was a testament to their resilience and an embodiment of their collective prayer for a better tomorrow. Their work was an act of worship, a testament to their faith in the promise of liberation. The destruction of these towns wasn't just an act of racism or economic aggression - it was a sacrilege, a desecration of the holy lands that these communities represented to those who dared to dream of a world unmarred by prejudice and hate.

Plantation economics is a system that echoes the ruthless, exploitative structure of the plantation era. It is a system that thrives on the subjugation and exploitation of the vulnerable for the advancement of the privileged. The term 'plantation economics' conjures up images of the brutal exploitation of enslaved African Americans for the economic prosperity of the white elite. In the modern context, it describes a system where wealth is concentrated in the hands of a few, while the majority labor under oppressive conditions with scant rewards.

This model of capitalism is referred to as evil because it prioritizes profits over people, stripping individuals of their dignity and devaluing their labor. It disregards the fundamental principles of fairness, equity, and humanity in its relentless pursuit of wealth. It relegates marginalized communities to continual hardship and struggle, and disposability, while the privileged continue to amass wealth. It erodes the fabric of the community, leaving despair and destitution in its wake. The real evil of this system is its dehumanizing impact - the creation of a society where some lives are deemed less valuable than others, a society where the rich get richer, and the poor are left to grapple with the scraps.

Just like the false prophet mentioned in the Book of Revelation, many modern-day evangelicals turn a blind eye to the ongoing apocalyptic reality of displacement and erasure endured by Africatowns, drowned towns and Gullah communities. Instead of standing up against these modern-day injustices, they preach a gospel of forgiveness and love, hoping to soothe the wounds inflicted through systemic racism and capitalist exploitation. But how can we truly forgive when the sin is ongoing, not a relic of the past but a continuous, living beast? How can we talk about love when our communities are being torn apart, our history erased, our very existence threatened? Their words become hollow echoes, a facade of reconciliation and unity, masking the uncomfortable reality of systemic oppression. It is not enough to simply 'get along' when our communities are being shattered – we must fight for justice, preserve our histories and ensure the survival and prosperity of the next generation.

Chapter 12

RIDE ON KING JESUS

Revelation 19 paints a vivid picture of our Savior-King, mounted on a white horse, ready to wage war against the forces of evil. This powerful image is not merely a call for divine intervention, but a rallying cry for us to stand firm in our faith, knowing that our Black Messiah is always ready to fight alongside us. He rides on a white horse, symbolizing purity and righteousness, against the exploitative elites and systems of oppression that seek to perpetuate injustice and inequality.

"Ride on King Jesus," an anthem of the enslaved ancestors, encapsulates a vision that parallels the depiction of the Savior-King in Revelation 19. This spiritual, crafted in the crucible of bondage, articulated a deep-rooted hope for divine justice and liberation. The enslaved envisioned Jesus as a warrior king who, riding to victory, would overturn the existent oppressive systems. Much like the present struggle of the Gullah people and other black communities, the enslaved sang these spirituals as an affirmation of their unyielding faith and a prophetic declaration of their imminent deliverance.

The implications of this vision are profound. It challenges us to reject the narrative of passive acquiescence often espoused by some faith leaders and instead, to embrace an active, militant faith that resists the forces of injustice and oppression. "Ride on King Jesus" is a call to action, a reminder that we are not simply passive recipients of God's deliverance but active participants in His divine plan. It compels us to resist the capitalist systems that erase and displace our communities and to reclaim the narrative of emancipation and liberation that lies at the heart of our faith and history. This is not just a fight for survival, but a fight for justice, for dignity, and for the preservation of our history and identity. Just as our enslaved ancestors sang in the face of oppression, we too must raise our voices, firm in the knowledge that our Savior-King is fighting alongside us.

This image should not be viewed as a distant, unreachable ideal, but rather, it should serve as a source of inspiration and motivation for us to actively strive towards a more equitable society.

In this envisioned world, every man will "sit under his own vine and fig tree," a biblical promise of peace and prosperity. It speaks to a future where each individual will have the right to enjoy the fruits of their labor without fear of exploitation or subjugation. This prophetic vision beckons us to work tirelessly till we create a world that reflects this divine blueprint - a world that is anchored in justice, where every individual has access to equal opportunities, and where our collective well-being is prioritized over capitalist greed. Indeed, the Savior-King on the white horse challenges us to actively partake in this righteous war, our faith being the weapon that shall render the systems of oppression powerless.

Participating in this work is a tangible embodiment of Jesus' prayer "thy kingdom come, thy will be done, on earth as it is in heaven." This is not merely a spiritual exercise, but a call to bring about God's kingdom here on earth, in the here and now. It is a divine mandate to rectify the injustices that pervade our society, to echo the outcry of the displaced Gullah people and the submerged black towns, and to ensure they do not fade into oblivion. This is a clarion call to reconstruct a world where all are valued, all are loved, and all are included - just as they are in the kingdom of heaven. This present-day effort is a continuation of the heavenly vision, a manifestation of the Almighty's will on earth. As we labor to restore justice and equity, we are not only aligned with but are actualizing Jesus' prayer, establishing His kingdom of love, justice, and peace right here among us.

Esau McCaulley, an eminent theologian, and author, provides potent insights into the nuances of Revelation 7. He underscores the envisioning of a heavenly congregation, rich in diversity, where all languages and kinship coexist harmoniously around the throne - their cultures unfettered and intact. This scene, as per McCaulley, is not just a distant celestial expectation, but rather a portrait of God's present-day desires and his inclusive future. The preservation of cultures around the throne is a profound testament to the value God places on our unique identities and cultural heritages. It signals that our diversity, far from being obliterated, is instead celebrated in His divine vision.[46] McCaulley's interpretation presents a compelling argument for us to strive towards crafting a world reflective of this heavenly blueprint - a world where differences are not merely tolerated but embraced, where every language, culture, and kinship is acknowledged and cherished. The divine intent revealed in Revelation 7 underscores the need for us to address and dismantle systems that hinder this inclusivity. In doing so, we not only affirm the inherent worth of every individual but also inch closer to actualizing the divine mandate of establishing His kingdom on earth.

This divine observation, however, starkly contrasts with the frightening indifference displayed towards the erasure of cultures and their lands. The Gullah people, hailing from the South Sea Islands, have endured the devastating blow of cultural erasure and displacement. Their lands and homes, symbols of their rich ancestry and cultural heritage, have been steadily encroached upon by the insidious forces of capitalism and racism, disguised under the banner of progress and economic development.

The biblical imagery of Revelation 7 acts as a sermon on page, a clarion call to the world, of how contrary these actions are to the divine vision. It is ironical and indeed tragic, that in a world where many tend to intertwine capitalism with Christianity, the displacement of the Gullah people and the destruction of their culture is seen as an acceptable consequence of economic growth. These actions are not merely unjust, but deeply antithetical to the teachings and vision of Christ. They are, in essence, a

---

[46] Esau McCaulley, *Reading While Black: African American Biblical Interpretation as an Exercise in Hope* (Downers Grove, IL: IVP Academic, 2020).

manifestation of the Antichrist, contravening the very tenets of love, justice, and peace that form the bedrock of Christianity.

Erasure of the Gullah people is not an isolated instance. Many black towns have been razed or submerged, their identity and history wiped off the map due to the prejudice and racism ingrained within our societal structures. These actions are a stark reminder of how far we have strayed from the divine intent of inclusivity, justice, and cultural preservation. It becomes incumbent upon us, therefore, to challenge and dismantle these oppressive systems, to see past the veil of ignorance, and to work towards creating a world that embraces the diversity and richness of all cultures, as envisioned in the heavenly congregation of Revelation.

This struggle against erasure and displacement is not unique to the Gullah people. The suppression of a myriad of marginalized black communities resonates with a shared experience of systemic inequity. From the bustling streets of Black Wall Street in Tulsa, Oklahoma, to the quiet corners of Seneca Village, New York, thriving black communities have been disintegrated, their legacy left in ruins. The echoes of these injustices reverberate through time, a painful reminder of the communities lost, and the potential unfulfilled. The intersection of capitalism and racism becomes a bulldozer, flattening the distinct identities of these communities under the guise of progress. Our collective memory must not forget these acts, for they form the narrative of innumerable black communities, underrepresented, and too often, overlooked. The revealing of this truth is not just a matter of justice, but of humanity, and a call to action for us all to uplift and honor the histories of these underrepresented communities.

Reflecting on Esau McCauley's potent words concerning Revelation 7 and its depiction of all cultures worshiping the Lamb-Jesus, he declared *God's eschatological vision for the reconciliation of all things requires my blackness and my neighbor's identity to endure forever. Colorblindness is sub-biblical and falls short of the glory of God...This means that the gifts that our cultures have are not ends in themselves. Our distinctive cultures represent the means by which we give honor to God. He is honored through the diversity of tongues singing the same song. Therefore, inasmuch as I modulate my blackness or neglect my culture, I am placing limits on the gifts that God has given me to offer to his church and kingdom.*[47] This speaks of the divine intent for the preservation of our diverse cultures and identities. It critically dissects the concept of colorblindness, emphasizing that our individual cultural richness and diversity are gifts from God to be celebrated and revered, not suppressed or erased.

Mainstream eschatology's reference to wars and rumors of wars as signs of the end can strike a tone-deaf chord, particularly from the perspective of African and Black history. This is because in this context, the 'wars' being fought are not conventional battles but a more insidious, relentless war on blackness that's been raging since the dawn of the Transatlantic slave trade. The very notion of equating these struggles with apocalyptic foretelling can be seen as a trivialization of the continuous, systemic injustices faced by Black communities. Moreover, the assertion contradicts Jesus' words in Matthew 24, where He states that wars, and rumors thereof, are occurrences to always expect, not signs of the end. This misinterpretation can be attributed to a lack of cultural competency, as it fails to recognize and honor the unique and ongoing tribulations faced by black communities. Thus, it is crucial for interpretations of eschatology to be made with sensitivity, inclusivity, and a thorough understanding of historical and ongoing racial struggles.

Jesus, in his profound wisdom and foresight, highlighted in Matthew 24:6 that we would hear of wars and rumors of wars. He warned us not to be alarmed, as such events are but the birth pains of creation, not the end. This statement serves as a powerful reminder to us, especially the Black community, that struggles, injustices, and battles, both overt and covert, are unfortunately a

---

[47] Ibid.

part of this world's flawed fabric. Yet, Jesus did not instruct us to passively accept this reality. Instead, His words were a call to action, to resist these injustices and work tirelessly towards a world rooted in love, peace, equality, and respect for all of God's creations. In the context of the relentless war on blackness, this means actively opposing systemic racism, advocating for the preservation of threatened Black communities like the Gullah people, and seeking justice for the numerous black towns unjustly destroyed or submerged. Thus, while the occurrence of these drastic events is, sadly, not the end, it is our Christian duty to ensure they do not define our future.

The right-wing argument that often responds to discussions around systemic racial injustice and apocalyptic suffering with deflections such as "What about Chicago?" reflects a deep-seated unwillingness to acknowledge and address the complex and pervasive nature of racism in America. This tactic sidesteps the issue at hand and instead, attempts to shift the focus onto isolated incidents of violence or crime within Black communities. The underlying implication is an insidious stereotype that suggests such communities are inherently violent or dysfunctional. However, such arguments fail to recognize that the issues plaguing cities like Chicago are not separate from the systemic racism and injustices being discussed; rather, they are a direct consequence of these larger, systemic issues. Years of segregation, disinvestment, and discriminatory policies have sown the seeds of instability and violence in these areas. Thus, the "What about Chicago?" argument is not only a diversion but also an oversimplification of complex socio-economic issues, rooted in systemic racism. As Christians, it's crucial to see beyond these diversionary tactics, and maintain our focus on advocating for justice, equality, and systemic change.

The "What about Chicago?" argument, while subtly reinforcing stereotypes about Black communities, conveniently ignores the reality of crime and violence in white communities. By focusing on crime in predominantly Black cities, these arguments create a misleading narrative that crime is an exclusively Black issue, effectively diverting attention from the high rates of domestic violence in white communities. As Christians, we must reject these skewed narratives that attempt to single out and stigmatize one community while conveniently ignoring the pervasive issues within others. It is incumbent upon us to recognize and address the sin and suffering that exist in all communities, advocating for justice, reconciliation, and healing as taught to us by Christ.

Too many times, we hear individuals wield the "What about Chicago?" argument like a weapon, using it to deflect from the broader conversation about systemic racism and the socio-economic challenges faced by Black communities. It's a favored tactic amongst those who harbor racial biases, often reaching into the hundreds or even thousands, depending on the forum. This argument frames Black communities as inherently dangerous or problematic, painting a grim, one-sided picture of our cities that devalues Black lives. It reinforces harmful stereotypes and perpetuates the false narrative that crime is endemic to Black communities, while ignoring the societal structures that breed such conditions. As believers, we need to counter this damaging rhetoric and continually affirm the inherent value of all Black lives.

The focus on crime within communities, a narrative often peddled to bolster stereotypes and justify systemic disinvestment, is fundamentally flawed and cannot be used to rationalize the generational injustice inflicted upon communities like the Gullah and other Black towns. This perspective dangerously misleads the idea that crime is the cause rather than a symptom of socio-economic disenfranchisement. The systemic deprivation of resources, opportunities, and rights, which is a form of structural violence, breeds despair and instability, which can, in turn, lead to crime. It is essential to understand this cycle to challenge the narrative that crime rates justify disinvestment. Remember, it is the disinvestment and systemic racism that set the stage for such devastating outcomes, not the other way around. As followers of Christ, we are called to seek truth and justice, to challenge these deceitful narratives, and to strive for equality, understanding that everyone, regardless of their community or history, is made in the image of God.

The story of violence in Chicago did not begin with the Black community. Long before modern political pundits began invoking the city's name as shorthand for urban pathology, it was the site of brutal organized crime, orchestrated not by impoverished youth of color, but by white men in fedoras with government connections. During Prohibition, Chicago was the domain of Al Capone and the Chicago Outfit—a violent syndicate that left blood in the streets over control of bootleg alcohol. The infamous St. Valentine's Day Massacre of 1929 was not an outlier but emblematic of an era when violence was the currency of business, and white criminality operated with both impunity and flair.

To racialize violence in the present while ignoring its white historical roots is a distortion. It is historical amnesia.

Equally disturbing is the narrative erasure of how modern gun violence has been facilitated—not simply by inner-city poverty, but by a national supply chain of destruction. In 2015, a train car parked in a Chicago railyard was broken into, and over 100 firearms vanished into the streets—.45-caliber handguns headed from New Hampshire to Washington state.[48] These weapons did not originate in Chicago. They were shipped through it, lost to poor security and weaker gun laws elsewhere, only to reappear in the hands of teenagers and on the bodies of the dead. What does it mean that guns can travel more freely across state lines than voting rights or healthcare?

The "Iron Pipeline"—that corridor of gun trafficking from states with lax laws to urban centers—is the artery of a silent war. It is a manufactured crisis that feeds on deregulation and political cowardice. And yet, when bodies fall, blame is assigned not to manufacturers, shippers, or legislators, but to Blackness itself.

This narrative about Chicago, however, overlooks the complex

---

[48] Paris Schutz, "Gun Theft in Rail Yard Raises Security Questions," WTTW News, August 3, 2015, https://news.wttw.com/2015/08/03/gun-theft-rail-yard-raises-security-questions

interplay of factors contributing to the city's challenges, including the influx of firearms through the so-called "Iron Pipeline."

A significant aspect of this issue is the role of certain evangelical communities in shaping gun policy. Within their cultural Christianity context, they are known for championing the second amendment with no limitations. While some evangelical leaders advocate for stricter gun control, studies indicate that white evangelical Protestants are among the most resistant to such measures. This resistance is often rooted in a cultural emphasis on individual responsibility and a skepticism of structural solutions, leading to a preference for personal over legislative approaches to social issues.

The juxtaposition of advocating for minimal gun regulation while highlighting urban gun violence creates a paradox. By opposing policies that could stem the flow of illegal firearms into cities and simultaneously pointing to the resulting violence as a moral failing of those communities, a cycle of blame is perpetuated without addressing the systemic contributors to the problem.

This is not merely a failure of policy—it is a theological crisis. When the systems designed to protect instead deliver death, and when public narrative blames the oppressed rather than the profiteers, we are living under an apocalyptic arrangement—where truth has been replaced by myth, and justice buried beneath political convenience.

From a biblical perspective, the gates of the New Jerusalem are symbolic of divine inclusivity and redemption. They offer access to those traditionally colonized and neglected - the left behind, the pushed aside, the least and the lost. In the Book of Revelation, the city is described as having twelve gates, each made of a single pearl, and at these gates, no one is turned away. This is a poignant metaphor for those who have suffered the most and been rewarded the least in an ongoing societal apocalypse. These gates symbolize the promise of a future where the 'last will be first', a reversal of the social order that has perpetuated inequality and exclusion.

These individuals, truly the ones left behind, are not only

welcomed through these gates but are also given the promise of a transformed existence inside. This reinforces the belief that no one is beyond the reach of divine love and redemption, and that societal structures that have perpetuated injustice and inequality will not have the final say. The gates of the New Jerusalem thus represent a profound biblical message of hope, justice, and inclusive community.

CONCLUSION: HOPE FOR THE LEFT BEHIND

From a preterist perspective, which interprets Revelation as a symbolic representation of first- century events, John's vision of the 12 gates in Revelation 21:12 carries significant meaning for the persecuted church. These 12 gates, each named after one of the tribes of Israel, symbolize the inclusiveness and protection of God's kingdom. They offered a message of hope and promise to the beleaguered believers, assuring them of God's covenant faithfulness and reminding them that, despite their present trials, they were part of a divine plan of salvation and restoration. John sought to inspire them with the vision of a perfect, secure city where righteousness dwells, offering a profound contrast to their current state of suffering. The promise embodied in these gates was a reassurance of their eventual deliverance and a call to endure in their faith.

Though John's vision of divine love and unity is deeply inspiring, it stands in stark contrast to the ongoing realities faced by the Palestinian people. In the context of Israel's policies, the walls are far from being a symbol of equality or unity. Instead, they serve as physical barriers that restrict the movement of Palestinians, disenfranchising them socially, economically, and politically. This reality resonates far from the ideal of a harmonious society where each individual, regardless of race or creed, has equal access to resources and opportunities. The inequality is evident in the disparate living conditions, access to essential services, and opportunities for growth between Israelis and Palestinians. The ongoing conflict and unequal treatment are a stark reminder of the need for societies worldwide to strive towards the values encapsulated in John's vision. It is a call for the walls of division to be transformed into bridges of connection, promoting equal rights, respect, and harmony among all people.

For African Americans, particularly during the era of slavery and civil rights struggles, Revelation 21:12 held profound symbolic significance. The passage describes a city enclosed by a wall with twelve gates, each representing one of the twelve tribes of Israel. This was perceived as a metaphor for unity, liberation, and divine protection, reflecting their own struggles and aspirations. The twelve gates were interpreted as a portal to their spiritual freedom and the promise of a better life, mirroring their journey towards social and civil emancipation. The inscription of the tribes' names symbolized recognition and equality, while the twelve angels stationed at the gates signified divine watchfulness and protection. These interpretations provided hope and a sense of empowerment amidst their historical struggles, paving the way for their relentless pursuit of justice and equality.

The twelve gates symbolized a pathway to an inclusive society, where every tribe, representing different races or groups, are equally recognized and protected. John was not just envisioning a geographical destination, but a spiritual realm of freedom, justice, and equality.

The promise of the twelve gates represents the community's collective spiritual journey towards emancipation. The inclusive nature of the twelve gates have always provided the community with a sense of hope and determination, reinforcing the belief that their struggle was part of a divine plan leading towards a society where each 'tribe' or race would enter the 'city' through its own gate, symbolizing equal recognition and protection for all.

The significance of the twelve gates remains profoundly relevant to our contemporary society. Each of these gates, my brothers and sisters, is a testament to the enduring struggle for justice and equality amongst diverse tribes of humanity. Just as the twelve tribes of Israel each had an entryway into the divine city, so too must every race, every culture, every marginalized community have its gateway into a societal city of justice and equality.

These gates are not mere architectural constructions, but symbolic passages through which we must all pass to reach a world free of oppression, segregation, and inequality. They represent our shared responsibility to acknowledge and address the systemic barriers that have historically hindered certain tribes from accessing their deserved gate. Today, we stand on the threshold of these gates, echoing the clarion call for justice and equality, and steadfast in our commitment to usher in a time when every tribe has their rightful gate to pass through. Let us not forget, we are on a divine journey, one that requires us to ensure each tribe, each race, each individual has a gate through which they can walk into our societal city, a city where justice is not selective but collective.

Allow the writer now to transition into sermonic language to draw a more impactful conclusion.

And so, my brothers and sisters, as we stand before these twelve gates, let us not be deterred by the magnitude of the task that lies before us. Rather, let us be inspired by the hopeful promise each gate represents. Each gate is a beacon of light, standing tall against the backdrop of our society's challenges. Each gate is a symbol of hope, a testament to the power of resilience and the triumph of unity over division. For just as the Israelites overcame adversity to each find their gate, so too will we overcome.

Let us remember, these twelve gates are not just our destination, they are our journey. They are our collective commitment to challenge injustice, to break down barriers, and to ensure every tribe, every race, every individual is seen, heard, and valued. For it is only when we all pass through our gates that we truly create a city that is free from the grasp of inequality.

The journey may be long, the road may be tough, but let us take heart, for we are not alone. Together, we can, we will, overcome. So, let us march on, until victory is won, until every gate is open, until every tribe is home. For it is in this city, our city, where we will find a society that is just, that is equal, and that is fair. Now is the time, my brothers and sisters, to cross the threshold, to pass through these twelve gates, and to usher in a new dawn of justice and equality. In the name of all that is divine, let us march on... till victory is won!

And so, we press on, my brothers and my sisters, each step a declaration of our determination, each breath a testament to our tenacity. We press on, not because it's easy, but because it's necessary. We press on, not because we are guaranteed success, but because we are grounded in faith. Yes, we press on, yes we do, knowing that every mountain climbed, every barrier broken, every gate crossed is a victory in the divine narrative of our journey.

We've come this far by faith, leaning on the Lord. We've come this far by grace, bathed in the unyielding light of His love. We've come this far by hope, anchored in the promise of a new day. We've come this far by courage, propelled by a spirit that says, 'Yes, we can!' And so, I say to you, we press on!

Press on, until every gate swings wide. Press on, until every tribe finds their home. Press on, until justice isn't just a dream whispered in the night, but a reality shouted in the light of day. Press on, until the melody of equality resonates in every corner, every crevice, every crack of this great city.

In that city, oh brethren and sistren, in that grand city of justice and equality, hope is more than a fleeting dream; it is the substance of our reality. In that city, we will find no gate barred, no tribe displaced. Yes, in that city, y'all don't hear me, the melody of equality reverberates, reaching every street, every alley, every park. In that city, the river of justice is not a mere trickle but a mighty torrent, flowing unabated, cleansing the path of every remnant of inequality and injustice. And in that city, I said, in that city, every tribe, everybody who has pressed on, will experience the joy of victory, the joy of homecoming. So, with faith as our guiding star, with hope as our compass, we press on toward that city!

Three gates to the north, three gates to the south, three gates to the east, and three gates to the west, in that city, love will be the cornerstone of every interaction and relationship. It will appear as empathy and understanding, bridging the gap between the diverse tribes that have journeyed from different corners of the earth. Love will be the shared laughter of children playing in the parks, the firm handshake of businessmen forging equitable deals, and the tender smiles exchanged between neighbors across the fence. Love will be reflected in the willingness of its inhabitants to lend a helping hand to those in need, and in the collective pursuit of justice and equality. It will resonate in the harmonious tune of respect and acceptance sung by every tribe, echoing through the city streets. As we enter through any of the twelve gates, we will be met with an overwhelming wave of love, a love that binds together, a love that heals, a love that inspires us to press on.

And when we reach that day, I said, when we reach that day, do I have a witness?, oh what a glorious day it will be! We'll lift our voices in unison, singing praises to the Most High. We'll dance in the streets, feet pounding out the rhythm of freedom. We'll rejoice in the dawn of a new era, where justice no longer lags behind, but leads the way. So, onward we trudge, with gratitude in our hearts and God on our side. In His name we march, in His name we strive, in His name we press on... till victory is won!

My brothers and sisters, as we stand on the precipice of promise and possibility, I want you to envision the 12 gates of Jerusalem. Each gate, a beacon of hope, a testament to God's unyielding love, and an embodiment of His divine purpose for us. As we face the turbulence of our individual struggles, these gates stand as an affirmation of faith and a promise of deliverance.

He has prepared a place for us, a city of refuge, a city of redemption, a city with 12 gates. It is for us to usher it in.

Remember, it is not about the destination but the journey. As we travel towards our goal and towards these gates, God is mending hearts, lifting spirits, renewing strength, and restoring hope. So press on, brothers and sisters, press on with hope, press on with faith, press on with love. For in His name, through His strength, we will reach those gates. We will overcome, we will triumph, we will stand victorious. Press on, till your victory is won!

Just like John, we aspire to be ready, prepared to stride into both the "this worldly" and the "other worldly" golden streets of Jerusalem, where all gates are open and the glory of God illuminates every corner.

Remember, the path may be rugged, the journey may be tough, but every step we take, every hurdle we overcome brings us closer to that bright city.

Three gates lie to the east, my brothers and sisters, three gates brimming with the radiant dawn of redemption. As we step through them, the weight of our burdens will vanish, replaced by a peace that surpasses understanding. Each gate, a doorway to grace, a testament to unwavering faith.

The first gate, the gate of joy. As our feet cross the threshold, laughter will bubble up like a melodic symphony, a sweet sound reverberating through the air. Sorrowful tears will be wiped away, replaced by indescribable joy and glorious moments.

The second gate, the gate of love. Stepping into its embrace, hearts once hardened by pain will soften, bathed in the divine love of our Creator. This is love that knows no limits, love that is boundless and unending.

The third gate, the gate of peace. As we enter, the inner turmoil of our souls will subside, giving way to a tranquility that transcends all comprehension. Here, in the presence of God, we discover the peace that surpasses all earthly struggles.

So, let us journey towards those three gates to the east. I feel the joy, I feel the love, I feel the peace that awaits us. For in this moment, through His grace, we shall find our solace.

Three gates to the west, my dear congregation, three gates shimmering in the golden hues of the setting sun. Each gate, a beacon of divine promise, a symbol of God's unfailing mercy.

The first gate, the gate of patience. As we step over its threshold, the rushed pace of our lives will slow, replaced by a serene rhythm in tune with the heart of the Almighty. This is patience born of trust, a trust that His timing is always perfect.

The second gate, the gate of endurance. Entering its archway, the frailty of our bodies will be fortified, strengthened by the enduring spirit of our Redeemer. This is the endurance that withstands every storm, the fortitude that does not falter in the face of adversity.

The third gate, the gate of hope. When we cross this final threshold, our fears and doubts will dissolve, replaced by a light of hope that outshines the darkest nights. Here, in the arms of God, we find the hope that breathes life into our weary souls.

So, press on towards those three gates to the west. Feel the patience, feel the endurance, feel the hope that is promised. For in His realm, under His mercy, we shall find our true strength. Amen, amen, and amen!

Three gates to the north, beloved ones, three gates bathed in the soft light of the North Star. Each gate, an emblem of God's eternal wisdom, a testament to His infinite love.

The first gate, the gate of understanding. As we walk through its portal, the veils of our ignorance lift, replaced by the clarity that comes from divine enlightenment. This is understanding that transcends worldly knowledge, a comprehension rooted in the mind of God.

The second gate, the gate of compassion. As we pass through its enthralling arch, the hardness of our hearts will soften, replaced by a tender love that mirrors God's own heart. This is the compassion that feels the pain of the world, the empathy that shares in another's joy and sorrow.

The third gate, the gate of humility. Upon crossing its hallowed entry, our pride and ego will crumble, replaced by a meekness that reflects the humility of Christ Himself. Here, in the shadow of God, we discover the humility that empowers us to serve others selflessly.

So, advance towards those three gates to the north. Embrace understanding, embody compassion, encapsulate the humility that is guaranteed. For in His realm, under His providence, we will find our true identity.

And so, the journey continues, through the three gates to the east, the west, and the north. But remember, dear ones, these represent only nine of the great twelve gates of the celestial city. So, let's step forward with faith and courage, for beyond these twelve gates, awaits the glory of God's eternal kingdom.

Three gates to the south, brethren and sisters, beckon us on our soul's pilgrimage. The first gate, the gate of grace. Swinging wide on it heavenly hinges

The second gate, the gate of gratitude. Step lightly over its threshold, and sense the surge of thanksgiving, a joyous jubilee jolting our being, a cascade of praise pouring forth from our hearts.

The last gate, the gate of glory. Glide graciously through its golden gateway and gaze upon the grandeur of God's majesty, an awe-inspiring spectacle splendidly spreading before our eyes, a radiant revelation of His divine dominion.

Brethren and sisters, these are the three gates to the south. They, along with the gates to the north, the east, and the west, form the sacred structure, the twelve gates of our celestial city. And through them, we march towards our magnificent Maker, experiencing an elevation, an elation, an ecstasy known only to the children of His kingdom. Through these twelve gates, we witness His glory, through these twelve we receive His grace, and Through these twelve gates we offer up our gratitude. Amen!

Through these twelve gates, we find fortitude in our daily fights, courage amidst the chaos of life. Through these twelve gates, we gather strength, drawing from their divine energy to stand unshaken in the face of adversity.

Through these twelve gates, we gain wisdom; wisdom that illuminates our path, making our way clear in the midst of life's storms. Through these twelve gates, we obtain love, the kind of love that binds us together as a community, a family, a nation.

Through these twelve gates, we achieve peace; the peace that surpasses understanding, bringing calm to our troubled hearts. And finally, through these twelve gates, we encounter hope; hope that sustains us through trials and tribulations, hope that anchors our soul in the midst of life's uncertain waves.

I'm passing through those gates with an air of audacity, an unwavering assertiveness that mirrors my resolve. I'm passing through those gates with a steadfast spirit, each stride reflecting the embodiment of bravery and valor. I'm passing through those gates with an unbothered poise, an emblem of the tenacity that resides within me.

I'm passing through those gates with a daring spirit, my courage as radiant as the golden dawn. I'm passing through those gates with an unyielding determination, a testament to the grit and endurance I possess. I'm passing through those gates with a holy boldness, my daring demeanor mirroring my resolute will. With my faith shining brighter

I'm passing through those gates with insuppressible confidence, a glorious display of the strength of my character. I'm passing through those gates with an indomitable boldness, my every motion an eloquent expression of fortitude within me. I'm passing through those gates, my spirit undaunted, my courage unflinching, my confidence untouched, standing as a testament to the strength that dwells within me.

I'm passing through those twelve gates with a humble heart; a heart that remembers the sacrifices of those who came before me. I'm passing through those twelve gates with the wisdom of Maya Angelou, who taught us that we are phenomenal. I'm passing through those twelve gates carrying the relentless spirit of Rosa Parks, who sat down so we could stand up. I'm passing through those twelve gates, channeling the audacity of Malcolm X, who taught us to fight for our rights, and the dreams of Martin Luther King Jr., who from a mountaintop envisioned a promised land.

I'm passing through those twelve gates, in fulfillment of the dreams of Thurgood Marshall, whose legal prowess helped topple the stronghold of segregation.

As I press toward those gates, I ain't gone let nobody turn me around because I stand on the shoulders of giants.

As I press toward those gates, I ain't gone let nobody turn me around because I carry the legacy of Harriet Tubman, whose courage carved a path to freedom.

As I press toward those gates, I ain't gone let nobody turn me around because I am fueled by the fire that Sojourner Truth set, speaking her truth against the oppression of her people.

As I press toward those gates, I ain't gone let nobody turn me around because within me resides the spirit of Frederick Douglass, who taught us that knowledge is the pathway from slavery to freedom.

As I press toward those gates, I ain't gone let nobody turn me around because I am a testament to the strength and resilience of my people.

As I press toward those gates, I ain't gone let nobody turn me around; I am standing firm, my gaze fixed on the horizon, my spirit unbroken, knowing the promised land is within reach.

In the context of our worldly lives, the equal dimensions of length, height, and breadth of the walls and gates serve as a metaphor for the inherent equality among all human beings. Just as every side of these walls and gates is equal, so too are all individuals in the eyes of divine love, with no distinction based on race, creed, gender, or social status. This equality is not merely physical but encompasses our potential, opportunities, and rights. The uniform measurements of the walls and gates symbolize a society where everyone has equal access to resources, opportunities for growth, and the freedom to express their individuality. The idea reflects a world where walls are not barriers of division, but bridges of connection and unity, mirroring the equality, respect, and harmony that should exist among all people.

The 12 gates of New Jerusalem, as described in the Book of Revelation, are viewed as portals to a world characterized by peace, unity, and divine love. These gates are made of a single pearl, symbolizing purity and perfection. Meanwhile, the crystal-clear walls of Jasper are interpreted as an emblem of clarity, transparency, and unblemished justice. These biblical metaphors offer hope and solace, especially to marginalized and oppressed communities such as African Americans and the south sea Island people, who have endured generations of systemic racism, displacement, and discrimination.

The hope that we may one day reach these metaphorical gates and transcend the walls of oppression is a powerful motivator for both individual and collective action. As these communities continue to endure the harsh realities of gentrification, segregation, redlining, over-policing, and natural disasters, the vision of the New Jerusalem serves as a beacon of light, motivating the pursuit of equality, justice, and dignity. It underscores the yearning for a new reality, one that transforms the walls of division into bridges of unity, and where the gates are open to all, irrespective of race or origin. It is this hope that fuels the ongoing struggle for social justice and equality, driving a commitment to dismantle oppressive systems and restructure societies centered on the values of unity, respect, and equality.

The vision of the New Jerusalem has the profound ability to inspire resilience in African Americans, who have weathered the storm of profound injustices for centuries. This metaphorical city, characterized by unity, peace, and divine love, stands as a beacon of hope, an affirmation that a future free of systemic oppression is possible. African Americans can cling to this vision during their ongoing fight against racial inequality, utilizing it as a source of strength to push forward in the face of adversity. This concept is not just a symbol of an ideal world, but also a call-to-action, prompting the community to strive for justice, equality, and unity. It instills a sense of purpose, fueling their courage to challenge discriminatory practices and norms, and to persist in demanding their rightful place in society. The New Jerusalem symbolizes a promised land, where the walls of racial prejudice are dismantled, and the gates of opportunity swing open for all. It is a powerful reminder that struggles, however daunting they may be, are not in vain and that triumph over adversity is not just a distant dream, but a future reality that is worth fighting for.

The vision of the New Jerusalem offers a potent antidote to the generational apocalyptic experiences of African American communities, who have suffered systematic marginalization, displacement through gentrification, and the profound trauma of racial violence. The concept of this envisioned city, founded on principles of unity, justice, and love, serves as a blueprint for the repair and rebuilding of these devastated communities. The promise of a city where all are welcomed and valued, regardless of race or origin, provides a hopeful contrast to the realities of gentrified neighborhoods and systemic disparity. This metaphorical city becomes a template for a future where communities are not just restored, but are transformed into havens of justice, equality, and enduring peace. The journey towards this New Jerusalem fuels collective action, prompting initiatives centered on community empowerment, preservation of cultural heritage, and proactive policy changes. In this respect, the vision of New Jerusalem is not just a comforting solace, but a motivating catalyst for actionable steps towards communal healing, social justice, and the creation of equitable spaces. It signifies that, in spite of the long history of adversity, a better future is not only envisioned but can be built with concerted effort, resilience, and a steadfast belief in the possibility of transformation.

From a biblical perspective, the gates of the New Jerusalem are symbolic of divine inclusivity and redemption. They offer access to those traditionally marginalized and neglected - the left behind, the pushed aside, the least and the lost. In the Book of Revelation, the city is described as having twelve gates, each made of a single pearl, and at these gates, no one is turned away. This is a poignant metaphor for those who have suffered the most and been rewarded the least in an ongoing societal apocalypse. These gates symbolize the promise of a future where the 'last will be first', a reversal of the social order that has perpetuated inequality and exclusion.

These individuals, truly the ones left behind, are not only welcomed through these gates but are also given the promise of a transformed existence inside. This reinforces the belief that no one is beyond the reach of divine love and redemption, and that societal structures that have perpetuated injustice and inequality will not have the final say. The gates of the New Jerusalem thus represent a profound biblical message of hope, justice, and inclusive community.

The city of New Jerusalem, as depicted in biblical scriptures, poses a stark contrast to the American ideal, particularly in its treatment of historically colonized, displaced and racialized groups, most notably African Americans. In the United States, the socio-economic hierarchy has been largely shaped by systemic racism and discrimination, with African Americans often positioned at the lower end of this structure. This societal structure significantly differs from the vision of New Jerusalem, a city symbolic of divine inclusivity and redemption, where no one is denied access. The promise of New Jerusalem, where 'the last will be first', is a direct rebuke to the American societal system that has perpetuated inequality and exclusion.

The biblical city serves as a mirror reflecting the deficiencies in American society, and its promise of inclusivity and equality stands in stark contrast to the socio-economic imbalances prevalent in the United States. The gates of New Jerusalem are not guarded by wealth, status, or race but are open to all, embodying a vision of community and equality that rebukes the socio-economic disparities that have historically characterized American society.

In essence, New Jerusalem stands as a witness against the American socio-economic hierarchy, and as a symbol of hope for those who have been historically marginalized and oppressed. The city's promise of transformation inside its gates offers a vision of a society where systemic prejudices are not only acknowledged but dismantled, and where justice and inclusivity are the foundational principles. It serves as a beacon of hope, a call for societal transformation, and a prophetic challenge to the American ideal.

In its essence, the model city of New Jerusalem contradicts the American legacy of greed and oppression that has perpetuated imbalances in wealth and opportunity. This legacy is deeply rooted in the enslavement of African people, the displacement of cultures such as the Gullah people, and the systemic denial of reparations and upward mobility. The American model has failed to fulfill the promise of the proverbial '40 acres,' emblematic of the broken pledges made to African Americans throughout history.

The vision of New Jerusalem is a challenge to America, a call for acknowledgment and reparation of the systemic injustices that have characterized its history. It prophesizes a society where justice and inclusiveness are the rule rather than the exception, a place where the scars of the past are not just recognized but healed. The contrast between the promise of New Jerusalem and America's socio-economic reality stands as a stark reminder of the need for transformation and justice.

Frederick Douglass' quote, "I prayed for twenty years but received no answer until I prayed with my legs," is a testament to the power of action in bringing about transformation. It calls for the active pursuit of justice, rather than passively waiting for divine intervention. Douglass emphasizes that prayers are more than mere words or thoughts; they are propelled by the actions that embody them. This concept is strikingly akin to the heart of Jesus' instruction in his model prayer, "thy kingdom come, thy will be done, on earth, as it is in heaven."

Jesus' prayer is not just a petition, but a call to action. Praying for the kingdom to come on earth as it is in heaven is an invitation to work tirelessly towards realizing the kingdom values of love, justice, and equity here and now. It is about fostering a society that mirrors the characteristics of the heavenly kingdom, a place of inclusivity, fairness, and mutual respect. In this sense, praying with our legs, as Douglass suggests, is a practical way of embodying Jesus' command. It's about taking tangible steps towards building a better world, a world that reflects the kingdom of heaven. When addressing the systemic injustices of our society, and by acting on behalf of the marginalized and oppressed, we are effectively 'praying with our legs,' and making the vision of New Jerusalem a manifest reality.

Come and go to that land,

Come and go to that land,

Come and go to that land where I'm bound, where I'm bound,

Oh' don't you want to go to that land where I'm bound.

Bibliography

Akenson, Donald H. Exporting the Rapture: John Nelson Darby and the Victorian Conquest of North-American Evangelicalism. Oxford: Oxford University Press, 2018.

Blount, Brian K. Can I Get a Witness? Reading Revelation through African American Culture. Louisville, KY: Westminster John Knox Press, 2005.

————. Revelation: A Commentary. Louisville, KY: Westminster John Knox Press, 2009.

Brown Douglas, Kelly. Stand Your Ground: Black Bodies and the Justice of God. Maryknoll, NY: Orbis Books, 2015.

Capital B News. "Developers Sue 93-Year-Old Woman Over Her Land. She's Fighting Back." June 27, 2023. https://capitalbnews.org/hilton-head-gullah-land/.

Centers for Disease Control and Prevention. "Health Disparities Experienced by Black or African Americans—United States." Morbidity and Mortality Weekly Report 54, no. 1 (2005): 1–3.

Charleston, Stephen. We Survived the End of the World: Lessons from Native America on Apocalypse and Hope. Minneapolis: Broadleaf Books, 2023.

Cone, James H. The Cross and the Lynching Tree. Maryknoll, NY: Orbis Books, 2011.

Cremer, Benjamin. "The Mark of the Beast." Into the Gray. Accessed May 23, 2025. https://benjamin-cremer.kit.com/posts/the-mark-of-the-beast.

Currie, David B. Rapture: The End-Times Error That Leaves the Bible Behind. Manchester, NH: Sophia Institute Press, 2003.

DeGruy, Joy. Post Traumatic Slave Syndrome: America's Legacy of Enduring Injury and Healing. Milwaukie, OR: Uptone Press, 2005.

Franklin, John Hope. Mirror to America: The Autobiography of John Hope Franklin. New York: Farrar, Straus and Giroux, 2005.

Gafney, Wil. "Holy Blackness: The Matrix of Creation." Sermon delivered at All Saints Church, Pasadena, CA, December 1, 2019. https://www.wilgafney.com/2019/12/01/holy-blackness-the-matrix-of-creation/.

Green, Gene L., Stephen T. Pardue, and K. K. Yeo, eds. All Things New: Eschatology in the Majority World. Carlisle, UK: Langham Publishing, 2019.

Hagee, John. Can America Survive? 10 Prophetic Signs That We Are the Terminal Generation. Updated edition. New York: Howard Books, 2011.

Jeffress, Robert. Perfect Ending: Why Your Eternal Future Matters Today. Colorado Springs, CO: Worthy Publishing, 2014.

Keller, Larry. "Pastor Asks God to Smite President Obama." Southern Poverty Law Center, June 25, 2009. https://www.splcenter.org/hatewatch/2009/06/25/pastor-asks-god-smite-president-obama.

Kendi, Ibram X. How to Be an Antiracist. New York: One World, 2019.

MacArthur, John. "How Should Christians Respond to the Riots?" Grace to You. June 7, 2020. YouTube video, 1:05:32. https://www.youtube.com/watch?v=WKXAykFtehY.

Malcolm X. The End of White World Supremacy: Four Speeches. Edited by Imam Benjamin Karim. New York: Arcade Publishing, 1989.

McCaulley, Esau. Reading While Black: African American Biblical Interpretation as an Exercise in Hope. Downers Grove, IL: IVP Academic, 2020.

National Association for the Advancement of Colored People (NAACP). Criminal Justice Fact Sheet. Accessed May 24, 2025. https://naacp.org/resources/criminal-justice-fact-sheet.

Olson, Carl E., and Sandra Miesel. The Rapture: The End-Times Error That Leaves the Bible Behind. San Francisco: Ignatius Press, 2003.

Park, Wongi. "The Blessing of Whiteness in the Curse of Ham: Reading Gen 9:18–29 in the Antebellum South." Religions 12, no. 11 (2021): 928. https://doi.org/10.3390/rel12110928.

Ruffin, Amber. "How Did We Get Here: Drowned Towns." The Amber Ruffin Show, Season 1, Episode 30. Aired June 25, 2021, on Peacock.

Schutz, Paris. "Gun Theft in Rail Yard Raises Security Questions." WTTW News, August 3, 2015. https://news.wttw.com/2015/08/03/gun-theft-rail-yard-raises-security-questions.

Scofield, C. I., ed. The Scofield Reference Bible: The Holy Bible, Containing the Old and New Testaments. Oxford: Oxford University Press, 1917.

Sellers, Bakari. "Developers Sue 93-Year-Old Woman Over Her Land. She's Fighting Back." Interview by Aallyah Wright. Capital B News, June 27, 2023. https://capitalbnews.org/hilton-head-gullah-land/.

Shepherd, Brodrick D. Beasts, Horns and the Antichrist: Daniel, A Blueprint of the Last Days. Grassy Creek, NC: Cliffside Publishing House, 1994.

Smith, Cherranda. "Amber Ruffin Exposes History Of Flooding Black Towns In Viral Clip." Black Information Network, June 30, 2021. https://www.binnews.com/content/2021-06-30-amber-ruffin-exposes-history-of-flooding-black-towns-in-viral-clip/.

Smith, David Michael. "Counting the Dead: Estimating the Loss of Life in the Indigenous Holocaust, 1492–Present." In A-NAS-2017 Proceedings, Southeastern Oklahoma State University, 2017. https://www.se.edu/native-american/wp-content/uploads/sites/49/2019/09/A-NAS-2017-Proceedings-Smith.pdf.

Van Impe, Jack. Revelation Rumblings. Troy, MI: Jack Van Impe Ministries, 2013. DVD.

Van Wyngaard, Cobus, Craig Stewart, Curtis Love, and Sarah Montgomery. "Statement from White South African Christian Leaders on Recent Actions by the United States Government." INFEMIT, February 28, 2025. https://infemit.org/south-africa-statement-feb2025/.

Wells, Ida B. Southern Horrors: Lynch Law in All Its Phases. New York: New York Age Print, 1892.

Williams, Chancellor. The Destruction of Black Civilization: Great Issues of a Race from 4500 B.C. to 2000 A.D. Chicago: Third World Press, 1987.

Yahoo News Staff. "93-Year-Old Woman Faces Lawsuit from Developer over Family Land in Hilton Head." Yahoo News, June 27, 2023. https://www.yahoo.com/news/93-year-old-woman-faces-lawsuit-from-developer-over-family-land-in-hilton-head-123456789.html.